The Essential Guide to Christianity

THE ESSENTIAL GUIDES TO RELIGION

This series introduces students to world religions in various contexts, from their origins and scriptures, through to contemporary issues such as religion and sexuality, economics, and politics. Experts in the field explore religious traditions such as Christianity, Buddhism, and Islam. Each book comes illustrated throughout and includes suggestions for further reading. Students benefit from a glossary of key terms and concepts to guide learning about the world religions.

Also available:
The Essential Guide to Buddhism, edited by Gwendolyn Gillson

The chapters in this book were first published in the digital collection *Bloomsbury Religion in North America*. Covering North America's diverse religious traditions, this digital collection provides reliable and peer-reviewed articles and eBooks for students and instructors of religious studies, anthropology of religion, sociology of religion, and history. Learn more and get access for your library at www.theologyandreligiononline.com/bloomsbury-religion-in-north-america

The Essential Guide to Christianity

**EDITED BY
DYRON B. DAUGHRITY**

BLOOMSBURY ACADEMIC
LONDON • NEW YORK • OXFORD • NEW DELHI • SYDNEY

BLOOMSBURY ACADEMIC
Bloomsbury Publishing Plc
50 Bedford Square, London, WC1B 3DP, UK
1385 Broadway, New York, NY 10018, USA
29 Earlsfort Terrace, Dublin 2, Ireland

BLOOMSBURY, BLOOMSBURY ACADEMIC and the Diana logo are
trademarks of Bloomsbury Publishing Plc

First published online 2021

This print edition published 2024

Copyright © Bloomsbury Publishing Plc, 2021, 2024

Dyron B. Daughrity has asserted his right under the Copyright, Designs and
Patents Act, 1988, to be identified as Editor of this work.

Cover image © Heritage Images / Getty

All rights reserved. No part of this publication may be reproduced or transmitted
in any form or by any means, electronic or mechanical, including photocopying,
recording, or any information storage or retrieval system, without prior
permission in writing from the publishers.

Bloomsbury Publishing Plc does not have any control over, or responsibility
for, any third-party websites referred to or in this book. All internet addresses given in
this book were correct at the time of going to press. The author and publisher regret
any inconvenience caused if addresses have changed or sites have ceased to exist,
but can accept no responsibility for any such changes.

A catalogue record for this book is available from the British Library.

Library of Congress Cataloging-in-Publication Data
Names: Daughrity, Dyron B., 1973- editor.
Title: The essential guide to Christianity / edited by Dyron Daughrity.
Description: London ; New York : Bloomsbury Academic, 2024. |
Series: The essential guides to religion | First published online in 2021. |
Includes bibliographical references and index.
Identifiers: LCCN 2023058376 | ISBN 9781350406742 (paperback) |
ISBN 9781350406735 (hardback)
Subjects: LCSH: Christianity.
Classification: LCC BR121.3 .E87 2024 | DDC 230–dc23/eng/20240220
LC record available at https://lccn.loc.gov/2023058376

ISBN: HB: 978-1-3504-0673-5
PB: 978-1-3504-0674-2

Series: The Essential Guides to Religion

Typeset by Integra Software Services Pvt. Ltd.

To find out more about our authors and books visit www.bloomsbury.com
and sign up for our newsletters.

Contents

List of Illustrations vi

List of Contributors x

1 Introduction to Christianity *Dyron B. Daughrity* 1
2 Jesus: A Jewish Messiah *Nicholas J. Zola* 28
3 The Bible: How Christians Use Their Text *Craig W.C. Ginn* 44
4 The Sacraments: The Lifeblood of Christianity *Ellie Gebarowski-Shafer* 63
5 Women in Christianity: An Emerging Story *Ellie Gebarowski-Shafer* 81
6 Christianity and Politics: From Constantine to Today *Darin D. Lenz* 102
7 Eastern Orthodox Christianity: A Vital Tradition *Gaelan Gilbert* 120
8 Roman Catholicism: A Tradition in Transition *Todd Hartch* 138
9 Protestantism: 40,000 and Still Counting *William T. Purinton* 154
10 Global Christianity: The Future of the Faith *William T. Purinton* 169

Index 184

Illustrations

1.1 Jesus teaching in the Jewish temple in Jerusalem as a boy 4
1.2 Christ and the Woman of Samaria 6
1.3 Jesus preaching the Sermon on the Mount 9
1.4 Paul's vision of Christ leads to his conversion to Christianity 12
1.5 Constantinople (now Istanbul): the great city of Constantine 15
1.6 Greenwich Observatory, London, United Kingdom 16
1.7 Prayer is a critically important part of Christian life 21
1.8 The Eucharist is an essential sacrament for Christians 22
1.9 Christ the Redeemer, Rio de Janeiro, Brazil 25
2.1 A Byzantine silver plate from c. 630 CE depicting the prophet Samuel anointing a young David with oil while David's father and two of his brothers observe 29
2.2 The caves near Qumran, where locals found the Dead Sea Scrolls, an unparalleled collection of Jewish manuscripts first discovered in 1947 and now hailed as one of the greatest archaeological finds of the twentieth century 30
2.3 The Arch of Titus in Rome, erected in 81 CE, depicting Titus' destruction of the Jerusalem temple in 70 CE to signify Rome's victory in the Jewish–Roman War; the panel relief highlights the spoils of war, including the Jewish menorah 31
2.4 A medieval illustration of the authors of the four Gospels (called Evangelists) from an Armenian Gospel book, c. 1300 32
2.5 Although the exact location of Jesus's burial is unknown, some consider this ancient rock-cut tomb in Jerusalem, called the Garden Tomb, to be similar to how Jesus's tomb may have appeared 34

ILLUSTRATIONS

2.6 A wall painting from the church of San Baudelio in Spain depicts Jesus healing the blind man (Jn 9) and raising Lazarus from the dead (Jn 11), c. early twelfth century 39

2.7 A diptych from early eighteenth-century Ethiopia illustrating Jesus crucified on the right panel (with Mary and John in sorrow on either side) and Jesus resurrected in triumph on the left panel (raising Adam and Eve to symbolize his victory over death) 41

3.1 Entire Tanakh scroll set 46

3.2 Codex Vaticanus 47

3.3 Greek orthodox mural of Apostle Paul 51

3.4 Lutherstadt Wittenberg 54

3.5 Sunday School 57

3.6 Franklin and Billy Graham in Cleveland Stadium, June 1994 58

4.1 Christians traditionally understand the Eucharist as having a precedent in the Hebrew Old Testament as well as in the Greek New Testament 65

4.2 In Eucharistic celebrations in today's churches, priests and ministers seek to carry out the command of Christ to "do this in remembrance of me" 66

4.3 Traditionally, participation in the sacrament of penance is believed to transmit divine grace to the believer 69

4.4 Luther defended infant baptism, which Anabaptists rejected as unscriptural 71

4.5 North American Protestant churches have changed radically in the last century 74

4.6 When baptizing a new believer, Pentecostals fully immerse the candidate in water 75

4.7 Average charismatic believers pray for one another for long periods of time, by laying on of hands 77

5.1 Women outnumber men as churchgoers in North America 82

5.2	Since the early modern period, Christian women have had greater access to printed Bibles in vernacular languages, for personal study and outreach 89
5.3	Music performed in North American churches has often been composed by women, and women often serve as charismatic worship leaders 93
5.4	Elizabeth Johnson 95
5.5	Shannon MacLean-Brown, the first African American female bishop of the Diocese of Vermont 98
6.1	Chi and rho are the first two letters for the Greek word for Christ (Χριστός) and the Greek letters alpha and omega mean Christ is the beginning and the end 103
6.2	Victory of Constantine at the Battle of Milvian Bridge 104
6.3	Martin Luther 107
6.4	Frederick the Wise, Prince-elector of Saxony, c. 1530–5. *Source:* Wikimedia Commons 108
6.5	Napoleon Bonaparte crowns himself emperor while Pope Pius VII watches 112
6.6	Archbishop Desmond Tutu 115
6.7	Yoido Full Gospel Church in South Korea, one of the largest Pentecostal churches in the world with approximately 800,000 members 117
7.1	Icon of Christ the Pantocrator, Sinai, c. fifth century 123
7.2	Icon of the First Ecumenical Council in 325 CE 125
7.3	Icon of the Theotokos 126
7.4	The Church of Hagia Sophia (as a mosque, in the nineteenth century) 127
7.5	Simonopetra Monastery, Mount Athos 130
7.6	Trinity-St. Sergius Monastery, Sergiyev Posad, c. 1890 133
7.7	Orthodox clergy in a worship service (bishop, priests) 134

ILLUSTRATIONS

8.1 Painting of Our Lady of Guadalupe, San Miguel de Allende, Mexico 139
8.2 Bishops gathered at the Second Vatican Council, 1965 141
8.3 Archbishop Oscar Romero in 1979 145
8.4 Catholic Mass in Harare, Zimbabwe, 2018 146
8.5 Syro-Malabar Catholics in Bhopal, India, 2016 148
8.6 Pope Francis in San Cristobal de Las Casas, Mexico, 2016 149
9.1 Jan Huss, a Czech reformer, was martyred in July 1415 156
9.2 The Separatist Pilgrims seeking Zion in New England 159
9.3 Methodists in prayer 161
9.4 First Baptist Church of Morelia, Mexico 163
9.5 A small Pentecostal (full gospel) church in Seoul 166
10.1 Student choir at the Asian Center for Theological Studies and Mission (Yangpyeong, South Korea) 172
10.2 St. Peter and St. Paul's Church, Ganghwa Anglican Church in Korea 173
10.3 Adventist baptism in Mozambique 175
10.4 A seventeenth-century Japanese depiction of St. Francis Xavier 177
10.5 The World Parliament of Religions in Chicago (1893) 179

List of Contributors

Dyron B. Daughrity is the William S. Banowsky Chair and Professor of Religion at Pepperdine University, California, USA.

Ellie Gebarowski-Shafer is an independent scholar from Vermont, United States.

Fr Anthony (Gaelan) Gilbert is Adjunct Professor of Literature & History at Hellenic College Holy Cross Greek Orthodox School of Theology in Brookline, MA, and Visiting Assistant Professor of Literature at Saint Vladimir's Orthodox Theological Seminary in Yonkers, NY.

Craig W.C. Ginn is an instructor at University of Calgary, Canada.

Todd Hartch is Professor of History at Eastern Kentucky University and is the author of five books on the history of Christianity.

Darin D. Lenz is Professor of History and Chair of the Department of History at Biola University, La Mirada, California, USA.

William Purinton teaches global Christianity at Columbia International University, South Carolina, USA.

Nicholas J. Zola is Associate Professor of Religion at Pepperdine University, Malibu, USA.

1

Introduction to Christianity

Dyron B. Daughrity

Introduction

It is difficult to comprehend a world without Christianity. Its impact on humanity is incalculable. It is today the largest religion in the world, with around 2.5 billion adherents. That is around one-third of the entire human race. Some have observed that Christianity is the largest human *institution* that has ever existed. It is difficult to imagine any single institution in history that can claim the allegiance of one out of three people on the planet.

There was a time when Christianity was understood mainly as a Western religion, but that is not exactly the case anymore. While it began as a Middle Eastern faith, over time it migrated into Europe, where it gained a stronghold and dominated the culture of that part of the world for many centuries. However, over the last couple of centuries, Christianity has spread rather quickly to non-Western parts of the world. Today it is no longer associated exclusively with the West. In fact, of the world's eight cultural blocks, Christianity is the largest religion in six of them: Africa, North America, Latin America and the Caribbean, Eastern Europe, Western Europe, and Oceania (Pacific). There are only two cultural blocks where Christianity is not the majority faith today: Asia and the Middle East. But Christianity has influenced those regions too. In Asia, Christianity has been growing over the last several decades to the point that it is now the religion of around 10 percent of the population. Although the Middle East has few Christians today, it is the land where Christianity was born. And it is a land that will forever be associated with Jesus, the apostles, the Christian scriptures, and the holy city of Jerusalem—ground zero for the Christian faith (Daughrity 2016).

This article is a basic overview of Christianity. It is organized into three sections that attempt to answer three basic questions:

1   Who was Jesus Christ?
2   How did Christianity become the world's largest religion?
3   What do Christians believe?

By understanding the answers to these three basic questions, readers will gain a broad overview of what exactly this faith is and why it has appealed to more people than any other religion in human history.

Who Was Jesus Christ?

Jesus Christ was a Jewish man who lived from about 4 BCE to 30 CE. He was born in the town of Bethlehem, located in modern-day Palestine, and he died in Jerusalem—the most important city of the nation of Israel.

His given name was "Jesus," which is a famous Jewish name. In Hebrew, his name is "Yeshua" (in English, Joshua). He was named after Joshua, the famous leader in the Hebrew Bible who took over leadership of the Jews after Moses died. Joshua—the namesake for a biblical book—is remembered as a warrior who was full of courage. He led the Israelites to victory after victory over the Canaanites. After several successful battles, the Israelites took over the land—the land that Jews inhabit today and consider to be their rightful homeland.

However, by the time Jesus was born, the nation of Israel was under the authority of the Roman Empire. The Jewish people were an oppressed people, under the control of the emperor and the powerful Roman government. They had some measure of individual freedom, but their nation was overseen by delegated Roman authorities.

The story of Jesus's life is recorded in the New Testament Gospels: the books of Matthew, Mark, Luke, and John. There are other Gospel accounts about Jesus, but they never achieved official, canonical status in the history of Christianity, as they were likely written much later than the four canonical ones. Each Gospel tells a slightly different story, but much of the information overlaps.

A composite of the canonical Gospels tells us that Jesus's mother was a woman named Mary—a Jewish virgin who was chosen by God to give birth to the long-awaited Christ, or the Messiah. The word "Christ" is not Jesus's last name. Rather, it is an honorific title, meaning "anointed one," and it could apply to kings, priests, or emperors anointed publicly as a recognition of their authority. Jesus Christ means "Jesus, the anointed one." There was a long tradition in Judaism that God would eventually provide a Messiah to his people—the Jews. The Messiah would liberate the people from oppression, bring lasting peace, and usher in a new age that would restore the Jews to their rightful place in the world, as God's chosen people.

The Gospels claim that Jesus's father is Yahweh, or the Creator God. This God—according to Judaism the *only* God that exists—miraculously impregnated the Virgin Mary so that she conceived and gave birth to Jesus. Thus, Jesus's mother was a human being, but his father was God—the creator of the world. Mary became married to a man named Joseph, a carpenter. Joseph raised Jesus until Jesus's teenage years or twenties. There is no word about how Joseph died, but by the time we read of the beginning of the ministry of Jesus around the age of thirty, Joseph has disappeared from the story.

Jesus's birth is one of the most significant events for Christians and is celebrated annually during the festival of Christmas. In the Gospels, Jesus's birth attracted the attention of the Jewish leader Herod the Great, who commanded that all baby boys in the vicinity of Bethlehem should be put to death. Jesus's parents escaped the violence and made their way to Egypt for a short period of time. Once Herod died—which happened shortly after they fled to Egypt—Jesus and his parents moved to Nazareth and settled there. Nazareth is located in the northern part of Israel, in the Galilee region, and for two millennia has been revered by Christians as the childhood hometown of Jesus.

Little is known of Jesus's childhood, with one exception. When he was twelve, his parents took a pilgrimage to Jerusalem to celebrate the Jewish Passover festival. When they departed and were headed back to Nazareth, they realized Jesus was not with them. They returned to Jerusalem, only to find him sitting with the rabbis, learning from them and thoroughly impressing them with his knowledge.

The story of Jesus then jumps to his baptism, by his cousin, a wilderness preacher known as John the Baptist. As Jesus emerged from the water, a voice from heaven exclaimed "You are my son, whom I love." And immediately the Holy Spirit descended upon Jesus "like a dove" (Mt. 3:16–17).

Shortly after the baptism, Jesus went into the desert for a period of forty days and was tempted by Satan. Jesus prevailed against these temptations, proving himself to be a worthy son of God, a fitting person to take God's message to the world. It was here that Jesus launched his ministry, duly ordained, and properly tested, having overcome the temptations that so often corrupt or stifle regular human beings. But this is precisely what the Gospels try to prove: that Jesus was no ordinary human being. He was uniquely from God.

Jesus emerged from the wilderness on a mission to choose his core followers, known in the Gospels as his "apostles." Jesus chose twelve men of rather ordinary situations in life, for example, men engaged in fishing, tax collecting, and one named Simon who may have been a political revolutionary—a zealot. The twelve apostles are extremely revered in Christian history, depicted on stained glass windows, iconography, in sculptures, and in paintings all over the Christian world. The names of the twelve apostles are: Simon Peter, Andrew, James, John, Philip, Bartholomew, Thomas, Matthew, James, Thaddeus, Simon, and Judas. The last one, Judas, betrayed Jesus just before the Crucifixion; he was replaced by Matthias. The apostle Paul—perhaps the most famous apostle of Jesus in history—was not one of the original twelve. In fact, he never met Jesus in the flesh. However, he was so respected as a follower of Christ that he, too, was eventually given the honorable title of "apostle." We will discuss Paul at greater length below, as he rose up to be the most prolific of the apostles and is commonly thought to have authored about half of the New Testament books. His impact on the Christian faith, as its greatest theologian and missionary, cannot be overstated.

FIGURE 1.1 *Jesus teaching in the Jewish temple in Jerusalem as a boy.* Source: *traveler1116/ Getty Images.*

Almost immediately into his public ministry, the people around Jesus started to call him "rabbi" (master teacher of the Jewish law). There was an authority exuded by Jesus that seemed unique, even in comparison with the other rabbis (Mt. 7:29). As were most Jewish groups of that age, Jesus and his followers were concerned with how to interpret the will of God according to the Hebrew Bible. Many of the stories in the Gospels involve Jesus debating other Jewish leaders on how best to interpret the Jewish scriptures.

Accompanied by his great learning and authority, Jesus also performed miracles, beginning with his act of turning water into wine at a wedding to protect the hosts from humiliation. His list of miracles is extensive. He frequently healed people from illness, disease, deafness, blindness, hemorrhaging, paralysis, and even raised people from the dead. Jesus showed power over nature by calming storms, walking on water, and multiplying food to feed thousands of people. On several occasions, Jesus cast demons out of people.

Jesus was also prone to break social taboos, usually to prove a point that the Jewish law was not being observed properly. For example, in the Parable of the Good Samaritan, Jesus told a story about a traveler who was robbed, beaten, and left for dead. Jesus described a situation that was terribly unflattering to Jews: the Jewish priests passed by the severely injured traveler without helping him. However, the Samaritan is the one who stopped to help the injured man. This story was shocking to the Jews since they considered Samaritans as inferior mixed-breeds, idolaters, and members of a rival religion. Jews claimed that Samaritans had intermarried with Gentiles (non-Jews). Samaritans argued that it was actually the Jews who intermarried and compromised their religion when they were conquered by Babylon. Jews tended to be suspicious of Samaritans, as both religions claimed to be the true Israel. What made the Good Samaritan story so offensive to Jews was that Jesus was saying that sometimes Samaritans behave more righteously than Jews—even Jewish priests! They became incensed at Jesus and even labeled him a Samaritan (Jn 8:48).

Jesus committed other social taboos as well. On one occasion, he was refreshing himself at a well during travel, and he had a very tender conversation with a Samaritan woman. Even the Samaritan woman was surprised because Jews and Samaritans did not associate with each other. On another occasion, Jesus publicly forgave a woman who had been caught in the act of adultery, whereas the official punishment was that she should be stoned to death. Jesus basically outwitted those who wanted to stone her by saying: "He who is without sin can cast the first stone at her." No one dared to cast a stone.

Jesus performed many other questionable acts that caused Jewish leaders to resent and even despise him. Several times he was accused of violating the Sabbath—the commandment that specified that no work was to be done on the seventh day of the week. He spoke with Gentiles and even befriended the hated Samaritans. He was accused of almost equating himself with God when he said, "I and the Father are one." They wanted to stone him for this claim. He caused outrage when he "cleansed"

FIGURE 1.2 *Christ and the Woman of Samaria.* Source: *duncan1890/Getty Images.*

the temple, driving out the moneychangers and merchants, saying "My house shall be called a house of prayer, but you have made it a den of thieves" (Mt. 21:13)!

In addition to his performing miracles, Jesus also attracted people through his teaching. Some of the parables have been mentioned, and there were many others. A parable is a fictional story used to teach a moral principle. For example, the Parable of the Good Samaritan emphasized the potential goodness of people, even if they are not like us. The Parable of the Prodigal Son emphasized God's forgiveness of people when they sin badly. The Parable of the Unmerciful Servant taught that people should forgive one another, and God will punish those who withhold their forgiveness. The Parable of the Talents teaches that people who use their talents for God will be commended by God, whereas those who "bury" their talents will be punished.

Another central teaching of Jesus relates to what he called the Kingdom of God. He did not have a place in mind; rather, by "kingdom of God" he meant living according to God's will. Those people who place themselves underneath the authority of God, willingly enter God's kingdom. Jesus taught that eventually he would return to Earth, but until then, his followers should live kingdom-centered lives where they follow Christ's teachings. If they obey Christ's teachings, then they will effectively enter God's kingdom in *this* life, and not just in the hereafter. Although Jesus certainly believed in an afterlife, his notion of the Kingdom of God meant that his disciples would live inside the kingdom *now*, and eventually, in a future time, they would experience the full Kingdom of God after their resurrection from death.

One of the earliest and most fundamental teachings of Jesus is the concept of repentance. There is in Jesus's teachings this notion that all people have sinned and need to turn their hearts toward God. However, they must seek forgiveness from God and then change their habits and thought patterns. The meaning of the word repentance is literally to change one's ways. Jesus urged his followers to abandon their selfishness, to abandon their sinfulness, and to embrace the righteous life of following God with all of one's heart, soul, mind, and strength (Lk. 10:25–7).

Perhaps Jesus's most famous teaching is found in the "Sermon on the Mount," in Matthew chapters 5–7. In that sermon, Jesus begins with the "beatitudes"—a series of blessings given by Jesus to the poor, humble, and righteous people. In the sermon he flipped some established Jewish teachings, such as when he said, "You have heard it said that you shall not murder, but I tell you that whoever is angry at a brother or sister will be subject to judgment." Similarly, he taught, "You have heard it said that you shall not commit adultery, but I tell you that anyone who lusts after a woman has already committed adultery with her in his heart." Jesus was saying that an improper attitude was at the root of improper action. Thus, his hearers should focus on the root cause rather than the consequential immoral action.

In the Sermon on the Mount, Jesus challenged standard Jewish interpretations of divorce, oaths, and concepts of vengeance, arguing that his disciples should "turn the other cheek" when harmed by another. In fact, Jesus argued, you should "love your enemies, and pray for those who persecute you."

Jesus also condemned hypocrisy in the Sermon on the Mount, arguing that we should give to the needy in private, not in such a way that would bring attention to our goodness. The same with fasting. We should fast (avoid eating to focus on God) without telling people we are fasting. Similarly, we should pray in secret, not in public so that people will admire our piety. Importantly, it is in the Sermon on the Mount that Jesus uttered that most famous of prayers, still recited by most Christians:

Our Father in heaven,
Hallowed be your name,
Your kingdom come,
Your will be done,
On earth as it is in heaven.
Give us this day our daily bread.
And forgive us our debts,
As we also have forgiven our debtors.
And lead us not into temptation,
But deliver us from the evil one.

The Sermon on the Mount is full of important teachings that are still sacred and fundamental to Christian faith, such as this one: "Where your treasure is, there your heart will be also." Jesus warned his followers to avoid the temptation of loving money, as it can corrupt a person. He urged them not to worry about life, since worrying will not help a person in any way, rather it shows a lack of faith in God. He commanded his followers to avoid judging other people, for "in the same way you judge others, you will be judged, and with the measure you use, it will be measured to you."

In the Sermon on the Mount Jesus uttered the famous Golden Rule: "Do unto others as you would have them do unto you."

In the conclusion to the Sermon on the Mount, Jesus told his followers that if they followed his teachings, then they would stand firm, like a house built upon a rock foundation. However, if they ignored his teachings, then their lives would collapse, like a house built on sand.

Scholars agree that Jesus's ministry lasted only a few years at most. The teachers of the law were highly offended by his ministry and his teachings, and took action to kill him. They hired Judas—one of the twelve apostles whom we are told was overcome with greed—to betray Jesus. They captured him in the city of Jerusalem while he was celebrating the annual Passover celebration—a famous Jewish feast celebrating Moses leading the Israelites out of Egypt.

After Jesus was captured, the Roman governor Pontius Pilate put him on trial. The accusations against him were based on the testimony of Jewish leaders who resented his ministry. After condemnation, Jesus was punished in a variety of ways—a series of tortures known by Christians as the Passion of Christ. Effectively it was a long execution that culminated in the common Roman practice of crucifixion—publicly nailing a naked person to a cross made of wood. It was a brutal form of execution that

FIGURE 1.3 *Jesus preaching the Sermon on the Mount.* Source: *duncan1890/Getty Images.*

was used mainly for notorious criminals and those who rebelled against the Roman government. Jesus was killed on a Friday, which is commemorated in the Christian calendar as "Good Friday."

However, on the following Sunday—the most important day for all Christians everywhere—Jesus is reported to have risen from the dead. He came to life and walked out of his tomb and appeared to many of his followers. This story has befuddled Christians and non-Christians for twenty centuries. But, as the apostle Paul argued, "If Christ has not been raised, then our preaching is useless and so is your faith" (1 Cor. 15:14).

The resurrection of Jesus—known by Christians as Easter Sunday—had a profound effect on Jesus's followers. While they were initially discouraged by his death, thinking his entire ministry had been in vain, the resurrection utterly changed their perspective, and they went out with great courage and determination to spread the "gospel," or the "good news." The "good news" is that Christ died for all, and people can have their sins forgiven if they place their trust in Christ. Life is not hopeless. Rather, life lived in God's kingdom has great meaning. People are never too far gone. Everyone is redeemable. We must never give up on people, and we must always have hope that things will get better.

Further, and perhaps most importantly, there is a resurrection coming for all people. Those who are part of God's kingdom will dwell together in eternal happiness in a new creation with God and all his people.

How Did Christianity Become the World's Largest Religion?

Christianity began in the city of Jerusalem, in the Roman-occupied region of Palestine. Jerusalem is the home of the mother church of Christianity, and all Christian roads depart from there. It is the city where Jesus was crucified and where he was resurrected.

It is common for people today to think of the origins of Christianity as being in Rome, the heart of the **Roman Catholic Church**. But Christianity did not really establish itself in Rome until a decade or more after the resurrection. While Rome became an extremely important city in the history of Christianity, the origins of the faith are best understood as being in cities closer to Jerusalem, such as Antioch, Alexandria, and Damascus. Rome's important role in the history of Christianity came a bit later. One scholar put it this way, "It was not until the end of the second century that western provinces began to be seriously Christianized at all" (Ehrman 2018: 168).

By the time Jesus ascended to heaven—about forty days after his Resurrection—his followers were encouraged and prepared to fulfill the Great Commission, one of the most important commands ever uttered by Jesus:

> All authority in heaven and on earth has been given to me. Therefore go and make disciples of all nations, baptizing them in the name of the Father and of the Son and

INTRODUCTION TO CHRISTIANITY

of the Holy Spirit, and teaching them to obey everything I have commanded you. And surely I am with you always, to the very end of the age.

(Mt. 28:18–20)

These words propelled his mainly Jewish followers to start evangelizing the people around them, witnessing to them, and carrying on missionary work, even to far-off places.

Tradition holds that the twelve apostles began traveling to distant shores to spread the Gospel, or the "good news," about Jesus the Messiah. One follower in particular, a Jewish Pharisee named Saul, took the Great Commission extremely seriously. He had visions about Jesus, and learned about Jesus from the apostles, but never actually met the Lord himself. Nevertheless, Saul—whose name was changed sometime later to Paul—became probably the greatest missionary in the history of the Christian faith.

Paul was a uniquely gifted man. He was a Roman citizen, but he was also a zealous Jew. In fact, before he became a Christian, he was actually a sworn enemy to Christianity. He was an active participant in persecutions going on at the time, which punished and occasionally executed Christians. At one point, Paul had an experience where he encountered Jesus in a vision, and this encounter completely changed him.

Paul is known to Christians as an apostle, even though he was not one of the twelve. He was quite different from them, in fact. For example, the twelve tended to be Palestinian Jews who were country people, rural folk. Jesus probably only visited one city in his lifetime—Jerusalem. Similarly, the apostles were rural men, familiar with fishing, acquainted with farming and village life. Paul, however, was a man of the city. He was comfortable in the big cosmopolitan areas of the Mediterranean Sea region: Corinth, Antioch, Ephesus, Athens, and eventually Rome—where he was confined to house arrest and executed.

Paul proved to be an extremely effective evangelist, although not without trials and tribulations. He tells us he suffered shipwrecks and lashings and all manner of persecution during Christianity's early era. He took seriously the Great Commission—that disciples of Jesus should go out and preach the Gospel to people. Without Paul, the Christian faith would look very different and likely be much smaller than it is today. Paul was the great impetus behind the early expansion of Christianity. His letters were already being called "scripture" in the early days of the faith. For example, the biblical book of 2 Peter (3:15–16) says:

Bear in mind that our Lord's patience means salvation, just as our dear brother Paul also wrote you with the wisdom that God gave him. He writes the same way in all his letters, speaking in them of these matters. His letters contain some things that are hard to understand, which ignorant and unstable people distort, as they do the other Scriptures, to their own destruction.

FIGURE 1.4 *Paul's vision of Christ leads to his conversion to Christianity.* Source: ivan-96/ Getty Images.

Some scholars argue that 2 Peter may not have been written by the apostle Peter. They claim it may have been written in the early second century. That does not forfeit, however, what this passage says about Paul: (1) his teachings were revered; (2) his teachings were quite scholarly for the average person; and (3) his teachings were believed to be scripture very early in church history.

Paul's writings are foundational to what Christians believe. Of the twenty-seven books of the New Testament, Paul is believed to have authored thirteen of them. As a side note, scholars debate authorship often, but suffice it to say that throughout church history, Paul is believed to have written: Romans, 1 and 2 Corinthians, Galatians, Ephesians, Philippians, Colossians, 1 and 2 Thessalonians, 1 and 2 Timothy, Titus, and Philemon. Some people believe Paul may have written Hebrews. We also know that most of the book of Acts—the second longest book of the New Testament—is largely about Paul.

Paul's impact on the Christian faith is incalculable. He set the tone for how churches are to be organized and shaped. He is the first great theologian of the church. Whether looked at from a Christian perspective or even a scholarly perspective, his writings are impressive, sophisticated, and very well reasoned. He explains throughout how Jesus's life, death, and resurrection have achieved salvation for those who believe. He explains how Christians are to connect to God and behave once they have entered into covenant with the Lord. Paul reinterprets Judaism in the light of Jesus to create a systematic organization of what we can call Christian belief.

Currently, we live in an age of antipathy to Paul. He comes across as overly patriarchal—for example by saying "the head of every man is Christ, and the head of the woman is man, and the head of Christ is God" (1 Cor. 11:3). People in the twenty-first-century, Western world find this complementarianism to be off-putting. Similarly, Paul's understanding of sexuality never became dislodged from his Jewish worldview: that sexual relations are to be between a man and a woman in marital covenant. In rather forceful terms, Paul condemns adultery, homosexuality, and all manner of fornication (sex outside of marital fidelity). However, Paul also comes across as a champion for human rights, as when he condemns slavery (1 Tim. 1:10) and actually goes to great lengths to defend a runaway slave in the book of Philemon.

For around three centuries, Christianity was despised in the Roman world and in some cases even illegal. Some of the Jewish and Roman authorities were harder on it than others, but the fact was that by converting to Christianity, you put yourself outside the mainstream culture. Some of the Roman emperors outlawed Christianity. Others enacted forced conversions or even persecution unto death for those who obstinately remained in the faith. Notorious persecutions were authorized by several emperors, including Nero (r.54–68), Domitian (r.81–96), Marcus Aurelius (r.161–180), Decius (r.249–251), Valerian (r.253–260), and especially Diocletian (r.284–305).

Christians persevered, however, and continued to expand prolifically. In the year 312, something happened that changed the course of history: the rise of **Constantine the Great** (r.306–337). Constantine was probably the strongest Roman emperor since Caesar Augustus (r.27 BCE–14 CE), the first Roman emperor. After having a vision of the cross, Constantine decided to make Christianity legal in 313 with the Edict of Milan. In addition, Constantine's mother, Helena, was an extremely zealous Christian who wielded great influence over her son. Over time, Constantine, too, became a Christian and went to great lengths to look out for the interests of his brothers and sisters of the faith. Christians went from being persecuted to privileged, almost overnight.

Did Constantine singlehandedly change the course of Christianity? Not exactly. He obviously joined himself to Christianity at a moment when it was winning the hearts and minds of the ancient Mediterranean world. Some argue that it was in his best interests—as a ruler—to become a Christian. It cannot be doubted that he truly became Christian. Historians quibble about how committed to Christ he actually was, but there can be no doubt that he joined the Christian faith and became the model for what a Christian ruler would look like in coming centuries. Eastern Orthodox Christians often refer to Constantine as Saint Constantine the Great— Equal to the Apostles.

One scholar of early Christianity put Constantine's conversion and the legalization of Christianity into perspective:

> It would be a mistake to think that it was Constantine's conversion alone that facilitated the Christianization of the empire. If Christianity had simply continued to grow at the rate it was growing at the time of the emperor's conversion—or even less—it still would have eventually taken over.
>
> (Ehrman 2018: 177)

Constantine gets a lot of the credit for changing the fortunes of Christianity. However, the truth of the matter was that Christianity's fortunes had *already been* changed. They changed because of the tenacity of those who held firm during persecution and the evangelism of ordinary—yet highly committed—people across the Roman Empire and even far beyond.

In the 300s and 400s Christianity spread far and wide, and in several directions. While the Western part of the Roman Empire was being sacked by waves of Goths, Christianity still grew. History shows that many of the Goths were *already* Christian when they infiltrated Rome. Saint **Augustine** (354–430) was deeply troubled by these Germanic invaders. As he wrote what would become the foundational theological texts for Western Christianity, he held tight to a kind of xenophobia—that the invaders were somehow less Christian, less authentic, than the Romans. Augustine's worst fear was coming true—pagans were conquering Rome. However, in reality, they were not all pagans. While Rome did "fall" in 476, it remained staunchly Christian for many centuries. Indeed, Rome is still a profoundly Christian city, receiving around nine million visitors a year, many of whom are there on Christian pilgrimage.

Emperor Constantine was prescient to move the capital city of his empire to a town called Byzantium—in modern-day Turkey—in the year 330. Just decades after he made that move the so-called barbarians ransacked Rome. The city of Byzantium became ground zero for the Byzantine Empire, or the Eastern Roman Empire. Constantine renamed the city, however, in his own honor: Constantinople—the city of Constantine. Most Western history books place less emphasis on the Byzantine Empire because it is today more closely aligned with the Balkans, Greece, Eastern Europe, and Russia.

FIGURE 1.5 *Constantinople (now Istanbul): the great city of Constantine.* Source: *Leo Patrizi/Getty Images.*

Indeed, Moscow is today called the "Third Rome" because it is the new nerve center for **Orthodoxy**—a form of Christianity that few Westerners relate to.

Christianity's advance continued almost unabated until the rise of Islam in the seventh century. Islam posed a considerable challenge to the Christian world, and at several points in history fought mightily for territory and souls. Like Christianity, Islam is an intensely missional faith. It had great success in converting most of the Byzantine Empire—later known as the Ottoman Empire—to Islam.

Ever since the rise of Islam, there has been a back and forth between these two leviathan faiths that today account for over half of the world's population. Around 33 percent of the world's inhabitants are Christians, and around 24 percent of the global population is Muslim. Indeed, from a scholarly perspective, many of the political conflicts happening today in the world have their roots in this fourteen-centuries-long contest between Christianity and Islam. While there are certainly eras where the two faiths coexisted fairly well, in reality there has been an awful lot of discord between these civilizations.

The Russian people adopted Christianity in the year 988. Except for the twentieth-century experiment with Soviet atheism, Russia has been one of the most important epicenters for world Christianity—largely because it is today the torchbearer for Eastern Orthodoxy. Around 10 percent of the world's Christians today identify with some form of Eastern Orthodoxy, whether Russian, Greek, Coptic, Armenian, Ethiopian, or Syrian, for example.

Christianity grew dramatically in the fifteenth century during the conquest of what we now call Latin America. The Spanish and Portuguese took the lead here and subjected nearly an entire continent to Roman Catholicism.

Ironically, the conquistador era was unfolding at the same time as Martin Luther was rebelling against the Roman Catholic Church. His famous "protest" created the "Protestant" movement—which now claims over 40 percent of the world's Christians. Catholicism continues to be the largest form of Christianity in the world, claiming the allegiance of around 50 percent of all Christians. In the aftermath of Luther's Reformation, western Europe was essentially rent into two: a Protestant north and a Catholic south. England, Scandinavia, and northern Germany dominated the Protestant world, while Spain, Italy, Portugal, France, and Poland dominated Roman Catholic civilization.

While the Catholics set their sights on South and Central America, the Protestants—led by the British—set their sights on North America. Here we have one of the great religious experiments in world history: two forms of Christianity took control of two massive territories around the same time. Catholics claimed the south, and Protestants claimed the north. To the present day, there is a sense that Latin America has a Catholic ethos, while North America tends to have a Protestant ethos about it.

The powerful European civilizations came near to dominating the entire world during the years 1500 to the 1950. This period is often called the era of **colonialism**.

FIGURE 1.6 *Greenwich Observatory, London, United Kingdom.* Source: *Joe Daniel Price/ Getty Images.*

The British, in particular, took possession of ports and civilizations all over the world: North America, the Middle East, China, India, Africa, and more. Around the year 1900 it was said that "the sun never sets on the British Empire" because it had land in virtually every time zone in the world. Even the world's basis for measuring time—Greenwich Mean Time (GMT)—is located in the Greenwich neighborhood of London to this very day.

The era of colonialism meant the globalization of Western ideas, Western languages, and of course, Western religion—Christianity. Missionaries, especially the Jesuits, from the Catholic nations set out in the 1500s and tried to convert their empire's subjects to Christ. The Protestants did the same, although they began much later in the early 1700s, with a Danish mission in south India. Over time, however, much of the world—Africa, the Americas, parts of Asia—came to accept Christianity as their religion.

One of the most important developments in the history of Christianity's global expansion happened in the year 1906 in Los Angeles, California. In a very small church led by a poor African American preacher, there was a revival—the Azusa Street Revival—that changed the contours of world Christianity. This revival lasted about a decade but had a profound impact on global Christian missions. With great zeal, Pentecostal missionaries fanned out all over the world and had unimaginable success in Africa. Over time, sub-Saharan Africa became a strongly Christian civilization. Indeed, today, Africa has more Christians than even Latin America. It is now the center of the Christian world.

Meanwhile, the Western world, the old European Christian stronghold, has seen declines in Christian adherence. It is not so much that people have abandoned Christianity; rather, their *practice* of the faith has declined substantially. What was once a powerful, rushing river is now a trickle. Christians from the Caribbean, Brazil, Africa, and Asia are now returning to Europe and North America to try to win people back to the Christian faith, a process known as "reverse missions."

What is most impressive about Christianity is not necessarily that it has the most adherents of all the world's religions. Rather, what is most striking is how *widespread* Christianity is. This fact is understandable, given the long era of European colonialism. Western powers were basically able to plant their flag and faith in most corners of the world. However, once independence started happening in the 1940s—beginning with India—some thought Christianity might die in those postcolonial societies. Rather, the opposite happened. Christianity has flourished, globally, over the last seventy-five years. Over half of Africa is now Christian. Latin America is strongly Christian. North America is still quite Christian. Western Europeans are not so actively practicing the Christian faith anymore, but a majority of them still identify with the Christian faith. Eastern Europe is emerging from the brutal Soviet era, and Christianity is making a huge comeback there. The Pacific region is highly Christian, as are pockets across Asia—for example, the Philippines and South Korea. Some reports show that Christianity is growing steadily in Asia, notably in China, Cambodia, and Nepal.

What Do Christians Believe?

First and foremost, Christians believe in the veracity of the Jewish story. Thus, Christians believe in the God of the Old Testament. They believe that God—Yahweh—is the one and only God. Christians are, therefore, monotheists.

Christians uphold the Old Testament, also known as the Hebrew Bible, as a relatively trustworthy account of the history of the Jewish people. There are disagreements between Christians, such as whether the six "days" of creation were 24-hour periods or perhaps consisted of millions of years. These are in-house debates, however. The big picture is that Christians believe that the story of the Jewish people is crucial for understanding the nature of God, the nature of man, and the reality of the world we inhabit.

Similarly, Christians uphold that the story of the Jewish people is central. God reveals himself through the Jewish story. A small tribe of people rise up and build an empire, only to be conquered and enslaved. They go through cycles of victory and defeat, yet God walks with them through all of the turbulence. The Jews eventually settle down in the land we know today as Israel/Palestine. It is in that land, on that soil, that Jesus Christ—the Jewish Messiah who comes to rescue humankind from its sin—is revealed.

Jesus's life is the dividing point in history: BC means "Before Christ" and AD means "Anno Domini" or "the year of the Lord." Some scholars replace AD/BC with BCE/CE (before common era and common era, respectively) but the principle is the same: Jesus Christ's life divides human history for billions of people in the world.

While Christians uphold the importance of the Old Testament, they believe the latest revelation from God came in the form of God's own son, Jesus the Messiah. Thus, in addition to the Old Testament, the Christian Bible consists of a New Testament that describes the life of Jesus and the work of the early church, for about a century or so after his death—which occurred around the year 33 CE.

Christians believe that the life, teachings, death, and resurrection of Jesus hold the key to Judaism and, indeed, to the human predicament. We are born into this world and, inevitably, we lose our way by falling into temptations. We realize that we cannot save ourselves from our human predicament. We have anxiety and suffering in our lives, and we eventually die and return to dust. The Christian tradition upholds, however, that we are spiritual beings. We are not *merely* meat and bones. Death is not the end of the road for a human being. Rather, human beings will be judged by God, and will spend eternity with God or will spend eternity under God's judgment.

It is a thorny issue in Christian theology about what happens after death. Many Christians believe in purgatory, place where people have to work out their sins to be purified. Some Christians believe heaven is actually on planet Earth, while others believe the "saved" will go to another place called heaven. Similarly, the concept of hell is not so clear. Some argue that hell is complete death—no life after God's judgment. Others argue that hell is a painful eternity where the person suffers forever, as if under an eternal curse from God.

What Christians agree on is that life does not end when one's heart stops beating. There is a continuation. The hope is that people will live good lives so they do not have to worry about the consequences. They will trust in God's grace and in Christ's atoning sacrifice to open a path to heaven and eternal bliss.

Early Christians discussed and debated what they thought was absolutely essential for a Christian to believe. We see evidence of creeds or lists of doctrine in the New Testament itself. During the era of the early church fathers—roughly the late first century to around the year 400 CE—the church discussed and debated the most crucial beliefs. One of the most important creeds—from the Latin word *credo*, I believe—was penned in the city of Nicaea in 325 by over 300 church fathers. It is called the Nicene Creed. About a half-century later, in 381, the bishops of the church gathered again in the city of Constantinople and updated the Nicene Creed. Today, it is known as the Nicene-Constantinopolitan Creed; it is almost universally recognized as the most authoritative list of what Christians should believe:

> We believe in one God, the Father-All-Governing, creator of heaven and earth, of all things visible and invisible.
>
> And [we believe] in one Lord Jesus Christ, the only-begotten Son of God, begotten from the Father before all time, light from light, true God from true God, begotten not created, of the same essence as the Father, through whom all things came into being;
>
> Who for us humans and because of our salvation came down from heaven, and was incarnate by the Holy Spirit and the Virgin Mary and became human;
>
> He was crucified for us under Pontius Pilate, and suffered and was buried, and rose on the third day, according to the Scriptures, and ascended to heaven, and sits at the right hand of the Father, and will come again with glory to judge the living and dead. His kingdom shall have no end.
>
> And [we believe] in the Holy Spirit, the Lord and life-giver, who proceeds from the Father, who is worshiped and glorified together with the Father and Son, who spoke through the prophets.
>
> And [we believe] in one, holy, catholic [universal], and apostolic church. We confess one baptism for the remission of sins. We look forward to the resurrection of the dead and the life of the world to come. Amen.
>
> (Leith 1982: 33)

There are four major topics addressed in the Nicene-Constantinopolitan Creed: God the Father, Jesus Christ, the Holy Spirit, and the church. The first three are known collectively as the Trinity—the unity of three. The concept of the Trinity is crucial, for it concisely summarizes the Christian faith: God the Father sent his son Jesus to the earth to rescue humanity from their sins. While Jesus was on the earth he gave the Holy Spirit to the church, or to those who would trust in him as Lord and as God. The church is the body of believers who take these core teachings seriously in their personal and corporate lives.

Throughout the generations, Christians built upon these core truths: the Bible, the Trinity, and the church to create a large corpus of teachings. As Christianity became enmeshed with the state in the fourth century, we see a blending of Christianity with politics that continues up to present times, although it plays out in different ways. Some nations are rather explicit in their melding of church and state. Others try to separate religion from politics—a task that is almost impossible to do. How can a judicial system make judgments without a common ethic? How can morality be defined without religion? How can religion be extracted from a society that espoused Christianity for centuries? European societies have tried to disestablish Christianity from the state for decades now, but residual Christianity lingers on, and probably will for centuries more. How can a culture possibly redefine its understanding of right and wrong without a vestigial framework for justice, law, morality, and human identity? Some nations tried to completely secularize their society in the twentieth century, but they are now coming back to an explicit embrace of Christianity—this is precisely the case in Russia.

As Christianity is the world's largest religion, it is probably the most diverse. It is difficult to quantify how much Christians share, but there are many beliefs and practices that are espoused by the vast majority of the faithful, such as the core ideas expressed in the great creeds. But there are many others.

For instance, Christians believe in prayer. It was modeled by Jesus and he taught his disciples to do it. A belief in prayer is fundamental to Christianity. A truly Christian life involves regular communication with God. Christians pray for the sick, for the poor, for personal requests, and for all manner of human concerns. The Christian who neglects prayer effectively ceases to communicate with the divine, which results in a spiritually impoverished life. Prayer is the mechanism by which Christians maintain their role in the encounter of human-divine.

Christians believe in regular Bible reading. Prayer is the primary way that Christians communicate with the divine, while Bible reading is the primary way that the divine communicates with the believer. In Bible reading, Christians listen to the stories of old, increase their faith, and receive daily spiritual sustenance from the teachings of God's chosen leaders throughout history.

Christians believe that periods of deprivation, such as fasting, are good for the soul. Suffering produces a sense of dependence upon God that is absent during times of plenty. The Lord fasted, as did the apostles. Fasting and occasional deprivation promote humility, as one is more inclined to depend upon the Lord during those times of sacrifice and want. In the third century, these ideas culminated in the monastic movement, where monks and nuns established monasteries and convents as places of meditation, work, and prayer. Monks and nuns were expected to devote themselves to simple living and to sexual abstinence. It was a sacrifice many found worthwhile as they gave the comforts of family life to serve the Lord. The monastic movement is still alive and well, especially outside of the Western world.

Christians believe in the reality of sin. They do not always agree on what should be called "sin," but there is universal agreement that sin exists, that there is a right and

FIGURE 1.7 *Prayer is a critically important part of Christian life.* Source: *People Images/ Getty Images*.

a wrong way, and that sin is corrosive to the soul. In the medieval world, Christians attempted to systematize sin. They came up with two broad categories: (1) mortal sins are serious, and can separate one from God; and (2) venial sins are lesser, daily sins that are to be avoided, but they do not separate a person from God. Medieval Christians also came up with lists of sins, such as the seven deadly sins: pride, greed, envy, anger, lust, gluttony, and sloth.

While sins can be very harmful to the soul, the Christian faith has a solution for this predicament: forgiveness. Jesus modeled forgiveness most effectively when he prayed to God while on the cross, "Father, forgive them for they know not what they do" (Lk. 23:34). Similarly, Christians are to be people who forgive, readily offering and receiving forgiveness on a routine basis. Forgiveness provides for functional, healthy relationships. Jesus explicitly condemned the sin of unforgiveness in Matthew, "If you forgive other people when they sin against you, your heavenly father will also forgive you. But if you do not forgive others their sins, your Father will not forgive your sins" (Mt. 6:14–15).

Christians believe in regular worship of God. This comes in a vast variety of forms, but typically there is singing, chanting, and various types of music. The corporate worship of Christianity is probably the most visible aspect of the Christian faith. When non-Christians attend a Christian worship service, they will witness two ideas in

FIGURE 1.8 *The Eucharist is an essential sacrament for Christians.* Source: *Hill Street Studios/Getty Images.*

particular: a deep love of God and a relational commitment to one another within the community. When corporate worship is done well, it can be beautiful and attractive to outsiders.

Christians believe in participating in the Eucharist, also known as the Lord's Supper or Communion. The Eucharist was instituted by Jesus just before he was killed. Christians typically take a bit of bread and a sip of wine as they remember the body and blood of Christ as he suffered on the cross. Roman Catholics and Eastern Orthodox Christians participate in the Eucharist often, sometimes even daily for the extremely devout. Protestants—who stem from the sixteenth-century reformer Martin Luther—tend to take the Lord's Supper less frequently, perhaps quarterly or monthly. There are some Protestants who commune weekly, but that is atypical.

Baptism is the entryway by which Christians join the Christian community, or the church. Most Christians baptize people when they are babies or toddlers. Water is usually poured onto the head of the child as a priest or pastor recites passages from the Bible along with prayers. There is a sizeable minority of Christians, however, who administer baptism to believers. Historically, these people were called "anabaptists." They argue that baptism is for the person who can make their own decision to become a Christian. In the New Testament, we do not read about babies being baptized, thus, they feel baptism should be reserved for cognizant believers. Many Christians practice "immersion" baptism, meaning they completely submerge the candidate under water. This method is used by the ancient Orthodox Christians, along with several Protestant groups such as Baptists, Restorationists (Churches of Christ as well as Mormons), and most Pentecostal Christians.

Baptism and Eucharist are usually identified as being two of the Christian sacraments, along with Confirmation (anointing), Confession (penance), Ordination, Marriage, and Extreme Unction (last rites). Not all Christians practice the seven sacraments, but most forms of Christianity hold to a version of them. For instance, in most cases, ordination is reserved for clergy and monastics. Similarly, monastics do not get married. Extreme unction can be performed on any sick person, but it is most commonly associated with someone who may be near death.

Most Christians in the world hold to a Christian calendar. We have already discussed the BC/AD system of dividing time. There are also many other holidays celebrated throughout the Christian year: Advent, Christmas, Pentecost, Lent, Holy Week, Easter, and many more specific holy days. In recent times Christmas (the birth of Christ) seems to have overtaken Easter (the resurrection of Christ) as the most celebrated holiday. Nevertheless, both of them are absolutely critical to Christian liturgical life, and most forms of Christianity encourage their members to *at least* celebrate these two important holidays. For many non-practicing Christians throughout the world—especially the Western world—Christmas and Easter are the two times that they show public support for the church.

When it comes to leadership, Christians espouse a variety of views. Roman Catholics revere the bishop of Rome—the pope—as the denomination's most important leader, by far. Eastern Orthodox Christianity is organized nationally in most cases, so the highest-ranking national bishop is the most important religious authority. Protestant authority is arranged in a host of different ways. For example, Anglicans look to the archbishop of Canterbury, in England, as their authority. Many Protestant churches are organized nationally, similar to the Eastern Orthodox. A large and increasing number of Protestants think much more locally; these churches revere their head minister who might be in charge of a network of churches. Some churches are strictly autonomous and congregational. Authority in these churches is determined by the local, individual church members, whether consisting of a thousand members or even as few as ten. These churches are disconnected from larger denominational institutions and typically steer away from the larger conversations taking place within greater Christendom.

When it comes to ethics and morality, Christian belief is as broad as can be imagined. For instance, let us consider the issues of marriage and sexuality. Some Christians argue that the New Testament is normative: either one remains single or one marries for life. Divorce is rare, and remarriage is essentially forbidden. Intimate relations should only take place within the confines of monogamous marriage between a committed man and woman, who both declare themselves as followers of Christ.

On the other hand, some Christians argue that issues related to marriage and sexuality have evolved significantly in the two millennia since Jesus. Divorce is not only permitted but even encouraged in certain cases. Remarriage is unproblematic. Intimate relations should not be policed by the church, and attempts to do so usually cause more harm than good. Sexuality is seen as fluid, and as long as relations are consensual then they are acceptable to God. This kind of interpretation views tradition as malleable, the Bible as adaptable, and religious authority as susceptible.

Conclusion

It is difficult to ascertain what might be called the genius of Christianity. Obviously, it has succeeded on a larger scale than any religion in history. It claims the allegiance of one-third of the world's population, and it is extremely widespread, ranking as the top religion in Africa, Latin America, North America, Oceania, Eastern Europe, and Western Europe.

Is the genius of Christianity its adaptable nature? In some cases, this might be true. For example, in the case of **Protestantism**, its 40,000 denominations are diverse enough that they offer a theology and ethic for virtually anyone. On the other hand, the largest form of Christianity—Roman Catholicism—is tightly structured. A clergyman in Rome leads it, it has a top-down structure, its liturgies are shared across the entire world, and the doctrines are quite fixed. So perhaps it is inaccurate to speak of Christianity's genius being its flexibility. While Protestantism tends to be easily adaptable, Eastern Orthodoxy and Roman Catholicism are quite structured.

Perhaps the genius of Christianity is its economic success? If this is true, then it would seem that Christianity has succeeded mainly due to political power, such as

FIGURE 1.9 *Christ the Redeemer, Rio de Janeiro, Brazil.* Source: *Jeremy Walker/Getty Images.*

the power of the Roman Empire and the dominance of the Western world in global affairs. Christianity happened to go along for the ride as these civilizations essentially conquered the world.

Or perhaps the genius of Christianity is its most fundamental convictions and teachings: love, compassion, forgiveness. Do unto others as you would have them do unto you. Love your neighbor as yourself. Faith, hope, and love. Perhaps these teachings make the most sense to the most people, and as new generations come along, perhaps these teachings resonate like nothing else can.

Aside from academic analysis, the genius of Christianity, in the minds of Christians, must be in its most central claims: that God sent his son into the world to offer forgiveness, and to save us from ourselves. Death does not have the last word. Since Jesus conquered death, then we can too. These central ideas continue to captivate the hearts and minds of people all over the world.

Further Reading and Online Resources

Daughrity, D. (2016), *Roots: Uncovering Why We Do What We Do in Church*, Abilene, TX: Leafwood Publishers.
Ehrman, B. (2018), *The Triumph of Christianity: How a Forbidden Religion Swept the World*, New York: Simon and Schuster.
MacCulloch, D. (2010), *History of Christianity: The First Three Thousand Years* [Video series], New York: Ambrose Video Publishing.
Wright, N.T. (2018), *Paul: A Biography*, New York: HarperCollins.

References

Ehrman, B. (2018), *The Triumph of Christianity: How a Forbidden Religion Swept the World*, New York: Simon and Schuster.
The Holy Bible, New International Version (1984), Grand Rapids, MI: Zondervan Publishing House.
Leith, J. (1982), *Creeds of the Churches*, Louisville, KY: John Knox Press.

Glossary Terms

Augustine Lived 354 to 430. Probably the most important theologian in Western Christian history. He lived a profligate youth, but converted to Christianity in his early thirties. He wrote several books that are classics in Western Christianity, such as *Confessions* and *City of God*. Augustine's teachings on original sin, justified war, and predestination impacted Western Christianity profoundly. He became bishop of Hippo in the 390s and is often considered the end of the era of the church fathers and the beginning of medieval Christianity. He is a saint in the Roman Catholic tradition.

Colonialism European colonialism began during the age of discovery in the late fifteenth century as European nations traveled the world in search of expanding their influence. From the late fourteenth to the mid-twentieth century, European nations exerted tremendous power over world affairs and became exceedingly wealthy in comparison with most other parts of the world. Colonialism is debated by scholars today due to profound European influence on major spheres of human civilization such as economics, government, politics, language, religion, health care, and technology.

Constantine the Great Emperor of the Roman Empire from 306 to his death in 337. He is considered the first Christian emperor of the Roman Empire. He dramatically changed Christianity's fortunes, from a persecuted faith to a favored faith. He took a leading role at the Council of Nicea in 325, and shaped the future of Christianity's relations with government for centuries to come.

Orthodoxy A family of Christian churches that are typically nation-based, for example, Greece, Romanian, Coptic (Egypt), Ethiopian, Syrian, Armenian. The largest Orthodox body is the Russian Orthodox Church, with nearly 100 million members. The Orthodox churches comprise around 10 percent of the world's Christians. They are the smallest of the three main families of churches: Roman Catholic, Protestant, and Orthodox.

Protestantism A loosely connected family of churches that began with the protests of Martin Luther, in the city of Wittenberg, in modern-day Germany. Protestants combined comprise around 40 percent of the world's Christians. They vary greatly in belief in practice but are united in the shared identity of being offshoots of the sixteenth-century Protestant Reformations.

Roman Catholic Church The largest Christian denomination in the world, with around 1.2 billion members in the world. Around half of the world's Christians are Roman Catholics. The church is based in the small nation-state of Vatican City, a neighborhood within the city of Rome. It is led by the bishop of Rome, also known as the pope.

2

Jesus: A Jewish Messiah

Nicholas J. Zola

The Anointed One

Jesus Christ is not the son of Joseph Christ and Mary Christ. "Christ" is a title, not a last name; it is an affirmation. A "Christ"-ian is one who declares that Jesus is the Christ, which comes from the Greek word *christos*, itself a translation of the Hebrew word *māšîaḥ*, or "messiah." Both terms literally mean "anointed one," that is, one over whom oil has been poured; however, Jesus the Oil-Head is not especially clearer. An explanation of the term and its historic application to Jesus is in order.

In the **Hebrew Bible** (the scriptures of the Jewish people), the term "messiah" primarily refers to a king (but sometimes to a priest and possibly to a prophet). An anointed one is a leader who has been expressly chosen or set apart. In a special ceremony in 1 Samuel 16, Samuel the prophet anoints a young David as king over Israel by pouring a horn of oil over him in the presence of his family. This act sets David apart as a leader. Nathan the prophet later confirms David's anointing with words from Yahweh (the Jewish God) that set the future messianic expectation in motion: "your throne shall be established forever" (2 Sam. 7:16, NRSV). Thus the later hope arises—particularly in times of distress—that a descendant of David, or a "messiah," would arrive to deliver the Jewish people.

There was, however, no consensus among Jews in the times leading up to Jesus regarding what this messiah would look like or do (or even if he would indeed be a son of David). After Babylon destroyed the Jewish temple in 586 BCE and brought the Jews into exile, there was no longer a Davidic king on the throne. In an ironic twist, when the Persians defeated the Babylonians and allowed the Jews to return home and rebuild their temple, one Jewish prophet referred to Cyrus—the king of Persia—as Yahweh's "messiah" (Isa. 45:1). The rebuilding of the temple initiated what we now call the **Second Temple Period**, during which new expectations for a messiah arose,

FIGURE 2.1 *A Byzantine silver plate from c. 630 CE depicting the prophet Samuel anointing a young David with oil while David's father and two of his brothers observe (1 Sam. 16:13).* Source: *Metropolitan Museum of Art. Public Domain.*

especially after first the Greeks and then the Romans took over Judaea. Subjugation to a foreign power makes a messianic deliverer an appealing image.

As a result, various messianic expectations emerged. Some texts imagined a royal military messiah who would liberate the people once again (*Psalms of Solomon* 17). Other texts looked forward instead to a priestly or prophetic messiah who would lead the nation back to holiness (4Q541 in the **Dead Sea Scrolls**). Some texts combined the two ideas and expected two messiahs, a priestly messiah descended from Aaron and a kingly messiah descended from David (Community Rule, 1QS 9:11). In the first century CE, the Jewish historian **Josephus** reported more than one ill-fated figure who fashioned

FIGURE 2.2 *The caves near Qumran, where locals found the Dead Sea Scrolls, an unparalleled collection of Jewish manuscripts first discovered in 1947 and now hailed as one of the greatest archaeological finds of the twentieth century. The Dead Sea Scrolls contain texts with multiple messianic expectations.* Source: Andy Wall.

himself as a king and gathered groups of people in the wilderness for rebellion, sometimes claiming miraculous feats such as parting the Jordan river (*Ant.* 17.273–4, 278–80; 20.97). When the Romans tragically destroyed the temple again in 70 CE, it stirred one Jewish text to reimagine a militaristic offspring of David who would rise up as a messianic lion of Judah and deliver judgment upon the oppressive eagle (*4 Ezra* 12).

Suffice it to say, expectations for a coming Jewish messiah were neither uniform nor universal. It is ironic that Jesus, perhaps the most famous Jew to be called a messiah, is not in obvious continuity with any of these known expectations. This disjunction returns us to our initial question: why then do Christians hail Jesus as the Christ?

Jesus the Anointed One

Jesus of Nazareth was a Jewish man born around 4 BCE and executed in Jerusalem by the Romans around 30 CE. The earliest surviving accounts of his life have come to be known as Gospels (meaning "good news"), four of which became part of the Christian

FIGURE 2.3 *The Arch of Titus in Rome, erected in 81 CE, depicting Titus' destruction of the Jerusalem temple in 70 CE to signify Rome's victory in the Jewish–Roman War; the panel relief highlights the spoils of war, including the Jewish menorah. The catastrophic destruction caused some Jews to renew their messianic expectations. Source: Nicholas J. Zola.*

collection of sacred writings, or the **New Testament**. All four of these, in one way or another, affirm that Jesus is the Messiah. The question is what that meant to the earliest followers of Jesus.

To answer that question, we must explore what each of the four Gospels says about Jesus. There are also other Gospels outside of the New Testament, but scholars generally agree that these offer us little if any reliable information on Jesus (save perhaps the Gospel of Thomas). So our focus will be on the canonical Gospels. First we will look at the story that each one tells individually; then we will consider their collective memory of Jesus. A brief overview of their origins will help set the stage.

The four Gospels were written roughly between 70 and 100 CE, about forty to seventy years after the death of Jesus. Although traditionally attributed to four specific

FIGURE 2.4 *A medieval illustration of the authors of the four Gospels (called Evangelists) from an Armenian Gospel book,* c. *1300.* Source: *Metropolitan Museum of Art. Public Domain.*

individuals (Matthew, Mark, Luke, and John) all four are technically anonymous, in that the authors never name themselves within their respective works. Only one of the four specifically claims to originate with an eyewitness of Jesus (Jn 19:35; 21:24). Another explicitly claims *not* to originate with an eyewitness but to have carefully investigated the testimony of eyewitnesses (Lk. 1:1–4). The other two Gospels make no internal claims about their origins; there is an early church tradition that Matthew was a **disciple** of Jesus but that Mark was not. While their outlines are broadly similar, each Gospel paints its own messianic portrait of Jesus. Since scholars generally agree that Mark was written first of the four, we will begin there.

Mark's Jesus: A Messiah Who Suffers

Mark's story of Jesus begins and ends abruptly. It presumes you know more than it tells you. It also presumes you know less than you think. The prevailing question lurking behind the scenes is, "Who is Jesus?" The answer, of course, is the messiah. But the second question hovering just beyond it is, "What kind of messiah?" Mark's answer confounds both the disciples (Jesus's followers) and the presumed reader.

There is thematic tension in how Mark's Jesus simultaneously reveals and conceals his identity. Scholars have come to refer to this dichotomy as the "messianic secret" motif. On the one hand, Jesus repeatedly demonstrates his power: power to heal diseases (Mk 2:29–34), to control the weather (4:35–41), to make food appear from thin air (6:30–44), even to raise the dead (5:35–43). These "powers" (which is the Greek word for "miracles") are to convey something of who Jesus is. A first-century Jew expecting a kingly messiah coming to free the people from their Roman overlords might be very pleased with such displays. The army is hungry? Jesus could provide. A soldier is wounded? Jesus could heal. The opposing force is advancing? Jesus could pelt them with hail. A fighter dies in battle? Jesus could bring him back to life. Although Jesus turns out to be different, at first blush, he could be the ultimate general. The Romans would not stand a chance.

On the other hand, there is a puzzling pattern of secrecy that pervades this Gospel as well. After Jesus miraculously feeds the five thousand gathered in the wilderness (and recall Josephus' messianic potentials who gathered a group in the wilderness), he immediately disperses the crowd, sends his disciples away in a boat, and goes off alone to pray (Mk 6:45–6)—hardly the actions of a would-be king. After he raises a dead little girl to life, he strictly orders her family to say nothing to anyone (5:43). When he drives out demons, he does not allow them to speak, precisely because they know who he is (1:34). Jesus apparently does not want his reputation to spread, even while he performs grand acts that reveal his identity.

No group is slower to appreciate the true identity of Jesus in Mark than the disciples themselves. In scene after scene, as Jesus offers clues to his messianic status, the disciples do not grasp it. They have eyes but do not see (Mk 4:12; 8:18; cf. Isa. 6:9–10). Halfway through the narrative, the Gospel reaches a climactic turning point when Peter responds to Jesus's question, "Who do you say that I am?" with the penetrative reply, "You are the messiah" (Mk 8:29). It would appear at that moment that the disciples have finally understood; but the scene does not end there. The question pivots immediately to what *kind* of messiah Jesus is, and here the disciples again fail to discern. Jesus teaches them that he must undergo great suffering, be rejected by the Jewish religious leaders, and ultimately be killed (and then rise again, but they seem to miss this part). Peter will have none of it. He rebukes Jesus, but Jesus reverses the rebuke:

Get behind me, Satan! For you are setting your mind not on divine things but on human things. […] If any want to become my followers, let them deny themselves and take up their cross and follow me. For those who want to save their life will lose it, and those who lose their life for my sake, and for the sake of the gospel, will save it.

(Mk 8:33–5)

The disciples are ready to endorse Jesus the victor. They are not eager to fall behind Jesus the "suffering servant," language drawn from Isaiah 52:13–53:12, which describes a righteous servant who will make many righteous by bearing their iniquities and dying unjustly in suffering, shame, and silence. The earliest Christians employed such images to explain Jesus's great self-sacrificial act (e.g., Acts 8:32–3). Here in Mark, Jesus is essentially retorting, "Peter, you don't understand. Yes, I'm the messiah, but not the one you were looking for."

In Mark, Jesus wants to provide his own definition of messiah. He seems aware that his reputation could quickly surpass him (indeed, it does in some places; cf. Mk 1:45). Jesus does not want potential messianic presumptions to derail his mission. Jesus is not that kind of messiah. Yes, he is waging a messianic war, but it is a spiritual contest against the dark forces that plague this world—not against Rome. Yes, he envisions a messianic kingdom, but one whose most honored citizens are those who give up their lives to serve others—not who lord it over their subjects. Yes, he is gathering a messianic following, but it is a mass of farmers and fishers, of tax collectors and sinners—not of soldiers. He is a messiah who "came not to be served but to serve, and to give his life as a ransom for many" (Mk 10:45), and he expects his followers to do the same: "whoever wishes to be first among you must be slave of all" (10:44).

Jesus's grand messianic reversal culminates in his death by crucifixion, a shameful punishment reserved in Roman culture for slaves and criminals. No one expected a *dead* messiah. Yet the astute reader of Mark will perceive that the entire Gospel has been leading to the cross. Like the disciples, the reader is tempted early on to see only Jesus's powers, not his path. But the Crucifixion is the defining event of

FIGURE 2.5 *Although the exact location of Jesus's burial is unknown, some consider this ancient rock-cut tomb in Jerusalem, called the Garden Tomb, to be similar to how Jesus's tomb may have appeared. According to the Gospels, a large round stone was rolled over the entrance to Jesus's tomb to seal it.* Source: Andrew Agerbak.

Jesus's messiahship. Jesus is a messiah who gives up his life for others. Even as his executioners mock him with sarcasm, "Let the Messiah, the King of Israel, come down from the cross now, so that we may see and believe" (Mk 15:32), he silently subjects himself to their will. He is the suffering servant to his last breath.

After the Crucifixion, the disciples are despondent and defeated. They have followed a failed messiah. But Mark does not end the story here. In the last scene, some of the female disciples return to Jesus's tomb to anoint his body, only to discover the tomb is empty. A divine messenger tells them Jesus has risen and gone ahead of them back to Galilee. Galilee, of course, is where the story began, and some interpret this angelic announcement as Mark's way of guiding the reader back to the beginning of the Gospel, now with eyes that see. The Gospel of Mark instructs the would-be follower of Jesus that suffering is part of the path of discipleship from the beginning and that anyone who wants to follow Jesus as messiah must follow him all the way to the cross. Jesus is not the messiah some desired him to be. Mark's only question left for the reader now is, "Will you follow *this* messiah?"

Mark's narrative provides a helpful overview of the core Jesus story. Each of the successive Gospels adds fresh color to Mark's baseline portrait, highlighting other features of Jesus's messianic ministry. We will move next to the Gospel of Matthew, where we encounter a Jesus founded on Mark's outline, but with added dimensions.

Matthew's Jesus: A Messiah for the Jewish People

Unlike Mark, the Gospel of Matthew opens its narrative with a rather slow launch: an extended genealogy listing forty-two generations from Abraham, the father of the Jewish people, to Jesus (cf. 1 Chron. 1–9). In the middle, the genealogy pivots around King David, who (as we have seen) is the origin of the messianic promise. To be the "son of David" is essentially to be a messiah (Mt. 1:1; cf. Rom. 1:3).

From there Matthew moves directly into a play by play of Jesus's birth, highlighting how each scene echoes some moment in Jewish scripture. The combination of a genealogy that begins with Abraham and over a dozen explicit references to prophetic fulfillment are not insignificant facets of Matthew's approach to the Jesus story. They likely indicate this Gospel's primarily Jewish audience and its concern for continuity with the Jewish scriptural narrative. While Matthew takes over much of Mark's characterization of Jesus, there is one notable enhancement: Matthew's Jesus is a distinctly Jewish messiah.

This is not to say, of course, that Mark's Jesus was not Jewish, since he most definitely was. But Mark did not emphasize that aspect of Jesus's identity to the degree that Matthew does, probably because Mark's audience was not Jewish (note Mk 7:3–4). Matthew, while not disagreeing with the essence of Mark's portrait, is appealing to a different community, one where the question of how Jesus functions as the *Jewish* Messiah is still a live question. Matthew's answer is that as Messiah, Jesus "fulfills" the Jewish law.

The programmatic section of Matthew's Gospel is Jesus's so-called Sermon on the Mount (Mt. 5–7), where Jesus lays out his vision for discipleship and life in God's kingdom. Most of this teaching material is not found in Mark, so it supplements the Jesus we have met thus far. In the sermon, we encounter a Jesus who is explicit about the role of the Jewish law in his mission: "Do not think that I have come to abolish the law or the prophets; I have come not to abolish but to fulfill. For truly I tell you […] not one letter, not one stroke of a letter will pass from the law until all is accomplished" (Mt. 5:17–18). This opening gambit serves as Matthew's declaration to those who would suggest that somehow Jesus's messiahship is incompatible with the current practicing of Jewish law (cf. Mk 7:19). The ensuing sections of the sermon address this point in detail.

Jesus next reviews some classic statements of Jewish law and reevaluates them in the light of his messianic ethic. He employs a repeated formula, "You have heard it said …, but I say to you …, " whereby he introduces his refinement of the commandment. Here are some paraphrased examples (see Mt. 5:21–48): "You've heard it said, 'Don't murder,' but I say to you, 'Don't even be angry with one another.'" Or again, "You've heard it said, 'Don't commit adultery,' but I say to you, 'Don't even look lustfully at another.'" Or, "You've heard it said, 'Don't break an oath,' but I say to you, 'Don't make an oath at all. Just do what you say.'" Or perhaps the most difficult, "You've heard it said, 'Do back to others what they did to you,' but I say to you, 'Do for others what you wish they would do for you.'"

Matthew would not say Jesus is "reinterpreting" the law here. Matthew would call it "fulfilling" the law, that is, completing or restoring the commandments to their full and original intent. Like Mark's Jesus, Matthew's Jesus despises religious hypocrisy. God, he says, desires "mercy and not sacrifice" (a citation of Hos. 6:6, which Jesus cites twice in Mt. 9:13 and 12:7, but not in any other Gospel). The heart of the Jewish law, Jesus says, is justice and mercy and faith, not tithes; one should practice the former without neglecting the latter (Mt. 23:23). Thus, the Jesus we meet in Matthew is a deeply Jewish messiah who emphasizes the heart of the law as the way to fulfill the letter of the law.

Again, this messiah defies some traditional expectations. He does not amass honor, he blesses the poor in spirit (Mt. 5:3). He does not seek power, he extols the meek (5:4). He does not attack his enemies, he loves and prays for them (5:44). He does not persecute his opposition, he praises peacemakers as children of God (5:9). All of these features, argues Matthew, are in keeping with where the Jewish scriptures have been pointing all along. Jesus fulfills the Jewish law, even if his contemporaries did not interpret it that way.

The Gospel of Matthew ends much as Mark's did, but with one significant addendum: an appearance of the resurrected Jesus. While Mark ended with the empty tomb, in Matthew the disciples return to Galilee and encounter the risen Jesus, who leaves them with directions to bring his teachings to all nations, Jews and **Gentiles** alike (Mt. 28:18–20). This commission sets the stage for the next Gospel we will consider, the Gospel of Luke.

Luke's Jesus: A Messiah for All People

The Gospel of Luke begins much like the Gospel of Matthew, with a birth narrative and a genealogy. But the birth narrative features Mary (Jesus's mother) as the main character instead of Joseph (Matthew's focus) and the genealogy traces Jesus's lineage not just to Abraham (the father of the Jews) but all the way back to Adam (the father of humanity). These differences illustrate Luke's broader scope and major theme: Jesus is the Messiah for all people, especially the marginalized.

As in Matthew, there is an early programmatic sermon in Luke. But it is not a sermon on a mount, it is a sermon in a synagogue, in Jesus's hometown of Nazareth. While this scene partially appears in Mark and Matthew as well, Luke expands it considerably and relocates it to the beginning of Jesus's public ministry (Lk. 4:14–30; cf. Mk 6:1–6; Mt. 13:54–8). Luke uses the sermon to define Jesus's core message.

Jesus begins his address with a reading from Isaiah 61:1–2, which he applies to himself. The passage describes one who has been "anointed" (using the same Greek root as *christos*) to bring good news to the poor, recovery of sight to the blind, and freedom to the oppressed. These are messianic invocations. Every eye in the synagogue is upon Jesus, but the lesson takes an unexpected turn. Instead of working to win the crowd over, Jesus recounts two stories of prophets from the Jewish scriptures (Elijah and Elisha) who, rather than aiding local Israelites, went outside the borders of Israel and ministered to non-Jews. This message so infuriates the crowd that they initiate the process of stoning Jesus (who manages to slip away). They are enraged because they have understood Jesus's implication. Jesus has come not (just) for the children of Israel, he has come to reach the outsiders, the oppressed, and the outcasts. Luke repositions this sermon as Jesus's public debut because it encapsulates who Jesus is in this Gospel: "a light for revelation to the Gentiles" (Lk. 2:32; cf. Isa. 49:6). God is enacting the salvation of all people through Jesus the Jewish Messiah.

One of Jesus's primary teaching techniques is telling parables. Parables are short metaphorical stories, built upon daily life, but propped up by halting truths. Mark, Matthew, and Luke contain well over three dozen parables between them, but there is a parable unique to Luke that also exemplifies Jesus's ministry in this Gospel. In Luke 10:25–37, a lawyer queries Jesus on what is necessary to inherit eternal life. The two agree that the whole of Jewish law can be summed up in two directives: to love the Lord your God with all you heart, soul, strength, and mind; and to love your neighbor as yourself (Lk. 10:27; cf. Mk 12:28–34; Mt. 22:34–40). Then the lawyer asks a follow-up question: "And who is my neighbor?" (Lk. 10:29). That is, whom do I have to love? Jesus answers with a story.

The story concerns a Jew traveling from Jerusalem to Jericho, whom thieves ambush and leave for dead. First a priest and then a Levite (both Jews with special temple functions) walk by, but neither stops to help the dying man. Then a Samaritan comes along. First-century Jews and Samaritans historically despised and avoided each other. Paradoxically, it is the Samaritan who shows the Jewish stranger mercy. The Samaritan dresses his wounds, ferries him to shelter, and pays for his extended recovery. Jesus then asks the lawyer which passerby acted as a neighbor to the man in need. The lawyer offers a roundabout answer: "The one who showed him mercy." Jesus rejoinders, "Go and do likewise" (Lk. 10:37).

Jesus has reversed the lawyer's question. The lawyer asks, "Who is my neighbor?" in hopes of limiting his circle of care. Jesus asks, "Who was a neighbor?" to redefine a neighbor as one who gives care, not one who receives it. This parable lies at the heart of Luke. In Luke, Jesus is a messiah who reaches out to the poor, the crippled, the lame, and the blind (Lk. 14:13). He is a messiah with female disciples as well as male (8:2–3). He is a messiah who literally receives his anointing from the tears and ointment of a sexually promiscuous woman (7:38). It is no coincidence that the star of Jesus's most famous parable in Luke is not a Jew at all but a Samaritan outsider. Luke's Jesus reaches the unreached.

Luke also has a slightly different take on the end of Jesus's life. Mark and Matthew include one spoken line from Jesus on the cross: "My God, my God, why have you forsaken me?," a quotation from Psalm 22:1, meant to stress Jesus's self-sacrificial suffering. Luke prefers to accentuate the care Jesus shows to his detractors, even to his last breath. As the soldiers beneath him barter for his clothes he prays for their forgiveness (Lk. 23:34); to the criminal crucified next to him he offers mercy (23:43); his final cry comes not from Psalm 22:1 but Psalm 31:5: "Father, into your hands I commend my spirit" (Lk. 23:46). For a man dying of asphyxiation (which is how crucifixion typically ends), Jesus is remarkably present and intentional.

In the Gospel of Luke, Jesus is the culmination of a grand salvific plan for all people. He makes this clear in his post-resurrection pep talk to his disciples:

> "These are my words that I spoke to you while I was still with you—that everything written about me in the law of Moses, the prophets, and the psalms must be fulfilled." Then he opened their minds to understand the scriptures, and he said to them, "Thus it is written, that the Messiah is to suffer and to rise from the dead on the third day, and that repentance and forgiveness of sins is to be proclaimed in his name to all nations, beginning from Jerusalem. You are witnesses of these things."
> (Lk. 24:44–8)

These final lines summarize how Luke envisions Jesus's messianic role. Jesus never loses sight of the cosmic plan. He is the Messiah for all people. As we shall see, this intentionality is augmented even further in the Gospel of John, our final Gospel to cover.

John's Jesus: A Messiah Who Reveals the Father

The Gospel of John paints a noticeably different portrait of Jesus than the composite picture we have glimpsed in Mark, Matthew, and Luke (which are collectively called the **Synoptic Gospels** due to their overt similarities). John's Jesus does not speak in parables or perform exorcisms. He executes a limited number of miracles, which John prefers to call "signs." The signs point to who Jesus is, and John includes an explicit purpose statement explaining their function: "these [signs] are written so that you may come to believe that Jesus is the Messiah, the Son of God, and that through believing you may have life in his name" (Jn 20:31). Such is the messianic function of John's Gospel as a whole.

John introduces its main themes through a prologue, whose opening line is one of the more profound biblical assertions: "In the beginning was the Word, and the Word was with God, and the Word was God. [...] All things came into being through him" (Jn 1:1, 3). John draws on an ancient Jewish tradition that God created the world through "lady wisdom" (Prov. 8:22–31), except here John substitutes wisdom with the philosophical concept of the "word" (*logos* in Greek, also meaning "reason"). The Word is the preexistent Jesus, through whom God fashioned all of creation and spoke it into existence (see Gen. 1). What happens next is remarkable: the Word becomes flesh (what Christians call the incarnation) and dwells within creation itself (Jn 1:14). According to John, Jesus becomes human specifically to make God known to the world (1:18), which is the culminating point of the prologue. In the Gospel of John, Jesus is the messianic Son who reveals God the Father.

For one of Jesus's more revelatory signs, he heals a man born blind (Jn 9:1–41). This healing functions archetypically in this Gospel. The blind can see Jesus for who he really is, whereas those with perfect vision are blind to his messianic status (9:39). Accordingly, the so-called "messianic secret" (Jesus's penchant in the Synoptics for keeping his identity under wraps) is entirely missing in John, replaced by what we might call a "messianic broadcast." On at least seven occasions, John's Jesus makes public "I am" statements that reveal the contours of his messianic mission: "I am the bread of life" (6:35); "I am the light of the world" (8:12); "I am the good shepherd"

FIGURE 2.6 *A wall painting from the church of San Baudelio in Spain depicts Jesus healing the blind man (Jn 9) and raising Lazarus from the dead (Jn 11), c. early twelfth century.* Source: *Metropolitan Museum of Art. Public Domain.*

(10:11); "I am the resurrection" (11:25); "I am the way, the truth, and the life" (14:6); and so forth. Those in the narrative who grasp these metaphors are understood to walk in the light, not in the darkness; they receive the life Jesus offers.

Like the other three Gospels, John ends with the death and resurrection of Jesus. But once again, the flavor is different. In John, Jesus is always in control of his fate; a recurring motif is that Jesus's "hour had not yet come" until he decides that it has (see Jn 2:4; 7:30; 8:20; 12:23; etc.). John's Gospel devotes almost its entire second half to the last week of Jesus's life and the arrival of that "hour." (Mark's Gospel devotes a third of its space to the same time span, which was itself considerable.) The proportion of the narrative that John sets aside indicates how integral—and distinctive—these final events are to the story. When Jesus prays his final prayer before his crucifixion, he does not ask God to remove his cup of suffering (as in Mark); he embraces it and prays instead for the unity of his future followers (Jn 12:27–8; 17:1–26). When soldiers come to arrest Jesus in the garden, his disciples do not flee; he negotiates for their release (Jn 18:1–12). When Pilate interrogates him, he reveals directly that his "kingdom is not from this world" (18:36). Jesus is in control; he knows his hour has come (13:1).

Perhaps the most instructive difference between John and the Synoptics is how John characterizes the cross itself. It is not Jesus's shame but his glory; the cross represents triumph, not defeat. Jesus's final words as he is lifted up are not "My God, my God, why have you forsaken me?" (as in Mark and Matthew) or even "Father, into your hands I commend my spirit" (as in Luke) but the victorious cry "It is finished!" (Jn 19:30; a single word in Greek: *tetelestai*). Jesus has accomplished what he came to do. The Son is returning to the Father who sent him, having made him known. Those who recognize the Son's messianic status will have a place in the Father's home forever (Jn 14:2–3).

The Memory of the Anointed One

Thus concludes our foray into the messianic landscape of the four canonical Gospels. Each of these accounts manifestly understands Jesus as a Jewish messiah, but each with its own approach and focus. At times they converge, at other times they diverge, like four artists' portraits of a single figure, each painted from a different perspective. The question naturally arises: how accurate are these Gospels? Do they actually give us direct access to the mind of Jesus, to the things he really said and did? Did Jesus himself think that he was the Messiah?

The efforts to distill undiluted history from the Gospels have come to be called "the quest for the historical Jesus." Whole eras and scholarly careers have been devoted to such investigations, with various and competing results. In short, it is difficult to answer modern historical questions with our current sources of information. Ancient historiographers wrote biography differently than we do today. They were far less concerned with chronology and minute detail; they focused on anecdotes and key events that conveyed the subject's character. There was an historical core, with rhetorical flexibility in its recounting.

Consequently, the Gospels often cannot answer the historical questions modern scholars like to pose. They are not designed to do so. If it is the *ipsissima verba* (very words) of Jesus that we are after, the Gospels by their nature cannot deliver. They are impressionist paintings, not video-camera diaries. If we are content with the *ipsissima vox* (very voice) of Jesus, this is what the Gospels, at least insofar as their genre is concerned, were written to supply. They report what Jesus was remembered for.

While scholars may never agree completely on the historical accuracy of the Gospels, most can agree on a larger point: the canonical Gospels represent the earliest surviving collective memories about Jesus from his followers. Our sources cannot easily tell us who Jesus thought he was, because he did not write them. Nor can they tell us precisely what he did and said in every instance and exact order, because they are not written at that level of detail. But they can tell us who his first known adherents thought he was and what they remembered he did and said. And on at least one point they agree: the earliest believers (who were virtually all Jewish) understood Jesus as a Jewish messiah.

FIGURE 2.7 *A diptych from early eighteenth-century Ethiopia illustrating Jesus crucified on the right panel (with Mary and John in sorrow on either side) and Jesus resurrected in triumph on the left panel (raising Adam and Eve to symbolize his victory over death).* Source: Metropolitan Museum of Art, Public Domain Image.

The Gospels also agree on a related point: the Romans executed Jesus as a messiah, that is, as a king of the Jews. Not only is this the notice of his crime posted over the cross in all four Gospels (Mt. 27:37; Mk 15:26; Lk. 23:38; Jn 19:19) but it is also the line of questioning that the Roman governor Pilate pursues when deciding Jesus's fate. In all four Gospels, Pilate asks directly whether Jesus fashions himself as the king of the Jews (Mt. 27:11; Mk 15:2; Lk. 23:3; Jn 18:33). This is an overtly messianic charge, as Jesus's accusers in Luke make clear: "We found this man perverting our nation, forbidding us to pay taxes to the emperor, and saying that he himself is the Messiah, a king" (Lk. 23:2). In John, the repercussions of Jesus's alleged sedition are inescapable: "If you release this man, you are no friend of the emperor. Everyone who claims to be a king sets himself against the emperor" (Jn 19:12). Thus, the earliest followers of Jesus not only understood him to be the Messiah, they also remembered him as having been crucified specifically for that reason.

About thirty years after Pilate's trial of Jesus, early Christians remembered another trial taking place: Paul before Governor Festus. Paul was on trial for his faith in Jesus, but Festus was apparently surprised by the charges: "When the accusers stood up, they did not charge him with any of the crimes that I was expecting. Instead they had certain points of disagreement with him about their own religion and about a certain Jesus, who had died, but whom Paul asserted to be alive" (Acts 25:18–19). There is subtle humor embedded in this conclusive statement. Paul and his Jewish accusers both agree on one thing: Jesus died. Where they differ is that Paul also thinks Jesus is alive. This is the claim that encapsulates Christianity: Jesus the crucified Jewish Messiah is alive again. Such is what it means for a "Christ"-ian to claim that Jesus is the Christ.

Further Reading and Online Resources

Allison, D.C. (2009), *The Historical Christ and the Theological Jesus*, Grand Rapids, MI: Eerdmans.

Borg, M.J. and N.T. Wright (1999), *The Meaning of Jesus: Two Visions*, San Francisco: HarperOne.

Charlesworth, J.H., ed. (1992), *The Messiah: Developments in Earliest Judaism and Christianity*, Minneapolis, MN: Fortress.

Collins, J.J. (2010), *The Scepter and the Star: Messianism in Light of the Dead Sea Scrolls*, 2nd edn., Grand Rapids, MI: Eerdmans.

Fisk, B.N. (2011), *A Hitchhiker's Guide to Jesus: Reading the Gospels on the Ground*, Grand Rapids, MI: Baker Academic.

Fredriksen, P. (2000), *From Jesus to Christ: The Origins of the New Testament Images of Christ*, 2nd edn., New Haven, CT: Yale University Press.

Keener, C.S. (2019), *Christobiography: Memory, History and the Reliability of the Gospels*, Grand Rapids, MI: Eerdmans.

Levine, A.-J. (2006), *The Misunderstood Jew: The Church and the Scandal of the Jewish Jesus*, San Francisco: HarperOne.

Wenham, D. and S. Walton (2011), *Exploring the New Testament*, vol. 1, *A Guide to the Gospels & Acts*, 2nd edn., Downers Grove, IL: IVP Academic.

Glossary Terms

Dead Sea Scrolls An unparalleled collection of Jewish manuscripts first discovered in 1947 in caves near the Dead Sea. The manuscripts represent both biblical texts (dating one thousand years older than the next oldest copies) and sectarian documents (revealing the great diversity of Second Temple Judaism). They were likely produced by a group of Essenes living in nearby Qumran, who split off from mainline Jewish society in protest over religious corruption.

Disciple Literally, a "learner" or student of a teacher; in a Jewish context, the followers of a rabbi; in the New Testament, the followers of Jesus.

Gentiles Those who are not Jews; from the Latin word for "nations," that is, those who are part of the nations surrounding the Jews (from a Jewish perspective).

Hebrew Bible The collection of holy writings, or scriptures, of the Jewish people, referred to by Christians as the Old Testament. It is traditionally divided into three parts: the Torah (Law), the Nevi'im (Prophets), and the Ketuvim (Writings).

Josephus A first-century CE Jewish historian who wrote about the history of the Jewish people and in particular the Jewish revolt against Rome of 66–70 CE. Initially a leader in the Jewish army, Josephus was captured by the Roman general Vespasian, with whom he soon found favor after predicting that Vespasian would become the next emperor of Rome. Josephus's writings, while hardly neutral, are still crucial for understanding this period of Second Temple Judaism.

New Testament The Christian collection of holy writings, composed by followers of Jesus and comprising several genres, including narratives (the Gospels and Acts), letters (from Paul and others), and an apocalypse (Revelation). Most of the documents were written between c. 65 and 125 CE, although the collection did not solidify until the mid-fourth century.

Second Temple Period The period initiated when the Jews returned to Jerusalem from exile and rebuilt their temple in 515 BCE (the Babylonians having destroyed it in 586 BCE—hence the *second* temple). This period produced significant literature and events that are vital for understanding both early Judaism and early Christianity, including the Greek translation of the Hebrew Bible (called the Septuagint), the production of the Dead Sea Scrolls, and the Maccabean Revolt. Scholars mark the end of the Second Temple Period with the Roman destruction of Jerusalem in 70 CE (and again in 135 CE).

Synoptic Gospels Because their structure and language are so similar, scholars refer to the first three Gospels in the New Testament (Matthew, Mark, and Luke) as the Synoptic Gospels (*synoptic* indicating they can be "seen together"). The parallels are so close that most scholars conclude these three Gospels are literarily dependent on one another in some way, although each has unique material and its own perspective. The Gospel of John stands apart from the Synoptics both in content and style.

3

The Bible: How Christians Use Their Text

Craig W.C. Ginn

Introduction

The Bible is a, if not the most, renowned literary work in the world. Guinness World Records refers to the Bible as "the world's best-selling and most widely distributed book" (Guinness World Records 2020). *A History of the Bible* (2019) by Oxford professor John Barton is subtitled, *The Most Influential Book of all Time*. The influence of the Bible is especially far-reaching in Western culture, impacting theology, philosophy, literature, music, ethics, law, politics, education, and entertainment. In the American context the influence of the Bible is present almost everywhere, from the mundane use on bumper stickers, T-shirts, and signage held up at football games, to the venerated usage on the Martin Luther King Jr. memorial inscribed with the ethical call to justice and righteousness inspired by the biblical prophet Amos. But what is the Bible? How did it come to be the sacred text of Christians, and how do Christians make use of it?

This article will explore the nature and purpose of the Bible in the Christian tradition. Various questions will be explored: What is the Bible? How did writings from the two religious traditions of Judaism and Christianity get merged into one book? Why do Christians take ownership of the Bible, believing that the merged book belongs to them? And how do Christians use the Bible? How was it used by the early Christians before they composed their own sacred text? The Christian approach to ownership of the Bible will be considered. Why did Christians change their practice of sharing the Hebrew Bible with Judaism to one of claiming inheritance and superior understanding of its meaning? Attention will be given to understanding how the Hebrew Bible (the Tanakh) was used by Jesus and his apostles, the canonization process, and the biblical mandate to use the "sacred writings" in 2 Timothy 3:14–17. Consideration will be given to the approaches to interpreting the Bible by the three main branches of Christianity: Orthodox, Catholic, and Protestant. Modern understandings of biblical usage by Christians will concentrate on the American context where the Bible has served as a foundational text for Protestants.

Who Are Christians?

A Christian may be defined as: (1) one who identifies with the religion of Christianity; (2) one who believes the teachings of Christianity; and (3) one who has been baptized into the Christian faith. Seeking a working definition in the study of global Christianity, Philip Jenkins defines a Christian as one who self-identifies as a Christian and believes that Jesus is a salvific figure, such as the Son of God or Messiah (2011: 111). But these definitions, while accurately identifying Christians generally, overlook the nuances of the earliest period in the rise of the Christian faith. For this study, it is helpful to consider the dynamics of the first-century setting, as much of the New Testament was written between the years 50 and 80 CE. The first followers of Jesus were Jewish and did not identify themselves as Christians until several decades after the death of Jesus. The term *Christian* is conspicuously absent from the Gospels. The Acts of the Apostles recounts the city of Antioch as the location where disciples of Jesus were first called Christians, yet no specific time frame is provided. Writing at the end of the first century the Jewish historian Josephus referred to the Christians as a tribe. In relation to the emergence of the Bible and its usage, it is important to note that the sacred texts of Judaism preceded the Christian tradition. In contrast, the Christian tradition (the church) preceded the New Testament.

What Is the Bible?

The Bible as understood by Christians is composed of two separate collections typically identified as the Old Testament and the New Testament. The Old Testament— more appropriately referred to as the Tanakh, Hebrew Bible, or Jewish scriptures—is a collection of individual writings that were eventually compiled into a single volume. The individual writings were situated in various historical periods and geographical contexts, such as: (1) Genesis narrating the Patriarchal period situated in Mesopotamia, Israel, and Egypt (*c*. 1800–1200 BCE); (2) the book of Kings as a record of the united monarchy under kings Saul, David, and Solomon with the establishing of Jerusalem in Israel (*c*. 1000–900 BCE); (3) the Assyrian conquest of the northern kingdom of Israel (*c*. 720 BCE); and (4) the Babylonian Exile (586 BCE), witnessing the defeat of the southern kingdom of Judah, the destruction of the first temple, and the exile of many Jews to Babylon. The Hebrew Bible, then, is a product of the Israelite-Jewish tradition written by many

FIGURE 3.1 *Entire Tanakh scroll set.* Source: *Photograph by Peter Unseth.*

authors over many centuries (c. 1500/1200–c. 400/150 BCE). Later the books were designated into one of three genres: (1) Torah (law, teachings), (2) Nevi'im (prophets), and (3) Ketuvim (writings/wisdom literature). The first letter of each genre—T, N, and K—became the consonantal root (TNK) for the word Tanakh.

The New Testament is also a collection of writings situated in various historical periods and geographical contexts, such as: (1) the Gospels that recount the life and ministry of Jesus in Galilee and Jerusalem; (2) the letters of the apostle Paul that instruct Christian communities throughout the Roman Empire; and (3) Revelation (The **Apocalypse** of John), allegedly written from the author's exile experience on the island of Patmos where he received apocalyptic visions and a glimpse into the heavenly realm. The New Testament, then, is a product of the early Christian tradition that included multiple authors writing from the late 40s CE to the early second century CE.

By the third century the codex replaced the scroll and the Tanakh was referred to as the Old Testament and copied as a single book (Ulrich 2013: 104). In the fourth century, Christian translators and copyists combined the Old Testament and the New Testament into a single work, for instance the *Codex Vaticanus*, the *Codex Sinaiticus*, and the *Vulgate*.

FIGURE 3.2 *Codex Vaticanus.* Source: *Photograph by Leszek Jańczuk.*

The Bible Made Sacred by Usage

Seemingly the individual authors of the Jewish scriptures and Christian New Testament were unaware that their writings would eventually be venerated and compiled in a book considered sacred scripture. In most cases (or perhaps all cases) writings were not deemed to be inspired during the lifetime of the author. Instead, writings were collected over time and their revelatory value was assessed by later generations of Christian leaders. The criteria of canonization in the Jewish tradition included language, age, and usage (Ehrman 2014: 377), therefore Hebrew texts that demonstrated their lasting value and broad appeal qualified as revelatory. The New Testament criteria included apostolicity, catholicity, and orthodoxy (380), therefore texts had to be written by an apostle or companion of an apostle, contain correct teachings, and be used universally to qualify as revelatory. Writings that met these criteria were believed to be authoritative and were eventually canonized (measuring up to the rule of inspiration). Ultimately both Judaism and Christianity placed a high value on usage as essential to canonization. The widespread usage of a text proved its revelatory value. Both Judaism and Christianity rejected the addition of writings once each canon of sacred writings had been closed.

The Bible or Their Bible?

The Bible as a book used by Christians can be identified in at least two ways. The first identification as *the* Bible serves as a general reference to a textual source without indicating possession. The second identification, *their* Bible, employs a possessive adjective attributing ownership to Christians. Assuming or claiming ownership of the Bible is a critical point (Pelikan 2005), as the relationship between authorship and ownership can vary. If one considers authorship as a **prerequisite** for ownership, then the **Christian Bible** must be limited to the New Testament. The Tanakh was completed well before the time of Christ and the development of the Christian tradition. However, Jesus's disciples did not approach the Bible with this mindset. Rather, they reinterpreted the biblical tradition of Judaism from the lens of inheritance. The earliest followers of Jesus came to view him as the fulfillment of messianic prophecies in the Tanakh. Evident in the Gospels, and Matthew's Gospel in particular, is an evangelistic impulse to demonstrate Jesus's continuity with the Jewish tradition. Matthew addressed readers who were experiencing "a contentious relationship with Judaism." They viewed Jesus as the "Jewish Messiah and authoritative interpreter of Torah" (Marc 2015: 152). Jesus and the disciples were Jewish. Seemingly, they had always followed the teachings of the Tanakh. And the Jewish textual tradition provided them with primary source material to inform their understanding of the messianic profile. Thus Jesus's disciples continued to use the Tanakh without any sense of contradiction. Though some of their Jewish contemporaries may have accused them of misusing or even hijacking the Tanakh, their usage of the Tanakh was not as outsiders borrowing from Judaism. Rather, they used the Tanakh as adherents of an emerging sect within Judaism, albeit from a different hermeneutical perspective.

The Bible Used in the Bible

The first place to explore the use of the Bible is in the Bible. The New Testament came to represent the Christian faith—a faith descended from Judaism but later divided from Judaism. It is unlikely, however, that the New Testament authors wrote their ideas knowing they would be canonized as scripture one day. As Jesus was Jewish, so too was the first generation of his followers. Their view of religious piety reflected first-century Judaism, with one important difference: that Jesus was more than just a rabbi. Instead, he came to be venerated as the Jewish Messiah, and may have regarded himself as such (Jn 4:28). The earliest impression of Jesus was one of an authoritative teacher who frequently cited the Tanakh in his teachings. As the New Testament was written long after the Tanakh, the New Testament writers were able to integrate material from the Tanakh into their writings. They did this by quoting the words of Jesus—who frequently quoted the Tanakh. In addition, they often referenced the Tanakh to make sense of Jesus's life and teaching.

Jesus, the exemplar for his disciples, set a precedent for using the Tanakh. In many episodes from his life the Gospel writers recount Jesus's words, including his references to the Tanakh. The vast majority of Christians over the centuries have read the Gospels with an assumption that what they were reading was true. The words of Jesus remain fundamental to how Christians understand and interpret the entire Bible. Yet some biblical scholars—notably John Dominic Crossan and other members of a scholarly group known as the Jesus Seminar—emphasize the possibility of invention and/or exaggeration by the Gospels writers. Representing the view that the Gospels contained corruptions, the edition of the Bible by President Thomas Jefferson (*The Jefferson Bible*) removed the supernatural claims and miracles of Jesus from the Gospels. At issue here is the authenticity of Jesus's words. To demonstrate the magnitude of Jesus's words, one need look no further than Bibles with the words of Jesus printed in red. The first Red-Letter Edition, published in the United States in 1901, shows the authority of Jesus's words at that time (Crossway 2006). Tony Campolo's 2008 work *Red Letter Christians* demonstrates the authoritative status that Jesus's words continue to hold for American Christians, particularly those Christians that identify as evangelical.

Representative episodes in Jesus's life show how he used the Tanakh as an authoritative source to address questions of belief and practice. On one occasion Jesus was asked to identify the greatest commandment in the Law (Torah). In response, Jesus identified two commandments from the Torah: to love God (Deut. 6:5) and to love your neighbor as yourself (Lev. 19:18). In another instance, Jesus referenced the Tankah as a corrective to admonish money changers in the temple declaring words ascribed to God recorded in Isaiah 56:7 "My house will be called a house of prayer," further condemning the money changers for making it a "den of robbers." While Jesus used the Tanakh to teach and admonish, he also used the Tanakh as a prophetic source to validate his own authority. The nature of his mission and being, depicted as messianic and preexistent, respectively, are recounted by Luke and John. Luke's Gospel recounts Jesus's declaration that everything written about him in the Law, the Prophets, and the Psalms must be fulfilled (Lk. 24:44). Recounted in the Gospel of John (ch. 8), Jesus refers to himself in terms of preexistence—he claimed to exist "before Abraham." He revealed his identity (somewhat cryptically) as "I AM," a possible reference to the episode of Moses and the Burning Bush (Levine and Brettler 2011: 177). The Burning Bush was recounted in the book of Exodus where God revealed his identity to Moses (somewhat cryptically) as "I AM WHO I AM" (Exod. 3:13–14 NRSV). In the account of Jesus's sojourn in the wilderness (Mt. 4:1–11) Jesus is depicted in a standoff with the Devil where Jesus is presented with three temptations. Jesus withstands each temptation, countering the Devil's attempt to entice him by exposing the statements made by the Devil as false in contrast to the truth of scripture. With each temptation Jesus quotes teachings from the book of Deuteronomy: "One does not live by bread alone but by every word that comes from the mouth of the LORD" (Deut. 8:3 NRSV), "Do not put the LORD your God to the test" (Deut. 6:16), and to fear God alone, and worship God exclusively (Deut. 6:13).

Jesus's usage of the Tanakh informed the way that his disciples used the Bible. Like a domino effect, they quoted from or alluded to the Tanakh throughout their writings. The New Testament is loaded with Tanakh quotations and allusions contributing to over 30 percent of the New Testament (Greidanus 1999: 185). The usage of the Tanakh can be summarized in six areas:

1. A *genealogical* source. As the Tanakh has an interest in genealogies, particularly to show descent from patriarchal and tribal families, the writers of Matthew and Luke use genealogies from the Tanakh to demonstrate Jesus's lineage to King David. The ancestral interest in David is important to validate Jesus's messianic profile. Genealogical records from the Tanakh are used to substantiate Jesus as a descendent of David and thus a qualified candidate to rule the throne of David.

2. An *apologetical* source. Jesus's disciples attempted to defend Jesus's messianic candidacy and demonstrate the fulfillment of salvation through his sacrificial death. The disciples of Jesus used prophecies from the Tanakh to show their fulfillment in Jesus. For example, Jesus was the son born to a virgin prophesied by Isaiah (Mt. 1:23, quoting Isa. 7:14). He was the one who was pierced (in his crucifixion) prophesied by Zechariah (Jn 19:37, quoting Zech. 12:10). Jesus was the sacrificial offering for the forgiveness of sins prophesied by Isaiah (various phrases from Isa. 53, quoted in Mt. 8:17; Lk. 22:37; Jn 12:37; Acts 8:32–33; 1 Pet. 2:22).

3. A *typological* source. Recalling the fallen nature of humanity depicted at the outset of Genesis, Jesus is presented as a salvific figure. In particular, Paul substantiates the efficacy of Jesus's sacrifice by the appeal to a binary of type

FIGURE 3.3 *Greek orthodox mural of Apostle Paul.* Source: *Photograph by Peloponnisios.*

and anti-type. For example, the reference to Adam as *the type* responsible for the reign of sin, in contrast to Jesus as *the anti-type* whose sacrifice would abolish the reign of sin (Rom. 5:14). The first Adam (*type*) who brought death is depicted in contrast to the last Adam (Jesus as *anti-type*) who brought life (1 Cor. 15:21, 22, 45).

4   A *hermeneutical* source. Various episodes in the life of Jesus are used to demonstrate a correct understanding of the law and application of ethics. For example, Jesus's understanding of the Sabbath as a day of rest while permitting works of mercy (such as healing) or his decision to grant mercy to a woman allegedly caught in the act of adultery. During the apostolic period, various episodes in the lives of apostles and church leaders show the correct interpretation of the Tanakh. For instance, the story of the Ethiopian eunuch who is only able to identify the sacrificial victim described in Isaiah 53 once instructed by the Christian evangelist Philip.

5   A *polemical* source. As the emerging sect associated with Jesus was increasingly polarized with Judaism, the views of the disciples were presented in contrast to teachings and traditions of Judaism. The apostle Paul taught that there was no value in circumcision nor uncircumcision (Gal. 5:6), and the death of the Messiah (the Christ) as a sacrifice of atonement (Rom. 3:25). Other departures from Judaism include dietary laws, the Sabbath observance, and inclusion of Gentiles.

6   A *homiletical* source. Following the death and alleged resurrection of Jesus, the disciples (students) became messengers (apostles). A primary role of apostolic teaching (didactic usage) was through preaching, such as references to evangelists and apostles preaching the Gospel (Acts 8:25, 40; Rom. 1:9) and preaching the word of God (Acts 16:6, 17:3).

Christian Ownership and Polemical Usage

By the second century, Christianity was emerging as a distinct religious tradition. Its membership was expanding beyond a Jewish ethnic-centeredness to include converts from the larger Roman (non-Jewish or Gentile) culture and its geographic centeredness in Jerusalem was shifting to other centers in the Roman Empire. The Christian understanding and usage of the Bible shifted also. While first-century Jewish Christians used the Tanakh, non-Jewish Christians used the Tanakh from a very Christian perspective—often in conflict with Judaism. By the mid-second century, Christians (many non-Jewish by this time) viewed Jewish interpretations to be flawed. As the interpretation of the Jewish scriptures by Jewish readers was rejected as contrary to Christian interpretation, the Christian view of the Bible shifted. Christians began to see themselves as the correct interpreters of the Jewish scriptures, resulting in the view that Christians deserved to be the new stewards of the Jewish scriptures. This view is demonstrated in *Dialogue with Trypho*, written by the Christian apologist Justin Martyr in argument with the Jewish writer Trypho. Referring to the teachings in the Jewish scriptures Justin Martyr writes, "They are laid up in your scriptures, or rather not in yours but ours, for we obey them, but you when you read, do not understand their sense" (*Dialogue with Trypho*: 29.2). The bifurcation of the Christian Bible into the Old Testament and the New Testament later appeared in the Western church by way of Latin designations (Ziolkowski 2017: 3). By the fifth century, the Christian tradition had gained almost full control of the Bible. Pelikan summarizes the shift to Christian possession of the Bible, in a functional sense Christians have assumed ownership of the text, "read[ing] the Tanakh as their Old Testament" (Pelikan 2005: 238).

The Bible Used in Tandem with Tradition

There are many denominations in Christianity, but the vast majority descend from one of the following three traditions: Orthodox, Catholic, or Protestant. The Orthodox and Catholic traditions both trace their respective lineage to the original apostles through an unbroken succession known as a **postolic succession**. In the Orthodox and Catholic traditions, the Bible is used in tandem with tradition. As described above, the canonization of the New Testament writings involved a process. Critical to the process was the need for criteria and adjudication. The criteria of apostolicity, orthodoxy, and universal usage was adjudicated by many theologians and church fathers during the first three hundred years of Christianity (c. 100–400 CE). Collectively these adjudicators represent *church tradition*. Their writings were composed of apologetical works, commentaries on biblical writings, and homilies (sermons). The **church fathers** became renowned for their usage of the scriptures, particularly the New Testament. In fact, their collective work relies so heavily on scriptural texts as primary source material and their usage of biblical texts so comprehensive, that the claim has been made that "if the New Testament were somehow lost or destroyed it could be reconstructed virtually in its entirety from its quotation by church fathers" (Wegner cited in Blomberg and Markley 2010: 4). The church fathers quoted the New Testament comprehensively in their writings. This type of usage demonstrates the authoritative role of the Bible as a didactic source and **homiletical** source. Further, the extensive knowledge of the New Testament witnessed in patristic literature equipped the church fathers to serve as adjudicators of the canonization process. Their expertise to assess writings leading to rejection or acceptance in the New Testament is not disputed. However, their role in determining the content of the New Testament situates them uniquely in a position of authority over the New Testament. The church fathers represent the collective wisdom of tradition. A tandem was created: tradition and text. For Orthodox and Catholic Christians, the text is used in tandem with tradition. If the question of primacy is raised, the tradition has the chronological advantage of predating the text. Thus, hermeneutical usage of the Bible is conducted within the parameters of tradition. Catholics have a term for this: the magisterium. This refers to the jurisdiction of teaching ministry derived from apostolic authority. In the Catholic view, the church has the authority to teach the writings of the apostles. "Authentic interpretation of the Word of God" is entrusted to bishops in communion with the pope (*Catechism of the Catholic Church*). For the Orthodox tradition, the church fathers (Patristic tradition) represent the precedent of exegetical authority. The church fathers are regarded generally as the authority of apostolic reception. Rather than authenticating interpretation through the papacy, the collective interpretation of the church fathers has traditionally been privileged as the "explication of recorded revelation" (Stylianopolus 2002: 336) received within church community.

The Bible Used above Tradition

Distinct from the Orthodox and Catholic traditions, the Protestant traditions trace their roots to the sixteenth-century Reformation, led by Martin Luther. While all three traditions value the Bible as an inspired and authoritative text, Protestantism is distinct for its emphasis on text *above* tradition. In opposition to the church tradition represented in the papacy, Protestant reformers promoted biblical authority expressed in the important phrase *Sola Scriptura* (the Bible alone). In contrast to the Orthodox and Catholic usage of the Bible, Protestants valued and used the Bible above tradition to *critique* tradition. This was emphasized in Martin Luther's criticism of papal authority.

FIGURE 3.4 *Lutherstadt Wittenberg.* Source: *Photograph by ullstein bild Dtl./Getty Images.*

Protestants rejected the supreme authority of the papacy, and Luther himself disputed the Catholic interpretation of Jesus's words recorded in Matthew 16:18–19 that (as believed by Catholics) assigned special status to the primacy of Peter as the foundational leader and first pope of the church. For Luther, the rock (*petra*) was not Peter but "solely the Son of God, Jesus Christ, of whom Scripture is full, and no one else" (Kling 2004: 79).

Luther's challenge to papal authority and dramatic elevation of the Bible eventually led to his excommunication, and the emergence of the Lutheran tradition. However, Luther's reform served to pioneer a larger movement. Other reformers shared in the view of biblical authority and followed in Luther's wake by founding additional denominations. While Protestants often disagreed among themselves, they agreed strongly on two matters: (1) the Bible is authoritative; and (2) the individual has the right to interpret the Bible. In the Protestant view, the "priesthood of all believers" (derived from 1 Pet. 2:5) authorized all Christians to read and to interpret the Bible for themselves.

The Nature and Purpose of the Bible in the Bible

In addition to the Bible being the first place to explore the use of the Bible, the Bible is the first source to explore the Bible's nature and purpose (**Bibliology**). This may appear to be circular reasoning: *the Bible is a source of revelation because it claims to be a source of revelation*, or, *the Bible is useful in x number of ways because it claims to be useful in x number of ways*. The quintessential biblical text used by Christians to inform their understanding of the nature and purpose of the Bible is found in 2 Timothy:

> But as for you, continue in what you have learned and firmly believed, knowing from whom you learned it, and how from childhood you have known the sacred writings that are able to instruct you for salvation through faith in Christ Jesus. All scripture is inspired by God and is useful for teaching, for reproof, for correction, and for training in righteousness, so that everyone who belongs to God may be proficient, equipped for every good work.
>
> (2 Tim. 3:14–17 NRSV)

This excerpt is from a pastoral letter allegedly written by the apostle Paul to his close helper Timothy. In its personal context, the writer refers to Timothy's awareness of the sacred writings from his childhood. In its historical context the letter predates the canonization of the New Testament, thus the writer is almost certainly referring to the Tanakh alone as the holy scriptures. While the writer refers to the person of Christ, it is likely in the prophetic sense discussed above. The disciples of Jesus mined the Tanakh for evidence to prove the messianic nature of Jesus. **Messiah**, a Hebrew term for "anointed one," is translated into Greek as *Christos*, the Greek term for *anointed one*. *Christos* is transliterated into English as *Christ*. The impact of the "sacred writings" is directed but not limited to Timothy. As Timothy's life has been shaped by the scriptures, so too can the life of any reader. Based on 2 Timothy 3:16, the church fathers emphasized the *usefulness* of scripture "for the spiritual benefit of humanity" (Graves 2014: 41). Similarly, the specific ways that the scriptures are useful are not limited to Timothy's time period but continuous. These ways include teaching faith to children, serving as a source of knowledge for salvation, a standard of truth to establish correct belief, and an ethical guide to establish a moral compass for virtuous living. Further, Christians came to apply Paul's description of the Tanakh to the New Testament. For Christians, the writings of the apostles are equivalent to the Tanakh—inspired and sacred.

Use of the Bible in the American Context

In early America, Protestantism was the most influential Christian tradition. In the early seventeenth century, Puritan leader John Winthrop preached his famous sermon *A Model of Christian Charity*. In his use of the Bible, Winthrop expressed the earliest concept of America's destiny as a "city upon a hill" based on the words of Jesus from Matthew 5:14. As a landmark event, Winthrop's sermon has been called the manifesto of America's founding—a nation founded on the Bible (Witham 2007: 18). This vision of America was disproportionately represented by Protestantism, and the Protestant impulse in the United States has been characterized as evangelical. Mark A. Noll describes Protestants as "self-consciously evangelical" (Noll 2002b: 5) and recognizes American Christianity from the late eighteenth century to the American Civil War as the period when Protestants were "in charge" (2002b: 50). According to Martin E. Marty the term "evangelical" fits for most Protestants up to the mid-twentieth century, even members of liberal churches (1984: 411).

David W. Bebbington associated evangelicalism with four defining characteristics: (1) biblicism, (2) crucicentrism, (3) conversionism, and (4) activism (2005: 23). Based on these characteristics the evangelical use of the Bible has championed literalism in interpretation and the belief in the inerrancy of the Bible. Conversionism, expressed in the missionary enterprise both domestic and foreign, is validated and conducted with an emphasized use of the Bible. The Great Commission (Mt. 28:18–20) instructs Jesus's disciples to "make disciples of all nations." Activism, understood as social justice initiatives, is also based on biblical imperatives to care for those in need. Social justice, if and when acted upon, is motivated by Jesus's teaching in Matthew 25:31–40 to feed the hungry, give water to the thirsty, welcome the stranger, clothe the naked, care for the sick, and visit those in prison.

The priority of teaching children the Bible is evident in the Sunday School movement. In the United States, the Sunday School movement was highly successful and quickly became an accepted American Institution (Boylan 1988: 166). Sunday School lessons focused on Bible stories and Bible memorization. The pedagogical motive of memorizing the Bible is summed up: "Their minds are led to reflection on [the Bible], while they commit the precious truths to their tenacious memories" (44). Other educational endeavors are notable, including vacation Bible schools, Gideon Bibles distributed to elementary school children, and the publication of children's Bibles. Biblical content was also extended to Sunday School songs. Bible stories and verses were used in lyrics to teach children, such as lessons from the prodigal son, devotion to Jesus as shepherd, and the nativity. Already in 1860, fifty years before *The Fundamentals* was written in answer of biblical criticism, *The New American Sunday School Hymn Book* was publishing songs that supported the nature and authority of the Bible. Its thematic categories included the comfort and instruction of the Bible, as well as its perfection and prized status. Further to doctrinal affirmation of the Bible's authority, children sang songs of heart-felt expression. Emotional attachment was nurtured in songs such as *Holy Bible*, *Well I Love Thee*, *O Blessed Bible*, and *Precious Words*. In the latter, children expressed determination to increase both their reading and love of scripture. Ultimately, hymns reinforced the belief in the Bible and encouraged children to pledge their loyalty to obeying its truth (Ginn 2009: 93).

The Bible is central to the missionary impulse. Revivals and crusades are well documented in American history, such as the Methodist camp meetings, the Moody-Sankey revivals, and the Billy Graham crusades. All of them made deep and lasting impacts. The use of the Bible was central to conversion; evangelists based their

FIGURE 3.5 *Sunday School.* Source: *Photograph by Tom Mandel.*

FIGURE 3.6 *Franklin and Billy Graham in Cleveland Stadium (Cleveland, Ohio), June 1994.* Source: *Photograph by Paul M. Walsh.*

preaching on the Bible. A notable example is the evangelist Billy Graham who used John 3:16 with its promise of eternal life as one of his central verses for preaching throughout his career. Alongside biblical preaching, American gospel hymns featured song lyrics that in some cases featured Bible-based song lyrics. Revelation 3:20 was one of the most prominent verses used, portraying Jesus as Savior who knocked at the heart of the sinner. The sinner, in turn, was saved by the act of opening their heart's door (Ginn 2009: 263). Biblical texts, both preached and sung, were highly successful in conversionism.

The emphasis upon biblicism also informs the commitment to truth. With the rise of higher criticism the authority of the Bible came under historical and textual scrutiny. The defense of biblical truth claims were defended by Protestants with the Millenarian Conference of 1879 and *The Fundamentals* published in 1910. Both of these conservative projects were reactionary toward the encroachment of liberal theology. Beliefs that were considered fundamental were: the virgin birth, the deity of Christ, the miracles of Christ, the inerrancy of the Christian scriptures, the substitutionary atonement, and the physical resurrection of Christ. Ultimately, Christians defended the truths of the Bible as their source of truth. The commitment to biblical truth has been advanced in many ways, including supplementary publications to support the study of the Bible, such as Bible commentaries and biblically focused devotional guides. In addition, many types of study Bibles are published for specific readers, such as the

Teen Study Bible, Women's Study Bible, Every Man's Bible, Orthodox Study Bible, and the Catholic Study Bible.

Christians use the Bible as a source of ethics with the Ten Commandments and the teachings of Jesus each serving to inform their sense of morality. The synthesis of moral teachings from the Tanakh and the New Testament represents the construct of Judeo-Christian ethics. The claim that American laws are based on the Ten Commandments in the Bible is commonly made by both public officials and religious leaders (Green 2000: 526). One of the more striking examples of biblical usage is by the Temperance movement that succeeded in legislating prohibition with the Eighteenth Amendment, though prohibition was later repealed. Images of temperance leader Carrie A. Nation holding a Bible and hatchet represented a force to be reckoned with. But the usage of the Bible as the basis for ethics has been challenged. In *The Sins of Scripture*, retired Episcopalian bishop John Shelby Spong criticizes the way that some Christians have used the Bible to justify slavery, subjugate women, and justify religious hatred of homosexuality. From another perspective, in *Can We Still Believe the Bible?* Craig L. Blomberg maintains the inspiration and authority of the Bible encouraging Christians to keep using the Bible to learn correct doctrine as well as to assist in "worship, confession of sin, prayer, lament, **apologetics**, evangelism, and overall godly living" (Blomberg 2014: 81). This demonstrates usage continuous with the Pauline imperative from 2 Timothy.

Conclusion

Jesus and his earliest followers were Jewish and used the Tanakh, the Bible of Judaism. Jesus served as an exemplar in his use of the Tanakh as a didactic source to teach, as a legal source to correct, as a truth source to withstand temptation, and as a prophetic source to substantiate his messianic candidacy. Jesus's disciples used the Tanakh and the teachings of Jesus as an apologetical source to validate Jesus's messianic claims, as a typological source to substantiate the efficacy of Jesus's sacrifice, and as a hermeneutical source to reinterpret the teachings of the Tanakh. When Christianity emerged as a distinct religious tradition, its relationship with the Tanakh shifted from one of inheritance to one of ownership. Christians combined the Tanakh with the Christian writings as the Old Testament and the New Testament. Both the Tanakh and the New Testament were textual traditions compiled through a canonization process. In both cases, the usage of text served to validate the authority of the text. Usage confirmed the revelatory value of the text.

As Orthodox and Catholic traditions developed, so too did the tandem of tradition with text. The Protestants challenged the Catholic belief that the Bible was under the authority of the papacy. Instead, they championed *Sola Scriptura*, the Bible alone. Christians used the Bible to inform their understanding of the nature and purpose of the Bible. Paul's advice to Timothy set important guidelines to be followed by all Christians. The Bible was useful for instruction, salvation, conversion, and a foundation for truth and morality. These areas of usage were demonstrated in the American context in line with the evangelical Protestant emphasis upon biblicism. The priority of using the Bible to teach children was institutionalized in the Sunday School movement. The Bible used in both sermons and songs was central to conversionism. As the cornerstone of truth the Bible was used to defend Christian beliefs. The Bible was used as a source of ethics for individual Christians and as a moral compass for the nation.

Further Reading and Online Resources

Barton, J. (2010), *The Bible: The Basics*, London: Routledge.
McDonald, L.M. (2017), *Biblical Canon*. Oxford Bibliographies. https://doi.org/10.1093/OBO/9780195393361-0017.
Museum of the Bible (2020), "Home." Available online: https://www.museumofthebible.org/museum/about-us (accessed November 15, 2020).

References

Bartholomew, C.G. (2015), *Introducing Biblical Hermeneutics: A Comprehensive Framework for Hearing God in Scripture*, Grand Rapids, MI: Baker Publishing Group.
Barton, J. (2019), *A History of the Bible: The Story of the World's Most Influential Book, The Bible the Basics*, New York: Viking.
Bebbington, D.W. (2005), *The Dominance of Evangelicalism: The Age of Spurgeon and Moody*, Downers Grove, IL: Intervarsity Press.
Bebbington, D.W. and E. Clark (1999), *Reading Renunciation: Asceticism and Scripture in Early Christianity*, Princeton, NJ: Princeton University Press.
Bebbington, D.W. and E. Clark (2010), *The Bible the Basics*, London: Routledge.
Blomberg, C.L. (2014), *Can We Still Believe the Bible?* Grand Rapids, MI: Brazos Press.
Blomberg, C.L. and J. Foutz Markley (2010), *A Handbook of New Testament Exegesis*, Grand Rapids, MI: Baker Academic.
Boylan, A.M. (1988), *Sunday School: The Formation of an American Institution 1790–1880*, New Haven, CT: Yale University Press.
Crossway (2006), "The Origins of the Red-Letter Bible." March 23. Available online: https://www.crossway.org/articles/red-letter-origin/ (accessed September 28, 2019).
Ehrman, B. (2014), *The Bible: A Historical and Literary Introduction*, New York: Oxford University Press.
Ginn, C.C.W. (2009), "Theological Authority in the Hymns and Spirituals of American Protestantism, 1830–1930," PhD diss., University of Leeds, UK.
Graves, M. (2014), *The Inspiration and Interpretation of Scripture: What the Early Church Can Teach Us*, Grand Rapids, MI: W.B. Eerdmans.
Green, S.K. (2000), "The Fount of Everything Just and Right? The Ten Commandments as a Source of American Law," *Journal of Law and Religion*, 14 (2): 525–58.
Greidanus, S. (1999), *Preaching Christ from the Old Testament: A Contemporary Hermeneutical Method*, Grand Rapids, MI: W.B. Eerdmans.

Guinness World Records (2020), "Best-selling Book." Available online: https://www.guinnessworldrecords.com/world-records/best-selling-book-of-non-fiction (accessed December 21, 2020).

Gushee, D.P. (2008), *The Future of Faith in American Politics: The Public Witness of the Evangelical Center*, Waco, TX: Baylor University Press.

Jenkins, P. (2011), *The Next Christendom: The Coming of Global Christianity*, New York: Oxford University Press.

Kling, D.W. (2004), *The Bible in History: How Texts Have Shaped the Times*, Oxford: Oxford University Press.

Levine, A.J. and M.Z. Brettler, eds. (2011), *The Jewish Annotated New Testament*, Oxford: Oxford University Press.

Lindenbaum, J. (2009), "The Production of Contemporary Christian Music: A Geographical Perspective," in T.L. Bell and O. Johansson (eds.), *Sound, Society and the Geography of Popular Music*, 281–94, New York: Routledge.

Marty, M.E. (1984), *Pilgrims in Their Own Land: 500 Years of Religion in America*, Boston: Little, Brown and Company.

McKnight, E.V. (1988), *Post-Modern Use of the Bible: The Emergence of Reader-Oriented Criticism*, Nashville, TN: Abingdon Press.

Moyise, S. (2001), *The Old Testament in the New: An Introduction*, London: Continuum.

Noll, M.A. (2002a), *America's God: From Jonathan Edwards to Abraham Lincoln*, New York: Oxford University Press.

Noll, M.A. (2002b), *The Work We Have to Do: A History of Protestants in America*, Oxford: Oxford University Press.

Noll, M.A. (2015), "The Bible in North America," in J. Riches (ed.), *The New Cambridge History of the Bible*, vol. 4, *From 1750 to the Present*, 391–426, New York: Cambridge University Press.

Pelikan, J. (2005), *Whose Bible Is It? A Short History of the Scriptures*, New York: Viking.

Popović, M., ed. (2010), *Authoritative Scriptures in Ancient Judaism*, Leiden: Brill.

Raymer, V. (2018), *The Bible in Worship: Proclamation, Encounter and Response*, London: SCM Press.

Rogerson, J.W. (2014), *An Introduction to the Bible*, London: Routledge.

Smith, J.M. (2015), *Why Bios? On the Relationship between Gospel Genre and Implied Audience*, London: T&T Clark.

Spong, J.S. (2005), *The Sins of Scripture: Beyond Texts of Hate to the God of Love*, San Fransisco: HarperOne.

Stylianopoulos, T.G. (2002), "Perspectives in Orthodox Biblical Interpretation," *Greek Orthodox Theological Review*, 47 (1–4): 327–38.

Ulrich, E. (2013), "The Old Testament Texts and Its Transmission," in J.C. Paget and S. Joachim (eds.), *The New Cambridge History of the Bible*, vol. 1, *From Beginnings to 600*, 83–104, Cambridge: Cambridge University Press.

Witham, L. (2007), *A City upon a Hill: How Sermons Changed the Course of American History*, New York: HarperOne.

Ziolkoswki, E., ed. (2017), *A Handbook of Biblical Reception in Jewish, European Christian, and Islamic Folklores*, Berlin: De Gruyter.

Glossary Terms

Apocalypse In a general sense an apocalypse is something that is revealed or uncovered, in particular a vision of destruction. Revelation (or The Apocalypse of John) the final book in the New Testament, reveals the final judgment of humanity.

Apologetics A formal defense or justification of a belief. An apologist is one who provides justification of a belief.

Apostolic succession The belief that the authority of church leadership is directly descended from one of the original apostles; unbroken succession to the spiritual authority of the disciples.

Bibliology The study of the nature and purpose of the Bible.

Canonization The process of selecting prominent literary or artistic works. In the case of the Bible, the canonical process refers to selecting prominent writings deemed by the religious community to be sacred or inspired by God.

Christian Bible The Bible used by Christians includes the Old and New Testaments. In the Roman Catholic and Eastern Orthodox traditions the intertestamental works known as the Apocrypha are included, though they are considered secondary in status.

Church fathers Leaders who flourish after the Apostolic era. The earliest fathers may have had direct associations with apostles, such as Ignatius of Antioch and Polycarp of Smyrna associated with the Apostle John. Later fathers were authorities in apologetics, theology, and philosophy. Their writings represent a large library of works.

Homiletics Homilies are sermons. Homiletics refers to the art or discipline of writing and delivering sermons.

Messiah A Hebrew term for "anointed one," is translated into Greek as *Christos*, the Greek term for "anointed one." *Christos* is transliterated into English as *Christ*. In the Jewish tradition, the Messiah is believed to be a descendent of King David who will usher in a reign of peace and establish the Jewish nation. The concept is alluded to in the Tanakh (Jer. 23:5) and discussed more thoroughly in Jewish literature such as the Talmud.

Tanakh An acronym based on the first letters of Torah, Nevi'im, and Kethuvim, each representing collections of writings based largely on literary genre. Torah represents law and teachings, Nevi'im represents prophetic literature, and Kethuvim wisdom literature.

4

The Sacraments: The Lifeblood of Christianity

Ellie Gebarowski-Shafer

Sacramental theology and practice have defined the faith journeys of many Christians, guiding them in meaningful stages from infancy and childhood to adult life and death. Most **Protestants** recognize two **sacraments**—**baptism** and the **Eucharist**—as having a sufficient biblical basis to demand active presence in the church community. Roman Catholics and Orthodox Christians recognize five additional sacraments: **confirmation**, **anointing the sick**, **marriage**, **confession** (also called reconciliation or **penance**), and Holy Orders. Bound together by a common faith in Jesus Christ as risen and returning Savior, thoughtful and devout Christians may vigorously oppose sacramental beliefs held within other denominations. In the twenty-first century, Roman Catholics outnumber Protestants and adherents of non-Christian faiths in Canada and Mexico, while Protestants outnumber Catholics in the United States 47 percent to 22 percent (Pew Research Center 2013, 2014a, b). Thus, sacramental belief and practice remain important aspects of North American religious culture, with disagreements about the number and nature of the sacraments and the implications for a believer's life decisions. An examination of the controversial history behind Western sacramental belief helps an observer of North American church rituals appreciate why sacraments, the lifeblood of Christian faith communities, are practiced so differently within the same religion.

Common Ground in Scripture

Until the development of liberal Protestantism in the nineteenth century, churchgoers and their theologians typically agreed upon the importance of a few shared Christian sacraments whose outward signs pointed to invisible things of utmost importance. Faith, as defined by the anonymous author of Hebrews, "is the realization of things hoped for and the evidence of things not seen" (Heb. 11:1, NAB). Although many believers throughout Christian history have claimed direct experience of the unseen world and of miracles, for the ordinary Christian, symbolic rituals such as the sacraments instill hope for salvation and give a foretaste of heavenly glory. The notion of a covenant between God and people, made manifest in a distinctive sign or ritual, dates back to ancient biblical times, as Christians have traditionally read the text of the Bible. Although there have always been multiple ways of interpreting sacred scripture, the following account presents a classic, premodern Christian view on origins of the sacraments in the Old and New Testaments, offered with a view to helping the student of religion appreciate later controversies and twentieth-century divisions in Christian belief and practice.

In the Pentateuch, traditionally attributed to Moses, God created humankind in a perfect state, then wrestled with the outcome of human choices to disobey God's specific instructions. Humans seemed trapped in an inevitable cycle of wanting God's love and approval, yet being unable or unwilling to follow instructions. Theologians from Paul to Augustine and Luther called this struggle sin. Part of God's solution in the Old Testament, before the coming of Jesus the Messiah, was the covenant marked by a sign. In the time of Noah, God sent a flood to wipe out sinful humanity except for one obedient family. Promising never to send such destruction again, God put the covenantal sign of a rainbow in the sky (Gen. 9:3). When God decided to raise up a special nation out of all the peoples of creation, God made a covenant with Abram, changing his name to Abraham and requiring him and all males in his tribe to become circumcised as a sign of participation in the covenant to become a divinely favored people and land (Gen. 17:5–14).

Seeing this human–divine relationship established in biblical texts, a pattern of sin and second chances marked by a meaningful sign, Christians have traditionally read other literary works in the canon of the Old Testament as foreshadowing sacraments instituted by Christ and early Christian communities. God commanded the Israelites when leaving Egypt to kill and eat a lamb, ritually celebrating the event as the annual Passover ceremony, which Christians saw as linked with the death of Jesus (MacCulloch 2010: 91). Moses received and implemented God's plans for a worship tent where priestly washing, ritual bread eating, candle lighting, and laying hands on an animal as it became a sacrifice would manage the sins of the people as they strove to keep the Abrahamic covenant. The Levite priests' washing in a giant basin outside the desert tabernacle tent, together with God's earlier parting of the Red Sea to allow the Israelites to escape the Egyptian army, foreshadowed Christian baptism as a sign of God's forgiveness and washing away of human sin. When the priests prepared and ate showbread in the tabernacle, and when the people in the wilderness camp ate daily manna provided by God, their actions pointed prophetically to the breaking of bread in the Christian Eucharist. A temple built later by King Solomon in Jerusalem, featuring two massive porch pillars, a brass sea for ritual washing, and the Ark of the Covenant containing God's word in the Ten Commandments, provided a grand home for the Levite priests' sacrifices to the God of Israel.

FIGURE 4.1 *Christians traditionally understand the Eucharist as having a precedent in the Hebrew Old Testament as well as in the Greek New Testament.* Source: *Debby Hudson/ Unsplash.*

Historically, Christian interpreters of scripture routinely read the animal sacrifices of the tabernacle and the temple as foreshadowing Christ's death as the "vicarious sufferer" for the sins of many, with the accompanying ritual of the Eucharist as the sacramental sign of God's eternal covenant, now made not just with Israel but with all of humanity (Reventlow 2001: 166).

For the earliest Christians and for Jesus himself, the temple of Jerusalem loomed large as a model of sacramental worship. A first temple, built in Solomon's reign, was destroyed by invading Babylonians in 586 BCE. With the building of the second temple, completed in 516 BCE, sacrificial offerings and related rituals of the Law of Moses were restored at Jerusalem. During the earthly life of Jesus, Jewish culture and religion with its various factions (Pharisees, Sadducees, Essenes), centered on the temple, where Jews came once a year to offer sacrifices for atonement of sin. According to the author of the Gospel of Luke, Jesus confounded his parents at age twelve on a Passover trip to Jerusalem by slipping away to his "father's house," the temple, for three days, where he learned at the feet of scripture teachers who were "astounded at his understanding and his answers" (Lk. 2:46–9). In his adult ministry, Jesus often taught near the temple (Lk. 19:47) and spoke of his own body as a temple that would be destroyed and raised up again in three days (Jn 2:19).

Early Christians such as the great theologian Paul, writing in the mid-50s CE, saw the sign of the new covenant as the Eucharist (1 Cor. 11:17–34). For Paul, Jesus was a sacrificial offering, whose shedding of blood, death, burial, and resurrection marked the end of God's old covenant with Israel and the beginning of a new covenant with all those professing faith in Christ and receiving baptism in his name. In 70 CE, the Romans destroyed the second temple, causing Jewish sects to concentrate the heart of religion on scripture, the community, and God in the hearts and lives of the faithful (Rowland 1985: 41).

Christian Eucharistic practice became even more important in the post-temple context. Expanding on the stories of Jesus after the destruction of the temple, Gospel writers included the Lord's Supper: on the night before his fateful arrest and crucifixion, Christ led his disciples in a meal of bread and wine, saying, "do this in remembrance of me" (Mt. 26:26–8). This ritual Christians celebrated in symbolic memory of their Lord, finding hope in their partaking as baptized members of the body of Christ that one day they would see the heavenly city where the Lamb is the temple and the light (Rev. 21:22–3). There, as worshipful servants of the Lamb, with their names written in the Lamb's Book of Life, they would reign forever (Rev. 22:3–5). Unique rituals developed in Orthodox and African Christianity, while in Western Christianity, canon

FIGURE 4.2 *In Eucharistic celebrations in today's churches, priests and ministers seek to carry out the command of Christ to "do this in remembrance of me."* Source: *Mateus Campos Felipe/Unsplash.*

law of the Roman Catholic Church codified sacramental beliefs and formed a legacy to be reshaped and passed on to the communities in its own orbit of influence.

European Reformation Divisions

Scripture interpretation debates since the time of the European Reformations underlie various views on the sacraments in twenty-first-century churches. Many European and American Christian groups since the sixteenth century have streamlined sacramental practice, eliminating two or more in belief and practice. For example, marriage and penance are no longer considered sacraments by many churches. Faith communities have rejected some of the medieval European church's sacraments typically because their leaders seek to align themselves with their understanding of the earliest Christian teachings and, specifically, with the plain text of scripture, translated directly from Greek and Hebrew. Meanwhile, the Roman Catholic Church has maintained sacramental views that closely resemble their sixteenth-century positions, affirmed at the Council of Trent (1545–63) and in the twentieth century at the Second Vatican Council (1962–5). Roman Catholic teachings on the sacraments had been proven metaphysically true via scholastic methods in the late Middle Ages, but as rival humanist methods gained ground, Martin Luther (1483–1546) and other intellectual giants of the age asserted compelling new truth claims about the individual's salvation by *sola fide* (faith alone) and sacramental practice validated by *sola scriptura* (scripture alone). In part due to this dramatic clash of biblical interpretation methods, Western Christianity split permanently, and divisions would be played out in colonial lands such as North America.

Western Europe in the late medieval period struggled to maintain any sense of unity in Latin Christendom, having split from Greek Orthodox Christianity and the remnants of the Eastern Roman Empire in 1054 CE. Best attempts at Latin unity came in the liturgy of the Roman Catholic Mass, centering on a mystical celebration of the Lord's truly present body and blood in the Eucharist, and in the medieval university system. Following in the footsteps of Peter Lombard of France (c. 1096–1160) and Thomas Aquinas of Italy (1225–74), university theologians, canon lawyers, and popes defended the sacraments of the Roman Catholic Church, borrowing systematic categories of reason from the ancient Greeks but working primarily in the Latin language and using the Vulgate as their main scripture version. The scholastic method provided that a sacred teaching or doctrine should be questioned meticulously and answered confidently with proof-texts from scripture and reason. Scholastic theologians engaged in earnest metaphysical debates with one another, arguing about what to make, for instance, of the sacrament of penance, which did not involve a corresponding material (*elementum*) of significance, such as water, oil, bread, or wine (Reynolds 2016: 21). Peter Lombard questioned the admittedly new (non-apostolic) sacrament of marriage. Defending church teaching, Lombard still listed marriage as one of the seven sacraments and devoted a treatise to each one in his *Sentences*, which became the standard textbook of theology in the 1220s onward and established the key methods and establishment goals of theological studies through the time of Aquinas and into the sixteenth century (Reynolds 2016: 5).

Scholastic scripture commentaries, copied out industriously by students, monks, and professional scribes, along with virtually all university teaching, supported the seven sacraments whereby the church administered God's grace to the people for the salvation of their souls. From the Passion of Jesus Christ flowed the sacramental graces, and with the unique grace conferred by each sacrament, medieval Christians had a complete system that provided a sure pathway to salvation (Reynolds 2016: 3). In the Eucharist, chief of sacraments, the clergy member, ordained by Christ, presided over bread and wine being mystically transformed (transubstantiated) into the body and blood of Christ (Nutt 2017: 77). Receiving the sacrament worthily, after confession to a priest and doing the assigned works of penance, baptized believers merit divine grace. If said in memory of a departed loved one, a Mass could cause God's grace to ease the soul's suffering in purgatory while awaiting the final Judgment (MacCulloch 2010: 555). But was this the original intention of Paul and the Gospel writers when they exhorted believers to reenact the Lord's Supper?

Humanism, a methodology aiming to uncover original intentions of textual authors, challenged the comprehensive sacramental system that would later be completely abandoned by colonists such as the New England Puritans. A rival method to scholasticism, humanism arose in the early fourteenth century, initially promoting the value of vernacular songs and liturgies, alongside a revival of classical Greek and Latin literature. Humanist scholars and poets composed new literature in Italian and other vernacular languages, and they made fresh translations of classic texts into Latin, emphasizing the need to interpret a text in light of its original meaning when it was composed. Although vernacular translations of the Bible existed, from Latin into German, English, and other languages, humanist principles applied to the study and translation of the Bible posed new problems for the Roman Catholic Church, especially in teachings on the sacraments. Luther, who trained in scholastic theology, became interested in humanist methods for the study of scripture. He concluded that the old theological commentaries that took up so much of the student's time should be sidelined in favor of scripture read in its original sense (or senses), and in the original Greek or Hebrew, or in a fresh translation.

Luther began with an attack on indulgences and watched disapprovingly as radicals took his sacramental reform ideas, widely disseminated in new print technology, much further than he intended. Luther's protest in 1517, the year he posted his Ninety-Five Theses, centered on the church's authority to sell fundraising indulgences—remittance slips stating the years off purgatory one might be granted in exchange for certain sacramental acts of penance. Intended for a worthy cause—the rebuilding of St. Peter's Basilica in Rome—Luther argued that indulgences had no support from a direct reading of scripture. Teaching in his widely published *The Freedom of a Christian* (1520)

FIGURE 4.3 *Traditionally, participation in the sacrament of penance is believed to transmit divine grace to the believer.* Source: *Grant Whitty/Unsplash.*

that salvation came solely from faith and not from any good works the church could tell a person to do, Luther soon found himself excommunicated (barred from taking the Catholic Eucharist) by Pope Leo X.

Wanting average German readers to understand his theological position from direct access to scripture, Luther published a German translation of the Greek New Testament in 1522 and of the entire Bible in 1534, also writing many hymns to encourage learning of theology via congregational singing. There had been prior printed German Bibles, translated from the Vulgate, and a significant new Latin translation in 1516 by Erasmus of Rotterdam (1466–1536), but Luther's version became more popular and differed theologically, especially in readings related to the sacraments. For example, a literal reading of the Gospel of Matthew reveals that John the Baptist (Mt. 3:2) and later Jesus (Mt. 11:21) called believers to "repent." Translated from the Greek *metanoeite*, the word "repent" pointed to the individual's independent, spirit-led turning away from sin and toward the Savior. This reading differed substantially from the Vulgate and from the Vatican-backed interpretation of the scholastic theologians, where the faithful are called to "do penance" as acts mandated by a priest after a believer's oral confession of sin, to receive grace and merit salvation (Gebarowski-Shafer 2016: 493–4).

Besides penance, other sacraments fell by the wayside in the Reform movements inspired by Luther and influential Swiss reformer Ulrich Zwingli (1484–1531). Echoing criticisms of errant clergy made by pre-Reformers John Wycliffe (1330–84) and Jan Hus (1372–1415), Luther lamented the corruption of some worldly Catholic popes and lecherous priests. He declared that even though "we cannot all publicly minister and teach [...] we Christians are all kings and priests and therefore lords of all and may firmly believe that whatever we have done is pleasing and acceptable in the sight of God" without approval from pope or clergy (Placher and Nelson 2017: 6–7). Thus, Luther demoted Holy Orders from sacramental status, and most Protestants accepted this deviation from the medieval system. Demonstrating his views on a personal level, Luther abandoned his Augustinian monastic vows and married a former nun, Katharina von Bora (1499–1552). Like Luther, Zwingli bypassed scholastic commentaries and the pope's interpretation of scripture in favor of an original, historical reading, but Zwingli deemed it contrary to the Word of God to hold that in the Eucharist, Christ's real body and blood become present (Placher and Nelson 2017: 11). Christ said in John 17:11, "I am no more in the world," so Zwingli reasoned that Christ was not really present in the Mass, as the doctrine of transubstantiation maintained. Luther disapproved of Zwingli's interpretation. He also rejected teachings of the radical Anabaptists who refused to participate in infant baptisms, due to there being only adult baptisms in scripture. Conservative Luther held that the sacraments of the Eucharist and baptism should still be celebrated essentially in the manner that they had been done in the medieval church. In part due to his theological writings and biblical translation work, but often in manifestations contrary to his beliefs, Luther's Protestant movement spread throughout Europe and became firmly established in Germany, Switzerland, Holland, Scotland, and England.

THE SACRAMENTS: THE LIFEBLOOD OF CHRISTIANITY

FIGURE 4.4 *Luther defended infant baptism, which Anabaptists rejected as unscriptural.* Source: *Josh Applegate/Unsplash.*

In the English Reformation, especially important for understanding English-speaking North American religious culture, progressive religious leaders applied methods popularized by Luther and inspired generations of readers from all social classes to read and seek God for themselves in the text of the English Bible. Roman Catholics lost the country politically with Henry VIII's founding of the Church of England in 1534. The Council of Trent, convening in 1545, provided the opportunity for Catholics to revisit core doctrines amid the Protestant crisis, and at a time when Catholic missionary expansion by colonizing countries Portugal, Spain, Italy, and France demanded a clarification of church teachings. On March 3, 1547, at Session VII, the Council of Trent declared that Jesus instituted seven sacraments: baptism, confirmation, the Eucharist, penance, extreme unction (anointing the sick), Holy Orders, and marriage (Reynolds 2016: 2). English Catholic theologians in the Tridentine era had the green light to propose new arguments in defense of the sacraments. They briefly gained the upper hand against Protestant theologians during the reign of Catholic Mary I (r.1553–8). However, when Protestant Queen Elizabeth took the throne in 1559 for a reign of over four decades, Catholics theologians went into exile in Europe, where they wrote scores of polemical books, trying to convince a growing English reading public to rejoin the Church of Rome for the best chance at eternal salvation via faithfully administered sacraments. The English literature on both sides of the debates was reprinted for centuries afterward, in England, Ireland, and North

America, because the detailed discussions of controversial doctrines remained useful for later generations who continued to debate the same points on the sacraments and other issues (Gebarowski-Shafer 2013: 57–68).

Although the Roman Catholic Church frowned on indiscriminate reading of vernacular scriptures, post-Tridentine England abounded with printed Bibles due to the 1526 first publication of the New Testament of William Tyndale (1494–1536), followed by the Great Bible of 1539 and many other editions in various sizes and formats (Campbell 2010: 10–31). Consequently, an important method of debating the sacraments was to publish a Roman Catholic English Bible, heavily annotated to explain in detail why Protestant translations erred in reducing the number of sacraments to just two. Gregory Martin (1542–82) of Sussex, in exile at the English Catholic College at Rheims, France, translated the Vulgate into English, publishing the New Testament in 1582 (Martin 1582). Educated at St. John's College, Oxford, Martin also wrote a companion text, *A Discoverie of the Manifold Corruptions of the Holy Scriptures by the Heretikes of Our Daies*, explaining theological flaws in Protestant English Bibles (Martin 1583). Martin's NT translation and *A Discoverie* were refuted by Cambridge theologian William Fulke (1538–89). In the text of these polemical works, discussion of whether Holy Orders was a sacrament loomed large, as Protestants' exclusion of penance, marriage, anointing the sick, and confirmation, depended on their rejection of the sacramental nature of priestly ordinations.

Gregory Martin and William Fulke debated many issues, including Holy Orders, a brief analysis of which will help to explain enduring differences between diverging European church practices (married vs celibate clergy) that were carried over to North American Christian communities and still remain noticeably different across denominations in the twenty-first century. Martin, a Catholic, centered his discussion on scriptural proof-texts, as an authoritative common ground with his religious opponents, since Protestants had rejected many traditional sources familiar in the scholastic tradition still cited by Catholics. Martin brought up 1 Timothy 4:14 and demonstrated how it should be translated and understood. Protestants beginning with Tyndale had translated the Greek *charismatos* (in the Vulgate, *gratiam*) as "gift" instead of "grace," seemingly to take away scriptural support that sacramental grace is given by imposition of hands in clerical ordination. A prominent English translation, the Geneva Bible (1560), presented Saint Paul's words to the reader as, "Despise not the gift that is in thee, which was given thee by prophecie with the laying on of the hands of the companie of the Eldership." Martin translated differently: "Neglect not the grace that is in thee: which is given thee by prophecie, with imposition of the handes of priesthod." With reference to this passage and citing ancient authorities, he argued that the ceremony of Holy Orders ritually transmits divine grace and is a true, sacramental action.

Fulke, in contrast, believed that the so-called sacrament of Holy Orders should be abandoned as a mere tradition of men, in favor of married clergy and a scripture teaching-centered, not ritualistic, role for clergy. "We see not how it doth give any grace, and much lesse that it is a Sacrament [...]. For it must be an element, and not an externall action onely, that maketh a Sacrament [...]. We say Baptisme and the Lords

Supper, are Sacraments" (Fulke [1589] 1601: 698). Similar points were exchanged literally between Martin and Fulke over 2 Timothy 1:16, where Catholics rendered the Vulgate's *gratiam Dei* as "grace of God" conveyed by the "imposition of (apostle Paul's) hands," while Protestant translations from the Greek such as the Great Bible and the Geneva Bible rendered *charisma tou theou* as Paul's stirring up "the gift of God." Did Holy Orders give grace that the priests could pass on in other sacraments? Catholics said yes and had scripture (the Vulgate and translations from it) to back their doctrine, while Protestants said no and had humanist translations from the original Greek on their side.

Adopting Luther's position from fifty years earlier, English Protestants and their North American counterparts rejected ordination as a divinely instituted sacrament, and with it the notion that related sacraments transmit grace from God, through clergy, to the people. Anglican (Church of England) priests and other Protestant pastors could now be married males rather than celibate males, a lasting difference between Protestant and Catholic faith communities. United in their belief that there were two sacraments, Protestant groups in England still disagreed with each other on many issues; for instance, Puritans rejected the elaborate clerical vestments worn by the clergy of the Church of England. Many immigrated to New England seeking religious freedom, setting up permanent settlements along the Atlantic coast and acquiring land from Native Americans.

Numerous in New England, Congregationalists in the Puritan tradition held a streamlined view of the sacraments that branded Catholics or Anglicans as outliers in early colonial years. Among the radical émigrés and colonists in the seventeenth century, English-speaking Baptists rejected infant baptism and found the safe havens they needed to practice their beliefs in full immersion body baptism—in the manner Jesus himself was baptized in the Gospels (Mk 1:9–11, Mt. 3:13–17). A proliferation of printed Bibles authorized by their respective church leaders ensured that Catholics from Canada and Mexico remained firm in their beliefs, while Protestants interpreted scripture according to their consciences and guided their faith communities accordingly. Together with the Evangelical, **Pentecostal**, and Modernist (Liberal-Progressive) movements of later centuries, the Reformation-era divisions over sacramental practice created the foundations for North American Christian communities that were built upon by later generations.

Sacramental Practice in North America

In the twenty-first century, observers at North American churches will notice that sacramental practice has developed along the lines of the Reformation divisions, with further differences in Protestantism arising from movements that have occurred since the sixteenth century. All Protestant churches hold in common a rejection of the Latin Mass and the Vulgate as an inspired biblical translation, of papal authority to interpret the Bible, and of any restrictions on who can read the scriptures. Protestants also

FIGURE 4.5 *North American Protestant churches have changed radically in the last century.* Source: *Keagan Henman/Unsplash.*

reject the Apocrypha from the canon of inspired scripture, and they tend to reject the notion of saying prayers for the dead, as Catholic often do. From Episcopalian to Baptist, Protestants share a visible commitment to baptizing new members, celebrating the Eucharist, ordaining married or single clergy, valuing married life among lay people (rather than encouraging monasticism), with less outward emphasis on reverence toward the Virgin Mary and saints. While Roman Catholic teachings have undergone some noticeable changes since the Second Vatican Council (such as embracing vernacular language masses and allowing translations of the Bible from Hebrew and Greek), Protestant churches have experienced striking changes, due to movements such as Pentecostalism.

Although not exclusive to North America, Pentecostalism has many important early roots in the continent and has given rise to church communities with distinctive practices that differ from churches with a centuries-old presence on the continent, such as the Episcopal Church. For example, an observer of a baptism ceremony at a traditional Episcopal church in the United States will have a vastly different experience attending a baptism at a Pentecostal congregation the next Sunday. A keen-eyed student attending the two services would appreciate the common ground due to a shared Western European Protestant background, such as the service being sung and said all in English, and the pastoral office being open to a married person. In an ordinary Episcopal baptism, a male or female priest leads the Eucharistic service from a book,

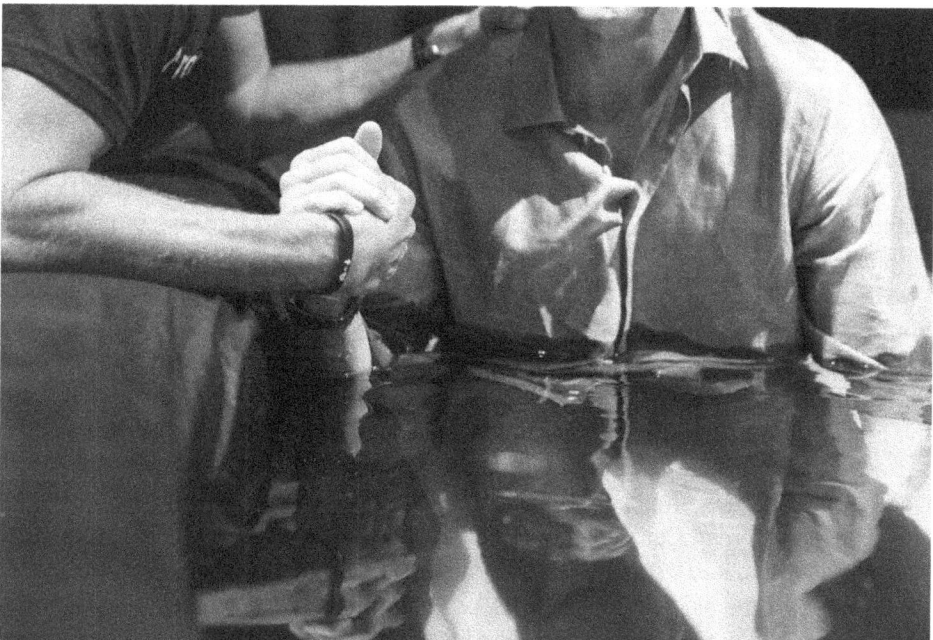

FIGURE 4.6 *When baptizing a new believer, Pentecostals fully immerse the candidate in water.* Source: *Kaleb Tapp/Unsplash.*

turning to the candidate for baptism (often a baby held by parents) to conduct a ritual of christening over a special bowl or fount, pouring a little water over the candidate's head. A routine Pentecostal baptism, in contrast, features a tank filled with water for a mature candidate (usually at least six years old) to be immersed in; or, alternatively, the congregation will move outside to a natural body of water for the ceremony. This is due to the insistence by Anabaptists and later Evangelicals that candidates for baptism choose the ritual freely and be fully immersed in water; Pentecostals continued this practice, viewing "sprinkling" baptisms as invalid. The Pentecostal pastor, who can be a married man or woman, may perform the baptism or delegate an elder of the church to perform it.

Further, at a Pentecostal baptism, the observer might be taken aback when the candidate, after being plunged in the water by the officiant and being lifted up to a standing position, raises her hands and face upward and begins speaking, with eyes closed, in an unintelligible, excited manner. This is because Pentecostals embrace the practice of speaking in tongues that was uniquely popularized as a second, spiritual baptism in late nineteenth-century and early twentieth-century revivals such as the Asuza Street revival of Los Angeles, led by African American preacher William Seymour (Anderson 2016: 28–35). Many fellow Evangelicals such as Baptists and Presbyterians would discourage speaking in tongues in a public church setting, but Pentecostals actively promote the spiritual manifestation, especially at a baptism ceremony, and some groups view spirit baptism as essential for salvation. Pentecostals, with nondenominational charismatic megachurch pastors, see their upkeep of spirit flow as a powerful antidote to godless secular culture and the "dead churches" where modernism and apathy have led to a decline in sincere belief. Pentecostal Christianity is often portrayed as being strange or quirky in the minds of more traditionally minded Christians who practice the sacraments in more traditional ways.

If the same observer of the Episcopal and Pentecostal baptisms visited a Roman Catholic church, the dignified Mass would seem to have more in common with the Episcopal service than with the emotional Pentecostal celebration. However, the controversial embrace of modernism and liberal theology in the Episcopal Church creates significant differences relating to sacramental practice. While in the Episcopal Church, women (even lesbian women) can become priests and preside over the Eucharist, the Roman Catholic Church maintains its traditional teaching that, after the order of Melchizedek and the example of Christ, only a celibate male can take the sacrament of Holy Orders and in turn become a faithful minister of the sacraments. Nor do Episcopalians emphasize rituals of confession before taking the Eucharist, as is common in Roman Catholic communities, where only baptized believers in good standing are permitted to receive Holy Communion. Catholics are known for elaborate, well-attended funerals where believers pray for the soul of the faithful departed, understood to be promised eternal life in a literal heaven where the saints are gathered and the risen Christ reigns as king and high priest.

Episcopalians, however, influenced by historical criticism of the Bible and questioning of the classic teachings, tend to view sacraments as beautifully symbolic but untenable as supernatural realities in light of a modern, scientific understanding of the world. Roman Catholics' continued practice of all seven sacraments thus puts this sizeable group of North American Christians at odds with liberal, progressive Episcopalians. Yet both groups christen babies, embrace social justice causes, change the color of table linens and vestments with the liturgical season, light many candles, recite the Nicene Creed, and worship amid stained glass windows with the organist playing an impeccable rendition of Schubert's *Ave Maria*.

For all their differences in observable church practices, Pentecostals and their charismatic brethren, together with Roman Catholics, all agree that a chief purpose of gathering together for worship is to be refreshed in one's spirit with a foretaste of heaven. They do this in different ways, with Pentecostals rejecting many of the traditional sacraments yet perhaps re-embracing some of the previously lost rituals in new forms. The expectation that a believer will speak in tongues—spirit baptism—in addition to water baptism, is one example. The adult conversion experience in Pentecostalism might amount to a reintroduction of the sacramental practice of confirmation. Adult conversions, although usually spontaneous rather than scheduled, often involve the spiritual laying on of hands for a life-changing time of charismatic prayer. Ministers sometimes participate in laying on of hands, but for Pentecostals, the presence of faithful lay people alone will bring to fulfillment Christ's promise in Matthew 18:20: "For where two or three are gathered together in my name, there am I in the midst of them" (NAB). Trembling in the spirit, the convert may feel completely changed and

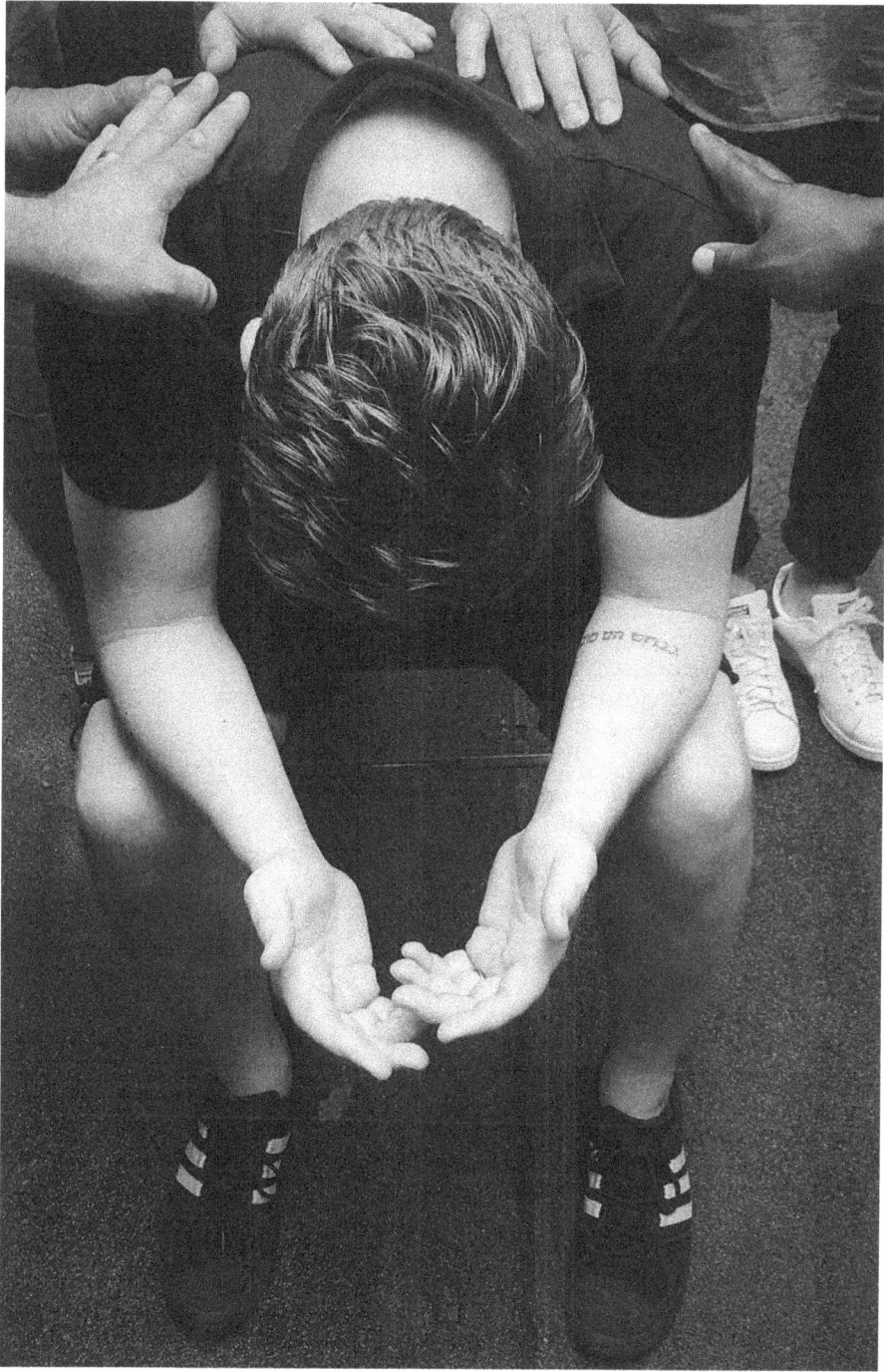

FIGURE 4.7 *Average charismatic believers pray for one another for long periods of time, by laying on of hands.* Source: *Jon Tyson/Unsplash.*

set on a new course in life, after experiencing Christ through laying on of hands in a charismatic or Pentecostal "altar call" setting. Without such a trance-like experience shared with fellow believers, a would-be convert may not yet feel one with Christ or bonded to the church group. Afterward, similar to a traditional confirmation ritual with laying on of hands by a bishop, the Pentecostal or charismatic believer may feel a joyful, permanent unity with the congregation as a full-fledged brother or sister in Christ. In this way, recognizable sacrament-like rituals have made a comeback in North American churches, among the many new and old ways of experiencing Christ and getting an early taste of heaven on Earth.

Further Reading and Online Resources

Assemblies of God (1995–2020), "Assemblies of God 16 Fundamental Truths." Available online: https://ag.org/Beliefs/Statement-of-Fundamental-Truths (accessed November 4, 2020).

Catechism of the Catholic Church (n.d.), "Part Two. The Celebration of the Christian Mystery." Available online: http://www.vatican.va/archive/ccc_css/archive/catechism/p2s2.htm (accessed November 4, 2020).

The Episcopal Church (2020), "What We Believe." Available online: https://episcopalchurch.org/sacraments (accessed November 4, 2020).

Evangelical Lutheran Church in America (2013), "Worship Formation & Liturgical Resources: Frequently Asked Questions." Available online: https://download.elca.org/ELCA%20Resource%20Repository/What_is_a_sacrament_for_Lutherans.pdf (accessed November 4, 2020).

Fulke, W. (1834), *Confutation of the Rhemish Testament*. Available online: https://books.google.com/books?id=zxQVAAAAYAAJ&printsec=frontcover&dq=inauthor:%22William±Fulke%22&hl=en&newbks=1&newbks_redir=0&sa=X&ved=2ahUKEwjvitrmjYTmAhVGU98KHValCR4Q6AEwBHoECAQQAg#v=onepage&q&f=false (accessed November 4, 2020).

Jacobsen, D., ed. (2006), *A Reader in Pentecostal Theology: Voices from the First Generation*, Bloomington: Indiana University Press.

MacCulloch, D. (2003), *The Reformation*, New York: Penguin.

M'Ghee, R.J. (1837), *The Complete Notes of the Doway Bible and Rhemish Testament*. Available online: https://books.google.com/books?id=AZkCAAAAQAAJ&pg=PR6&dq=rhemish+testament&hl=en&newbks=1&newbks_redir=0&sa=X&ved=2ahUKEwiRyLDXjoTmAhXwTN8KHVXoBx8Q6AEwAHoECAAQAg#v=onepage&q=rhemish%20testament&f=false (accessed November 4, 2020).

References

Anderson, A. (2016), *An Introduction to Pentecostalism: Global Charismatic Christianity*, 2nd edn., Cambridge: Cambridge University Press.

Campbell, G. (2010), *The Bible: The Story of the King James Version, 1611–2011*, Oxford: Oxford University Press.

Fulke, W. ([1589] 1601), *The Text of the New Testament of Jesus Christ, Translated out of the vulgar Latine by the Papists of the traiterous Seminarie at Rheims*, London: Christopher Barker.

Gebarowski-Shafer, E. (2013), "The Transatlantic Reach of the Catholic 'False Translation' Argument in the School 'Bible Wars',″ *US Catholic Historian*, 31 (3) (Summer): 47–76.

Gebarowski-Shafer, E. (2016), "The Bible in Roman Catholic Theology to c. 1750,″ in E. Cameron (ed.), *The New Cambridge History of the Bible*, vol. 3, *The Early Modern World, c. 1450–1750*, 489–517, Cambridge: Cambridge University Press.

MacCulloch, D. (2010), *Christianity: The First Three Thousand Years*, New York: Allen Lane.

Martin, G. (1582), *The New Testament of Jesus Christ, Translated Faithfully into English, out of the Authentical Latin …*, with annotations by W. Allen, R. Bristow, and T. Worthington, Rheims: John Fogny.

Martin, G. (1583), *A Discoverie of the Manifold Corruptions of the Holy Scriptures by the Heretikes of our Daies …*, Rheims: John Fogny.

Nutt, R.W. (2017), *General Principles of Sacramental Theology*, Washington, DC: Catholic University of America Press.

Pew Research Center (2013), "Canada's Changing Religious Landscape,″ June 27. Available online: https://www.pewforum.org/2013/06/27/canadas-changing-religious-landscape/ (accessed October 13, 2019).

Pew Research Center (2014a), "On Religion, Mexicans Are More Catholic and Often More Traditional than Mexican-Americans,″ December 8. Available online: https://www.pewresearch.org/fact-tank/2014/12/08/on-religion-mexicans-are-more-catholic-and-often-more-traditional-than-mexican-americans/ (accessed October 13, 2019).

Pew Research Center (2014b), "Religious Landscape Study." Available online: https://www.pewforum.org/religious-landscape-study/ (accessed October 13, 2019).

Placher, W.C. and D.R. Nelson (2017), *Readings in the History of Christian Theology*, vol. 2, Rev. edn., Louisville, KY: Westminster John Knox Press.

Reventlow, H.G. (2001), "The Early Church,″ in J. Rogerson (ed.), *The Oxford Illustrated History of the Bible*, 166–91, Oxford: Oxford University Press.

Reynolds, P. (2016), *How Marriage Became One of the Sacraments: The Sacramental Theology of Marriage from Its Medieval Origins to the Council of Trent*, Cambridge: Cambridge University Press.

Rowland, C. (1985), *Christian Origins: An Account of the Setting and Character of the Most Important Messianic Sect of Judaism*, London: SPCK.

Wosh, P. (1994), *Spreading the Word: The Bible Business in Nineteenth-Century America*, Ithaca, NY: Cornell University Press.

Glossary Terms

Anointing the sick Christians have specific rituals of prayer for sick, distressed, or dying believers, which may include putting oil and laying hands on the person, with the intent of invoking divine healing or easing of suffering.

Baptism A Christian ritual where a new believer is initiated into the faith, either by splashing of water on the forehead or by full immersion into a body of water.

Confirmation Rituals that involve a clergy member laying hands on a baptized believer and signaling the believer's receiving of the Spirit and commitment to lifelong Christian practice.

Eucharist A spiritual re-enactment of the Last Supper, where a clergy member prays over bread and wine and distributes the same to churchgoers.

Marriage In Christian churches marriage involves a program of music, a sermon, and sometimes the Eucharist, celebrating the romantic union of two adults.

Penance Also called Confession and Reconciliation, Penance rituals involve a baptized believer meeting privately with a clergy member to confess sin and receive prayer and instructions.

Pentecostals Protestants who emphasize divine healing, immersion baptism, scripture memorization, and gifts of the spirit, especially receiving the Holy Ghost as evidenced by speaking in tongues.

Protestants Christians in a wide range of churches that originated in a split from the Roman Catholic Church in the sixteenth century, including Lutherans, Anglicans, Episcopalians, Congregationalists, Presbyterians, Methodists, Baptists, and Pentecostals.

Sacraments Christians recognize at least two and up to seven rituals as beneficial for the believer's spiritual journey and the good of the church, and some sacraments are often thought to be necessary for salvation of the soul and preparation for eternal life in heaven.

5

Women in Christianity: An Emerging Story

Ellie Gebarowski-Shafer

Introduction

Women and girls hold a place of prominence in the historical Christian religion, from the time of early missionary expansion to European Reformation divisions and today's church communities around the world. In the twenty-first century, North American churchgoers find greater numbers of female than male parishioners, and women report believing in God at higher rates than men and are more likely to believe in hell (Pew Research Center 2014). Female pastors with seminary degrees are common in **Protestant** churches such as Pentecostal, **Congregational**, and **Episcopalian**. Since the 1980s, Elizabeth Johnson (b.1941), a prolific **Roman Catholic** theologian and nun, with other feminist Christian thinkers, has challenged the previously male-dominated institutions and methods of published academic theology and university teaching of religion. Such developments were made possible in part due to the pioneering work of North American women especially since the nineteenth century, who have publicly guided seekers to Christ, overcome significant obstacles and opposition, and at times made regrettable mistakes. Grounded in a shared tradition of biblical teachings and religious history, women in North American Christianity believe and practice diverse interpretations of Christianity, exemplifying key divisions in the worldwide faith today.

Women in the Christian Bible

While the human Jesus and his twelve apostles were all men, giving the religion a male-dominated image, the contributions of women are well documented in scripture and have been continuously valued in Christianity, despite the particular sexist

FIGURE 5.1 *Women outnumber men as churchgoers in North America.* Source: *David Diaz/Unsplash.*

attitudes and misogynistic cultures that have arisen throughout the religion's long history. Traditionally revered as God's word revealing the loving Creator's plan for the salvation of humankind, the Bible and its representation of women influenced early Christians' perceptions of female followers of Christ. Faith in Christ carried imminent risks of persecution and death, and first-generation believers were joined together in a theological worldview where miracles could happen to anyone and through the faith of any believer God chose to use. Even today, Christians remain grounded in a shared tradition of biblical stories, whether or not the leadership of their denomination has accepted the principles of historical biblical criticism, whereby new arguments are made for church leadership of straight, lesbian, or transgendered women. The biblical stories, with accounts of the holiness and failures of women are important to consider in their own right and as a basis for understanding today's divisions in Christianity, since with the passage of time and the careful study of scripture, readers of the Christian Bible have found much to honor and to malign about women.

Significant portions of Hebrew scripture portray women in error, sometimes pointing to a sexist worldview where men deserve a higher level of respect and obedience as more reliable human guides on the pathway to salvation. Tempted by the serpent in the idyllic Garden of Eden, Eve leads Adam to eat of the forbidden fruit of the tree of the knowledge of good and evil, and afterward God curses Eve with pain in childbirth and the rule of her husband over her (Gen. 2:16–3:16). Adam, for his part in disobedience to God, lost access to the abundant food growing in Eden and was cursed with hard labor to grow his own crops, infested with thorns and thistles (Gen. 3:17–19). In the stories of the Patriarchs of Israel (Abraham, Isaac, and Jacob), deceit within families runs rampant, especially in portrayals of women. Rebekah, mother of Jacob and Esau, upon hearing that Isaac planned to give the patriarchal blessing and inheritance to manly Esau, masterminded a deception of the elderly, blind Isaac whereby Jacob appeared for the blessing wearing Esau's clothing and goatskins on his arms to appear hairy like his brother (Gen. 27). Seductive Potiphar's wife (Gen. 39), cunning Delilah (Judg. 16), and wicked Jezebel, Queen of Israel (1 Kgs 16), stand out as deplorable women who still loom large in sexist stereotypes within Bible-believing Christianity.

Miriam, sister of Moses who delivered the Israelites out of slavery in Egypt, illustrates how the blessings and judgment of Yahweh fall upon women in sacred history recounted in Hebrew scripture. Miriam co-led a victory song after the Egyptian army drowned in the Red Sea (Exod. 15), favored by God with a leadership role and a ministry of music. Miriam would have benefited from protections for women and girls in the law God gave to Moses on Mount Sinai and that was enacted in sacred rituals in the tabernacle, a holy tent in the desert where the priests offered animal sacrifices to God. Exempt from participating in the painful covenant sign of circumcision, Miriam could not serve as a priest like her brother Aaron, for all women were barred from entering the tabernacle area of the wilderness camp during their monthly menstrual flow and after childbirth (Lev. 12:1–8). Notwithstanding her calling as a worship leader, God struck Miriam with leprosy when she opposed Moses over his marriage to a Cushite woman (Num. 12), while Aaron who had also grumbled against Moses was not afflicted with the flesh-eating skin disease.

Other women and girls portrayed in Hebrew scripture and the Greek Septuagint (an ancient Jewish translation from roughly the third century BCE) testify to the saving power of the God of Israel, who favors the faithful of all nations, regardless of gender, and with a particular interest in blessing the weak and vulnerable. The Law of Moses forbade prostitution, yet when the Israelites reentered the Promised Land, Rahab the prostitute was rewarded with safety for herself and her family, for helping Joshua and Caleb by hiding them on the roof of her home in the city wall of Jericho before its destruction by God (Josh. 2, 6). Widowed Moabite woman Ruth, who proclaimed to her Israelite mother-in-law Naomi, "your people shall be my people, and your God, my God" (New American Standard Version, Ruth 1:16b) was blessed for adopting the religion of Israel, becoming the great-grandmother of King David.

In the same pre-monarchic period, Israel had one female judge, Deborah (Judg. 4), and centuries later, a prophetess Huldah gave spiritual counsel when approached by the advisors of King Josiah (2 Kgs 22:14–20). God heard and answered the anguished prayer of Hannah for a son, causing her to conceive and give birth to the prophet Samuel and ending the mockery of sister-wife Peninnah, who already had children from their husband Elkanah (1 Sam. 1:1-20). General Naaman of Aram was cured of leprosy thanks to his Israelite servant girl's insistence that he go see the prophet Elisha for healing by plunging himself seven times into the river Jordan (2 Kgs 5:1–14).

Esther, Jewish wife of Persian king Xerxes I, saved the Jewish exiles in fifth century Persia, when she discovered Haman's genocidal plot and defied propriety notions for a queen in begging her husband to intervene (Est. 5). God commanded the prophet Hosea to marry a prostitute named Gomer, and they had several children together (Hos. 1), while Joel foretold that one day after a great pouring out of the Holy Spirit, both young men and women would prophesy (Joel 2:28). In the Greek additions to stories in the Exilic and Second Temple periods, pious and beautiful Judith beheaded Assyrian general Holofernes with the help of God (Jdt.). In the Greek literature of the New Testament, Anna of the tribe of Asher prophesied about the coming of Jesus at the Temple in Jerusalem (Lk. 2:36–8). These women of scripture carry out the will of God, and as read by many traditional Christians, they are an important part of the salvation story that centers on the coming of Christ as Savior of the world.

Jesus has meaningful relationships with several women in the Gospel narratives, most notably his Middle Eastern mother Mary, who raised him to speak the Aramaic tongue and to love and honor Jehovah God. As Christian Gospel narrative traditions developed in the first century CE, Mary the mother of Jesus was venerated as the virgin who gave birth to the Savior, heralded by the angel Gabriel announcing her divinely ordained pregnancy, "Hail, favored one! The Lord is with you" (Lk. 1:280). According to the earliest Gospel, Jesus attracted female followers—his mother and many other women—who believed and supported his ministry from his early days of teaching and healing in Galilee through his crucifixion and burial in Jerusalem (Mk 15:40–7). In his parables where he showed knowledge of Hebrew scriptures, Jesus included female characters, such as in the "widow's mite," where he commends the generosity of a poor woman who gives her last two coins as an offering to God, while rich men gave out of their wealth and abundance, which was no sacrifice for them (Mk 12:41–4, Lk. 21:1–4). In another parable, a woman loses a valuable coin and vigorously cleans her house until she finds it, calling all her friends to help celebrate, just as heaven rejoices when a sinner repents (Lk. 15:8–10). No wonder that women loved to hear Jesus teach, finding time amid their daily tasks to sit with him and listen. Jesus encouraged such female disciples in their learning, defending loyal follower Mary when her sister Martha complained of her neglecting household chores (Lk. 10:38–42).

In his first-century healing ministry, Jesus helped women and girls such as the seeker with "an issue of blood," whose healing by touching Jesus's garment hem is mentioned by all three Synoptic Gospel writers (Mt. 9:20–2, Mk 5:25–34, Lk. 8:43–8). Moments later, in the account from the Gospel of Mark, Jesus arrives at the home of synagogue official Jairus, whose twelve-year-old daughter has just died. Jesus says to her in his mother-tongue Aramaic, "*Talitha koum*," meaning, "Little girl, I say to you, arise!" And she lived again, but Jesus gave strict orders that no one outside the room should know what had happened (Mk 5:35–43). Challenging the austere Law of Moses and advocating its loosening for the benefit of women, Jesus ignored the Pharisees' condemnation of a woman caught in adultery, telling her only to go and sin no more rather than approving the law's punishment of death by stoning (Jn 8:1–11). According to all Gospel accounts, Jesus included women in his ministry and considered them an essential part of God's creation who he had come to teach, heal, and save.

But after his resurrection into heaven, as traditional Christians believe, did Jesus sitting at the right hand of the Father want godly women to teach, preach, prophesy, and lay hands on the sick, pointing souls to salvation? Moreover, was this the Father's will, and would the Holy Ghost lead and guide women into spiritual leadership roles equal to or even greater than the callings noted in Hebrew scripture? Some **canonical** New Testament writers, deemed by generations of church leaders to be inspired by God, opposed female church leadership. Fundamentalist Baptist preacher Steven L. Anderson (b.1981) of Tempe, Arizona, cites 1 Timothy 2:11, "I do not permit a woman to teach or to have authority over a man," against the trend toward Protestant female pastors (Anderson 2014). Anderson's online popularity reflects a widespread agreement with his literal interpretation of the passage. Biblical scholars in the Western academic tradition, however, maintain that although traditionally attributed to the apostle Paul (c. 5 BCE–c. 64 CE), 1 Timothy was written by a later, unknown Christian writer, indicating that the NT book lacks apostolic authority. Paul writing elsewhere, but possibly as an interpolation from a later writer, says to the church at Corinth, "women should keep silent in the churches" (1 Cor. 14:34), and a literal interpretation of this verse has also reinforced views that women should not preach or pastor in Christian churches. On the other hand, the apostolic history attributed to Luke, a follower of Paul, claims that Joel's foretelling of young women prophesying has come to fruition at the Day of Pentecost (Acts 2:16–17), and this text in particular has empowered women throughout Christian history to hear, speak, and write at the urging of the Holy Spirit.

While Paul's own letters, in contrast to Gospel writings and the book of Acts, may promote a negative view of women's leadership in Christianity, he nevertheless taught **Christological** views that included women as full members of the body of Christ, and he valued their contributions to early Christian missions and formation of communities. Paul acknowledged that women (with their heads properly covered) prayed and prophesied aloud in churches (1 Cor. 11:5), and as baptized believers, they participated equally in the new covenant sign of unity with Christ, replacing the old covenant sign of circumcision (1 Cor. 12:13). Departing controversially from his Jewish legal and religious roots, Paul rejected the Levite tribe's monopoly on the priesthood and argued that Jesus had offered himself as the final sinless sacrifice, and that the blood of Christ the Savior cleansed humanity of the sin that Adam, not Eve, brought upon them (Rom. 5:6–12). Due to this view of Christ as sacrificial lamb and savior of all human souls, sacrifices offered at the temple in Jerusalem were no longer necessary, removing some of the prejudice against women who could neither enter the holy place nor serve as priests. Women could serve in church communities, where spiritual servant or slave status was embraced even by a leader like Paul (Rom. 1:1; Gal. 1:10). In Paul's **soteriology**, God graciously grants eternal salvation of the human soul equally to all baptized believers, so that Mosaic legal distinctions between nationalities, slave versus free, and male versus female were abolished, "for you are all one in Christ Jesus" (Gal. 3:28). Paul wrote appreciatively about the women who served with him, such as Phoebe in Corinth (Rom. 16:1), and today's academic scholars concur that women of all social classes made essential contributions to early Christianity, whether hosting religious gatherings in spacious homes or serving as perpetual virgins in Christ's service (Mullin 2014: 24, 42).

Paul's view of scripture also paved the way for spiritually anointed biblical preaching by women once Christian Bibles became available in countless translations and in an extended, relatively fixed literary *canon* unknown to the earliest Christians. When Paul wrote his Greek letters to congregations he had visited or intended to visit on his missions trips, he delivered teachings he would ideally have communicated in person (Rom. 1:13) and that were a concise distillation and reinterpretation of Hebrew scriptures as being fulfilled with the coming of Christ. The Law of Moses, the prophets, and the wisdom teachings and psalms were passed down to each new generation in carefully maintained scrolls, written in archaic Hebrew language that had become distant from the Aramaic, Greek, and Latin speech of Israel's inhabitants in Paul's day. So Paul's Greek theological writing, in engaging letters such as Galatians, Romans, and 1–2 Corinthians, made thinking about God in Christ more accessible to all interested people, especially those who had already been reading the Septuagint translation of the Hebrew scriptures. Gospel writers, compiling their texts after Paul's time, applied his Christological views—that Christ was truly the wonder-working Son of God foretold by prophets such as Isaiah and who offered himself as a final blood sacrifice in atonement for human sin—to the chronological earthly life and ministry of Jesus and his followers, including women who were the first to see the empty tomb. One could through the sign of baptism (not circumcision) become a heaven-bound member of a Christian community, where specialized knowledge of the Law of Moses lost its former prestige and usefulness. In centuries to follow, with the canonization of Christian literature into a specific set of Greek books, attached in convenient codex form to the traditional writings translated in Greek, a Christian Bible emerged and could be translated into many languages and published as evolving technologies allowed (MacCulloch 2010: 158, 627). Women were subsequently able to preach and teach from scripture in an unprecedented way, in large part due to the theology of Paul and other early Christian apostles such as Peter. In the meantime, Christian women called into God's service distinguished themselves in other admirable ways.

Women of Faith in Late Antiquity and the Latin Middle Ages

Women of the post-apostolic era served as foundational, essential members of Christian communities and sometimes became respected figures who courageously endured martyrdom. Christian communities of late antiquity provided favorable conditions for women to thrive, in that they rejected female infanticide, preached against divorce, and denounced incest, infidelity, and polygamy (Mullin 2014: 42). Christian women were supported in commitments to chastity before marriage and could expect sexual faithfulness from their husbands in marriage. While not promoted to the highest church offices, they could serve as deaconesses, assisting in baptism of women and otherwise ministering to women, and they were valued as witnesses of important events, in contrast to prevailing views in the cultures of antiquity (Rowland 1985: 191). Women could discern a holy calling to perpetual virginity as an alternative to marriage and childrearing; if widowed, the church did not pressure them to remarry, in contrast to expectations of Roman society (Mullin 2014: 42). Particularly gifted women could dream prophetically and be believed after seeing holy visions, and in the face of persecution, they could expect a martyr's reward for death: immediate entry into eternal paradise, skipping the wait in slumber of death for final judgment. North African saints and young mothers Perpetua and Felicitas (d.202 CE) demonstrated this in the early third century by refusing to recant to escape execution, defying social expectations of putting love of family before faith, according to Perpetua's authentic account, edited posthumously by her friends. Prior to her passion, Perpetua, a **mystic**, saw herself in a vision fighting wild beasts and the devil, which strengthened her resolve to endure death by mauling in a Carthage arena rather than renounce Christ. At a time of intense persecution, she championed the moral high ground of martyrdom instead of apostasy: "Stand fast in the faith, and love ye one another" (quoted in Mullin 2014: 45). Such women who gave their lives for the faith found great respect in close-knit Christian communities as saintly conduits of God's miraculous love and grace.

In the **Roman Catholic** and Eastern/Ethiopian Orthodox traditions, where only men can become priests, women's contributions as saints, patrons, and mystics were known and revered throughout late antiquity and the Middle Ages. Sarah and Syncletica, fourth-century women of ancient Egypt, embraced holy desert living, inspiring other women to join them in lives devoted solely to prayer. Egyptian men also formed religious communities, and together, male and female models of Christian monasticism perpetuated a rich Orthodox spiritual tradition and heavily influenced the development of religious orders in Europe (Isichei 1995: 29). In monastic houses and convents, many women had a culturally rare opportunity to discern a call to a life of prayer, study, and service, with institutional support to live out such a calling. The Emperor Constantine's mother, Helena (c. 250–330), contributed to the rise of pilgrimage and the cult of saints and shrines in the early Middle Ages, visiting the Holy Land in the 320s. She had an impressive church built in Bethlehem and a second on the Mount of Olives in Jerusalem (Mullin 2014: 55). Veneration of the ascended Virgin Mary, Mother of God and Queen of Heaven, also grew in Eastern and European Christianity during the medieval period, with statues erected where the faithful could pray for her to intercede with Christ on their behalf (MacCulloch 2003: 17–18). In the Latin liturgy of the Mass, the Song of Mary or the *Magnificat* (Lk. 1:39–56) reminded European churchgoers of her importance as glorified being already rejoicing in heaven and of God's promise to safeguard and reward devout women. As European universities developed from monastic foundations, women stayed fixed in roles of prayer and service, denied the opportunity to become academic theologians, schooled in the methods of classical reason and metaphysical proof. Great intellects such as

Thomas Aquinas (1225–74) used complex Aristotelian methodology to defend the Roman Catholic Church's doctrine of transubstantiation, the miraculous change of bread and wine into the body and blood of Christ during the sacred Mass. Unorthodox Christians (heretics), Muslims, and Jews found their views refuted eloquently in Latin by scores of prolific scholastic medieval theologians, none of them women.

As in the past, gifted medieval women earned profound respect as mystics and spiritual authors, battling sexist stereotypes among an increasingly more biblically literate population who were in early stages of monumental religious change. Julian of Norwich (1342–c. 1420) wrote of her visions during sickness of God as kindly father and "God all-wisdom" as "our kindly Mother: with the love and goodness of the Holy Ghost; which is all one God, one Lord" (quoted in Placher and Nelson 2015: 179). Her book, *Revelations of Divine Love*, became the earliest surviving book in English written by a woman. As medieval European institutions abused and excluded women, literature such as the *Malleus Maleficarum* (1486) depicted women as feeble-minded and prone to using witchcraft. Many women considered whether early modern religious Reforms and colonial migration opportunities would allow them to serve Christ with even greater sincerity and truth. Although early modern reforms caused devastating fragmentation in Christianity and in European political institutions, the rise of the printing press and vernacular translations of scripture, coupled with colonial expansion's new political havens for religious freedom, allowed for the rise of powerful female **evangelists** and even priests in some denominations.

When Martin Luther (1483–1546) called for reform of Roman Catholic doctrines of purgatory and the Mass, and of papal primacy (MacCulloch 2003: 10–15, 26–34), women of great piety and conscience found themselves on each side of the Reformation divide. Ex-monk Luther's bride, Katharina von Bora (1499–1552), an ex-nun, embraced Protestant teachings and assumed the role of pious, dutiful, and learned German pastor's wife. Literate women studied the printed Latin or vernacular scriptures carefully in newly available portable Bibles, to grow in faith, teach their children and household members, and understand religious controversies about how to bring the faith back into alignment with apostolic doctrine and practice. Anne Boleyn (1501–36), famous second wife of Henry VIII of England (1491–1547) and mother of Queen Elizabeth I (1533–1603), promoted the Reformation cause, reading the New Testament newly translated by William Tyndale (1494–1536) and encouraging her household to embrace ideas of salvation by faith only, not through merit-based works such as pilgrimage and prayers to the saints (Daniell 2003: 152). Saint Teresa of Ávila (1515–82), a Carmelite nun and mystic who wrote powerfully of her dreams in *Way of Perfection* (1583), exhorted fellow Roman Catholics in Spain and beyond to a life of prayer as a response to the dramatic turning away from traditional piety in Protestant areas such as England, Germany, and the Netherlands. Anne Bradstreet (1612–72), New England colonist and devout Protestant, applied her biblical learning to the writing of poetry, significant sections of which "moved in and out of Scripture and expect the reader to recognize this" (Daniell 2003: 551). Whether maintaining a belief in salvation through full sacramental participation in the Roman Catholic Church

FIGURE 5.2 *Since the early modern period, Christian women have had greater access to printed Bibles in vernacular languages, for personal study and outreach.* Source: *Kelly Sikkema/Unsplash.*

or by faith only through grace in Bible-centered Protestant churches free from papal control, women in the early modern period gained greater knowledge of scripture and were poised to communicate ideas or visions directly to a growing reading public that included potential new converts in the Americas.

North American Christian Women through the Twenty-First Century

Whether nuns, wives, and mothers or writers and preachers, North American women since colonial times have shaped Christianity while facing controversy in a divided Christian world. Roman Catholic women, bound to observe the conservative, anti-Protestant decrees of the Council of Trent (1545–63), looked to the church to receive sacraments faithfully administered by priests and reading the Bible when given permission. Mexican women established a legacy of prayerful piety and chastity inspired by a Saint Teresa of Ávila and other saintly women and men, and lay women sometimes voluntarily lived alongside nuns in convents. Whether serving at a convent as a slave or committed involuntarily by family members to learn obedience, women participated in colonial Mexican religious culture through reserved but strategic engagement with rituals and authority figures (Delgado 2018: 6–13). From French

Quebec to Mexico, Catholic women saw access to duly administered sacraments as the pathway to eternal salvation, while Boston Puritans and Virginian Anglicans viewed their interpretation of Christianity as a more dignified way to journey toward heaven. Each literate Protestant woman read extensively from vernacular scriptures such as the Geneva Bible (1560) or King James Version (1611) and discerned her soul's salvation directly with God, accepting authority of husband and king as divinely ordained.

In the seventeenth century, permanent New England colonies of a distinctively English Protestant character emerged, where women such as Anne Bradstreet demonstrated the growth of English-speaking culture, a by-product of the English Reformation and emphasis on scripture (not Roman Catholic tradition) as the sole source of Christian truth. Puritan women read the Bible extensively and with cultural approval, cultivating a private, intellectual piety and prayer modality distinctive from that of lay Roman Catholic women who confessed their sins to a priest and might not know the language of scripture to pray it extemporaneously themselves. When a Protestant woman's thinking became too controversial, a New England woman such as Anne Hutchinson (1591–1643) could migrate to less regulated territory in Rhode Island and persist in what many contemporaries deemed theological error. Reversing medieval views assuming the worst about women's readiness to consort with the devil, famous Massachusetts minister Cotton Mather (1663–1728) concluded that women were more spiritual than men, leading to eventual abandonment of witch trials that had often been directed against women (MacCulloch 2010: 793). Insofar as the major intellectual institutions of Europe and the various American colonies were still dominated by men, whether Catholic clergy or learned Protestant divines, women continued to be excluded from the highest level of scriptural reflection and theological argument, despite their sophisticated engagement with vernacular scriptures.

By the early eighteenth century, Roman Catholics lived in the Atlantic colonies in greater numbers, and together with Protestants, they faced new challenges from Enlightenment critics of traditional belief. Emphasizing reason and science as the foundation of truth and questioning the divine authority of kings and of scripture itself, Deists rejected the Scholastic method and laid the foundations of the modern scientific method of observation and experimentation. In an era when transatlantic slavery reached its highest volume, Enlightenment thinkers argued for the inherent dignity of the human person and the universal right of free people to govern themselves. Some of these ideas inspired American revolutionaries to overthrow British colonial rule, while other notions provoked a spiritual backlash in Evangelicalism and the Great Awakening.

Where Enlightenment reason and its theological manifestations in **liberal Christianity** questioned the existence of literal heaven and hell, Evangelicals insisted on apostolic Christology and the necessity of the individual developing a personal relationship with the truly risen Savior. Missionaries from Moravia spread religion of the heart throughout the transatlantic slave triangle route, inspiring British brothers John Wesley (1703–91) and Charles Wesley (1707–88), educated at Lincoln College, Oxford, to adopt lives of fervent prayer and intense study of vernacular scripture in preparation for their own missionary callings. The Wesleys ministered to American slaves and helped increase rates of conversion to Protestantism where believers prayed extemporaneously at great length to Jesus Christ who they believed worked miracles of deliverance and healing. By the nineteenth century when Sierra Leone and Liberia were founded as for freed slaves, some Black colonists who returned to West Africa had converted to Evangelical Protestantism and learned to read the Bible, laying the foundations for Pentecostal revival with some Black women leaders in the twentieth century.

Evangelicals also formed Bible societies to distribute scriptures to the masses, pushing back against liberal critics of the Bible who saw the text as a product of human invention, written by anonymous authors rather than real historical figures such as Moses, David, or Peter. The favored translation of English-speaking Evangelicals was the King James Bible, often produced containing just the New Testament due to the print cost savings. Prior to the eighteenth century, complete Protestant Bibles (Old and New Testaments) included the Apocrypha, also known as the deuterocanonical books. Apocryphal Old Testament texts (1–2 Macc., Jdt., Tob., and others) were found only in the Greek Septuagint, without a Hebrew original known at that time. Evangelicals omitted the Apocrypha in their missionary Bibles. Thus, streamlined further, the canon of scriptures in a familiar version became ever more manageable for **charismatic** preachers to expound upon to open-air audiences, passionately calling for sinners to repent and for the unbaptized to join the family of God down by the river. On the American frontier, Evangelical revivalism created a favorable climate for inspired and knowledgeable women, called by God, to lead seekers to deeper Christian faith.

Maria Beulah Woodworth-Etter (1844–1924) of Ohio felt a call to preach the Christian Gospel soon after her sudden Evangelical conversion in 1879, serving as an itinerant American revivalist for the next forty-five years. She defied contemporary expectations for a wife and mother, not less due to her education being limited to self-study of the King James Bible in its shorter, 66-book Evangelical canon. Woodworth-Etter reported that at the beginning of her ministry, she saw a vision of grain ready for harvest, immersed in "liquid fire" of God's healing presence (Jacobsen 2006: 19). Protected by American religious freedom, the visionary's integrated meetings reached crowds of 25,000 by the 1880s and featured widely reported biblical preaching, followed by an altar call with strange physical phenomena such as spellbinding trances experienced by believers and non-believers alike. Her husband, Philo Harrison Woodworth, a Civil War veteran with a traumatic head injury, had no interest in the ministry. He sold concessions at the back of her tent revival meetings from the Midwest to California until the two divorced (Warner 1986: 7–21). She faced opposition for refusing to segregate her southern meetings where at altar benches blacks and whites together sought healing and salvation. Woodworth-Etter insisted that "God made the whole human family of one blood. Christ had died for all" (quoted in Warner 1986: 215). Some opposition came from those who objected on principle to women preachers. In early 1890, she brought harsh criticism on herself with a false prophecy in Oakland, California, where she claimed that on April 14, tidal waves would destroy the Pacific coast city and simultaneously Great Lakes cities Milwaukee and Chicago (Warner 1986: 100–1). Supporters sold their homes and headed for the hills only for the date of doom to come and go without incident. For positive and negative reasons, her prolific ministry generated a great deal of news coverage and influenced denominations and churches, especially in the early Pentecostal period.

Pentecostal revivals became prominent around the globe at the turn of the twentieth century, with poor and disadvantaged seekers embracing Evangelical religion of the heart, together with spirit-possessed behavior in public meetings, such as rolling on the ground and unintelligible shouting. Women and people of color often led local revivals, among them African American William J. Seymour (1872–1922) in Los Angeles. Participants at Pentecostal services sang lively Gospel hymns, listened to lively sermons, and proceeded to fall under the power of God for hours, witnessing charismatic manifestations of the Spirit exactly as they believed the apostles had experienced on the day of Pentecost (Acts 2). Seminary trained Seymour preached an interracial revival on Azusa Street, training missionaries including African American Lucy Farrow (1851–1911), who traveled to Liberia in 1907. Farrow and others brought the charisma and Bible-centered teaching of the Pentecostal outpouring with them and helped introduce new service formats where converts could share testimonies in vernacular languages and contribute to the praise music with traditional instruments such as calabash rattles.

Woodworth-Etter continued to hold meetings as the Pentecostal movement gained attention and converts, noticing with disapproval the theatrical style of younger **evangelist** Aimee Semple McPherson (neé Kennedy, 1890–1944) of Ontario, Canada. Aimee Kennedy converted to Pentecostalism after hearing the preaching of Irish evangelist Robert Semple, and the two married and set off for China as missionaries (Shaefer 2004: 3). At age twenty, she found herself widowed and a mother to baby Roberta. She and her child traveled alone from China to New York City to live with her mother, Minnie Kennedy, just nineteen years her senior. Marriage to Harold McPherson and the birth of a son, Rolf, could not tie McPherson down (the two would divorce in 1921). Sensing a call to preach, she left with the children for Canada in 1916 and led successful revivals, soon starting a publication and publishing house, *The Bridal Call*. In 1918, she drove to California with her mother and children, possibly the first woman to drive herself across the continental United States (Epstein 1993: 95). So far, her life's story somewhat paralleled Woodworth-Etter's, but the two Pentecostal leaders kept a distance from each other due to stylistic differences in preaching and outreach methods. At least once in Indianapolis, the two were in the same city, and Woodworth-Etter's evangelistic party reported that the elder preacher expressed concern about the direction McPherson's ministry was going, with theatrical performances that took attention away from the simple Gospel of repentance and deliverance from sin and disease (Warner 1986: 292). Both *Evangelical* and Pentecostal, and both opposed to liberal Christianity and secularism, the women remained at odds over issues they felt were important for the integrity of God's great revival, anticipating divisions in the charismatic movement that continued throughout the twentieth century.

By 1923 when McPherson put down roots in Los Angeles, she had preached in more than a hundred cities and towns, staying from one or two nights to more than a month in some cities (Epstein 1993: 95–6). Angelus Temple, built with funds raised from her supporters, held daily crowds of 5,000 people, and the newspapers reported on her activities as well as her many scandals from 1926 onward. A kidnapping and disappearance, possibly faked to mask an affair with her married sound man, followed by a second failed marriage to a different man, tarnished her reputation significantly. McPherson rebounded after each setback, claiming she preached more sermons than any other living preacher of her time, with a ministry total of 40,000 converts baptized, 400 branch churches formed, and 178 mission outposts planted around the world (Barfoot 2011: 1). The two legendary yet flawed female evangelists published major works of around 600 pages within a few years of each other: McPherson's *This is That* (1919), followed by Woodworth-Etter's *Marvels and Miracles* (1922). Together, their ministries offered generations of North Americans and their audiences a meaningful Christian experience—a lively, powerful faith in which divine promises of scripture really came true and a glimpse of heavenly glory could be seen in this life.

Women in twentieth-century Evangelical and Pentecostal leadership continued to gain prominence in North America and throughout the world, sometimes known for their modern music ministries. Gloria Gaither (b.1942), together with her husband

FIGURE 5.3 *Music performed in North American churches has often been composed by women, and women often serve as charismatic worship leaders.* Source: *Edward Cisneros/ Unsplash.*

Bill Gaither (b.1936), built an American-based media empire, fueled by their original songwriting and successful marketing of performance recordings. Beginning in the 1960s, Ms. Gaither wrote songs and Christian musical scripts that drew upon her life circumstances. She composed lyrics expressing the calm assurance she found in Christian faith, producing popular songs, for instance "Something Beautiful" (Harper 2017: 108). As longtime husband and wife musical team, the Gaithers wrote over 700 songs, some of them becoming standard worship songs that Evangelicals know by heart, such as "He touched me," "Let's just praise the Lord," "The Family of God," and "Because He Lives." From the late 1990s, Australian Pentecostal singer-songwriter Darlene Zschech (b.1965) rose to worldwide fame as a worship leader and Contemporary Christian Music recording artist, with a significant impact on North American church music cultures. Hillsong United is a band and global outreach ministry featuring popular female lead singers Brooke Fraser (b.1983) of New Zealand and Taya Smith (b.1989) of Australia. The Hillsong franchise has performed worship concerts all over the world and planted missionary churches in North America, including a branch in New York City. The American-based global media empire of Joel and Victoria Osteen and other evangelistic associations formed by notable male and female preachers carry on the work begun by charismatic pioneers Woodworth-Etter and Semple McPherson.

Since the middle of the twentieth century, feminist theologians more in alignment with Enlightenment ideals than with fundamentalist Pentecostal faith have demonstrated keen intellect in traditionally male positions of Christian authority while facing opposition and misunderstanding within their own churches. Sidestepping full-on secularism, feminist theologians embrace feminist social principles such as pushing for reform of male-dominated institutions, advocating for equal women's rights in society, and understanding gender roles and behaviors as learned from culture, not assigned by nature or God. Feminist biblical scholarship analyzes and critiques the portrayal of women in biblical stories while extolling the virtues of female "characters" who have emerged since biblical times, especially the past two centuries: "Sojourner Truth, Anna Julia Cooper, Elizabeth Cady Stanton, Mary Wollstonecraft, Emmeline Pankhurst" and others (Sherwood 2001: 296). Embracing these values, many intellectually gifted women have asserted their right to first-class theological education in the Western philosophical tradition, taking on prominent roles as theologians and bishops, criticizing traditional ideas and in turn facing criticism for their understanding of scripture.

Catholic theologian Elizabeth A. Johnson forged an important pathway for women as heirs of the scholastic tradition of writing and teaching university-level Roman Catholic theology. Catholic women have an impressive spiritual writing legacy, including works by Perpetua, Julian of Norwich, Teresa of Ávila, and many others, yet pious women in Catholicism were not widely known as authors of systematic theology. In 1981, Johnson became the first woman to receive a doctoral degree from the Catholic University of America. In part due to reforms in the Catholic Church enacted at the Second Vatican Council (1962–5), where an official stance since the nineteenth century against modernism was set aside (Mullin 2014: 269–72), Johnson could engage with feminist ideas in theological work. A member of the Sisters of St. Joseph of Brentwood,

FIGURE 5.4 *Since the 1980s, Elizabeth Johnson's teachings and publications have promoted the dignity of women in Christianity and the world.* Source: *Elizabeth Johnson.*

Johnson wrote critically in her first published book, *She Who Is* (1992), of the persistent use of masculine pronouns for God in Christian worship. Such use gives believers the impression that "God is male, or at least more like a man than a woman, or at least more fittingly addressed as male than as female" (Johnson 1992: 4). Exclusive speech about God "support[s] an imaginative and structural world that excludes or subordinates women. Wittingly or not, it undermines women's human dignity as equally created in the image of God" (4–5). Advocating new speech about God that upholds the dignity of women, Johnson has emphasized the unknowability of God as explored in classical Western theology, while being appreciative of the ineffability of God as understood in cultures outside of North America and outside of Christianity (112–19). At times facing opposition from Roman Catholic leaders, she continues to enjoy a positive reputation as a leading North American Christian theologian and professor.

Despite the accomplishments of intellectual Catholic women such as Johnson, the Roman Catholic Church bars women from top leadership positions such as priests and bishops, refusing to modernize along the lines of the American Episcopal Church and most Pentecostal churches. At the Second Vatican Council, a Latin-based tradition gave way to sweeping modernizations, as conciliar decrees declared the church's openness to biblical translation from original languages, vernacular masses, and more involvement of the laity, including women, in the worship and catechesis of the church. Yet the priesthood was still reserved for celibate men who had discerned a call from God. Sex abuse scandals and cover-ups seemed to indicate that in North America and elsewhere, a celibate male priesthood, corrupt and aging, was not meeting the spiritual needs of parishioners. Neither historians' claims that women served as priests in the early church nor feminist theologians' urging for equal representation of women in church leadership have opened doors for women to become priests in the Roman Catholic Church. The Vatican has, however, clarified its unwavering spiritual support for natural born women and all they do for their families, the world, and the Kingdom of God, often under much more difficult conditions than the men around them. Pope John Paul II wrote in a special letter to women dated June 29, 1995:

> Thank you, women who are mothers! You have sheltered human beings within yourselves in a unique experience of joy and travail [...]. Thank you, women who work! You [...] make an indispensable contribution [...] to the establishment of economic and political structures ever more worthy of humanity. Thank you, consecrated women! Following the example of the greatest of women, the Mother of Jesus Christ, the Incarnate Word, you open yourselves with obedience and fidelity to the gift of God's love.
>
> (Helman 2012: 198)

Thus, even while holding to its traditional soteriological teachings, that a male priest in the image of Christ must perform the sacraments for the cooperative salvation of church members, the Roman Catholic Church welcomes and appreciates women and their multifaceted contributions. It remains to be seen whether the next council will feature rigorous debate and potentially new conciliar decrees allowing for the ordination of women called by God to the Catholic priesthood.

Women in clerical leadership, in denominations that have accepted them, have no guarantees of a smooth tenure during their time in office. The Most Reverend Katherine Jefferts Schori, the first woman to serve in the highest leadership position of the Episcopal Church, came to the position with an impressive academic background as a biologist and was awarded an honorary D.D. from Oxford (the highest degree in the medieval university system) in 2014. Yet the year before, she experienced condemnation for a controversial sermon on Acts 16:16–34 while visiting the Episcopal Diocese of Venezuela. Preaching in Curaçao, Jefferts Schori interpreted Luke's account of Paul casting a demon out of a fortune-telling slave girl as the renowned evangelist's failure "to value diversity, to see the slave girl's beautiful 'difference'" (Oppenheimer 2013). She preached that in the account, the slave girl proclaims apostolic truth, but Paul was "annoyed perhaps for being put in his place, and he responds by depriving her of her gift of spiritual awareness. Paul can't abide something he won't see as beautiful or holy, so he tries to destroy it" (quoted in Oppenheimer 2013). Such exegetical remarks seemed to reject the possibility of a demon-occupied world, where possession sometimes occurs and a man or woman of God can rebuke the unclean spirit and cause a person to be delivered by the power of God. Episcopalians and other Christians questioned the bishop's exegetical skill and even whether she was an authentic Christian. Under her leadership, many congregations left the Episcopal Church, often to affiliate with organizations holding more traditional views on sacred scripture and on social issues such as gay marriage for laity and ordination of women, gays, and lesbians to the clergy.

Episcopalians notably enact reforms in the spirit of equal opportunity for women in global leadership, sometimes falling out of synch with peer churches in the worldwide Anglican Communion, particularly in the Southern Hemisphere. Mpho Tutu, daughter of famed former South African Archbishop Desmond Tutu, experienced firsthand the challenges of navigating a global church where the American branch turned out to be more progressive than the church in her native country. Tutu was ordained in 2004 by the Episcopal Church in Alexandria, Virginia. Her father presided over the ceremony, and Mpho Tutu returned for a ministerial career as a licensed priest in the Anglican Church in South Africa. The father–daughter duo coauthored *The Book of Forgiving: The Fourfold Path for Healing Ourselves and Our World* (2014). By 2016, Tutu had divorced the father of her children and married her long-term girlfriend, Dutch atheist philosophy professor Marceline van Furth. In the Episcopal Church, where lesbians had been ordained since 1991, Tutu's remarriage to a woman would not have caused her to give up her license. Likewise, in the Church of England, where ordination of gays and lesbians began in 2005, she could have carried on with parish ministry as a priest. Pressured by the more conservative South African Church, she gave up her ministerial license and moved to the Netherlands. Known as the Rev. Canon Mpho Tutu van Furth, she continues to be held in high regard by Christians sharing her values of inclusivity, gay rights, and preservation of the environment.

In the same global church as the Tutus, the Very Reverend Shannon MacLean Brown, first African American bishop of the Episcopal Church of Vermont, has accepted the challenge of shepherding a dwindling flock in the least religious of all fifty American states. An artist with interests in environmentalism, she took office in May 2019

FIGURE 5.5 *Shannon MacLean-Brown, an artist with interests in environmentalism, became the first African American female bishop of the Diocese of Vermont.* Source: *Maurice Harris, the Episcopal Church in Vermont.*

and promised "she would be 'looking at numbers.'" Her main focus as bishop will be conservation, with an emphasis on "creation care, conservation and alternative energy" (Wertlieb and Rosen 2019). During the COVID-19 crisis of 2020 when all churches closed for an extended period of time, she moved quickly to offer online prayer services. The daily services, available to parishioners or anyone interested, featured Bishop Shannon on Zoom or via telephone conference, from a publicly posted number and pin on her website. The need to adapt to circumstances thus shifted a progressive leader of a traditionally liturgical (formal Eucharist, with pre-written prayers) a bit more into alignment with Pentecostal-charismatic leaders, who have ministered effectively through global communication technologies for decades.

While onlookers of the emerging story of women in Christianity admire what they see in the Episcopal Church, according to the numbers of weekly attendees and members in good standing, Roman Catholics and Pentecostal-charismatics have the larger numbers in North America and throughout the world. Diverse women have shown themselves to be intellectual heirs of Paul and Aquinas as well as spiritual descendants of musical Miriam, visionary Perpetua, and prayerful Teresa of Avila. Yet critics of particular women in leadership or of the appropriateness of any women in Christian leadership will continue to draw attention to mistakes and errors of judgment that women leaders, being human, will continue to make. Facilitating salvation of lost souls for heaven and preserving welcoming, green spaces on Earth, women in North American Christianity will keep shaping the faith at home and throughout the world.

References

Anderson, S.L. (2014), "'Women Preachers' Preached by Pastor Steven L Anderson at Faithful Word Baptist," *YouTube*, March 24. Available online: https://www.youtube.com/watch?v=j921XOqiQ7o (accessed October 20, 2019).

Barfoot, C.H. (2011), *Aimee Semple McPherson and the Making of Modern Pentecostalism, 1890–1926*, London: Equinox Publishing.

Daniell, D. (2003), *The Bible in English: Its History and Influence*, New Haven, CT: Yale University Press.

Delgado, J. (2018), *Laywomen and the Making of Colonial Catholicism in New Spain, 1630–1790*, Cambridge: Cambridge University Press.

Epstein, D.M. (1993), *Sister Aimee: The Life of Aimee Semple McPherson*, New York: Harcourt Brace Jovanovich.

Harper, R.P. (2017), *The Gaithers and Southern Gospel: Homecoming in the Twenty-First Century*, Jackson: University Press of Mississippi.

Helman, I.A., ed. (2012), *Women and the Vatican: An Exploration of Official Documents*, Maryknoll, NY: Orbis Books.

Isichei, E. (1995), *Christianity in Africa*, London: SPCK; Grand Rapids, MI: Eerdmans; Lawrenceville, NJ: Africa World Press.

Jacobsen, D., ed. (2006), *A Reader in Pentecostal Theology: Voices from the First Generation*, Bloomington: Indiana University Press.

Johnson, E. (1992), *She Who Is: The Mystery of God in Feminist Theological Discourse*, Chestnut Ridge, NY: Crossroad.

MacCulloch, D. (2003), *The Reformation*, London: Allen Lane.

MacCulloch, D. (2010), *Christianity: The First Three Thousand Years*, New York: Allen Lane.

Mullin, R.B. (2014), *A Short World History of Christianity*, Rev. edn., Louisville, KY: Westminster John Knox Press.

New American Bible (2010), Rev. edn., Totowa, NJ: Catholic Book Publishing Corp.

Oppenheimer, M. (2013), "For Episcopal Church's Leader, a Sermon Leads to More Dissent," *New York Times*, June 21. Available online: https://www.nytimes.com/2013/06/22/us/for-episcopal-churchs-leader-a-sermon-leads-to-more-controversy.html (accessed November 5, 2020).

Pew Research Center (2014), *Religious Landscape Study*. Available online: https://www.pewforum.org/religious-landscape-study/gender-composition/ (accessed October 13, 2019).

Placher, W.C. and D.R. Nelson, eds. (2015), *Readings in the History of Christian Theology*, vol. 1, Louisville, KY: Westminster John Knox Press.

Rowland, C. (1985), *Christian Origins: An Account of the Setting and Character of the Most Important Messianic Sect of Judaism*, London: SPCK.

Shaefer, S.A. (2004), *Aimee Semple McPherson*, Philadelphia: Chelsea House Publishers.

Sherwood, Y. (2001), "Feminist Theology," in J. Rogerson (ed.), *The Oxford Illustrated History of the Bible*, 296–315, Oxford: Oxford University Press.

Warner, W.E. (1986), *The Woman Evangelist: The Life and Times of Charismatic Evangelist Maria B. Woodworth-Etter*, Metuchen, NJ: The Scarecrow Press.

Wertlieb, M. and S.G. Rosen (2019), "Vt. Episcopal Bishop Shannon MacVean-Brown on Inclusivity, Community, and 'Creation Care,'" *VPR*, October 11. Available online: https://www.vpr.org/post/vt-episcopal-bishop-shannon-macvean-brown-inclusivity-community-and-creation-care#stream/0 (accessed November 5, 2020).

Glossary Terms

Canonical The contents of sacred scripture at a particular point in history or for a specific denomination, as opposed to works considered secular, uninspired, or heretical. In Paul's time, the canonical scriptures included the Law of Moses, the prophets, and the writings, but not his own letters or the Gospels. Pentecostals reject the Apocrypha from their canon of inspired scripture.

Charismatic Devout Christians, often Evangelical, Pentecostal, or Roman Catholic, who exercise the gifts of the spirit as alive and working through believers today.

Christology Debates and theological arguments regarding the identity of Jesus and the role of his life, death, and resurrection in God's salvation plan for humanity.

Episcopalian American hierarchical liberal Protestants in the Anglican lineage who emphasize representation of women and gays in the clergy, the importance of caring for God's creation on Earth, and the value of exploring questions about traditional beliefs on miracles, heaven and hell, and sin.

Evangelical A broad term for especially devout Protestants who emphasize personal crisis conversion, responsibility for proselytization, belief in literal heaven and earthly return of Jesus, daily individual scripture reading, and daily extemporaneous prayers said aloud.

Evangelist A preacher, ordained or self-appointed, who proclaims the Gospel in public gatherings, seeking to revive complacency among believers and bring new converts to sincere Christian faith and practice.

Liberal Christian A broad term for thinking Protestants who emphasize science, reason, the earth's future, equality of men and women, inclusivity toward the lesbian, gay, bisexual, transgender, and queer/questioning (LGBTQ) community, and historical biblical criticism as the proper lens through which to understand scripture.

Mystic In Christianity, a believer who has an intense, personal relationship with the Divine, often reported to see visions and experience miracles of healing and heavenly knowledge, sometimes writing about the experiences for a larger audience of spiritual seekers.

Pentecostal Especially devout Evangelical Protestants who emphasize the imminent return of Jesus to Earth and practice gifts of the spirit, such as prophecy, discernment, speaking with tongues, and laying on hands for miraculous healing and deliverance from oppressive spirits.

Protestant A term encompassing hundreds of Christian denominations and independent churches emerging since the European Reformation, having similar beliefs in two sacraments (baptism and the Eucharist), sole authority of scripture for establishing doctrine, salvation solely by individual belief, and the value of married clergy.

Roman Catholic Refers to the large, hierarchical Christian church affirming traditional beliefs in the resurrection and second coming of Jesus, the authority of scripture, miracles of healing, papal doctrinal authority, the value of monasticism and clerical celibacy, the necessity of the sacraments, the reality of transubstantiation, and a literal heaven already populated with saints.

Soteriology The branch of theology dealing with questions about how the eternal human soul becomes saved. Classic biblical theology teaches that the eternal soul (which is neither male nor female) becomes saved from eternal damnation and ready for the final judgment and entry into heaven by belief in Christ and obedience to the Gospel.

Women Adults naturally born girls, typically experiencing menstrual cycles by the teenage years and who continue to identify as female and to be socially recognized as such; or adults who self-identify as women and have gained social recognition to live as women.

6

Christianity and Politics: From Constantine to Today

Darin D. Lenz

Since Christianity appeared in the first century, the religion's relationship to politics has remained contentious. Christians have rarely agreed about how their faith should interact with politics. Politics is essential to all human communities and is concerned with the rules, laws, and relationships that govern a group or society. The term originates from the Greek word *polis* meaning "city" or "state," and came to describe how the affairs of the city or state could best be managed. Christianity originates with Jesus of Nazareth, the promised Messiah, found in the Hebrew scriptures more commonly known as the Old Testament. Throughout Jesus's three years of ministry in the first century, he was a highly polarizing figure and his arrest, trial, execution, burial, and resurrection were, according to the accounts in the New Testament, treated as political events by Jewish leaders and Roman authorities.

In the decades that followed the time of Christ, Christianity separated from Judaism and Christians began to suffer erratic bouts of persecution from the Romans. Christians were viewed as a new sect practicing an immoral superstition that was subversive to Roman rule. The worst period of persecution erupted at the end of the third century when Christians serving in the Roman army began to be viewed as disloyal and were executed if they did not recant their faith in Christ. Even though many Christians served as Roman soldiers, there was no uniform agreement about the stance that Christians should take toward military service, and this made them appear unpatriotic. Roman authorities feared that a lack of religious unity focused on the worship of traditional Roman deities would undermine the favor bestowed upon the empire by the pantheon of gods. Upon the orders of the Roman emperor Diocletian, Christians were expelled from the army. In 303, a new edict removed Christians from all roles in government and demanded that Christian books and places of worship be destroyed,

FIGURE 6.1 Chi and rho are the first two letters for the Greek word for Christ (Χριστός) and the Greek letters alpha and omega mean Christ is the beginning and the end. Source: Svantassel/Wikimedia Commons.

FIGURE 6.2 *Victory of Constantine at the Battle of Milvian Bridge.* Source: *Philadelphia Museum of Art/Wikimedia Commons.*

along with requiring Christians make sacrifices to the Roman gods. Many Christians refused to comply with this order and were persecuted because of their loyalty to Christ. Thousands died for their faith as martyrs.

The first reprieve from persecution came under Galerius in 311 when he issued an edict of toleration for Christians. Galerius's edict was followed by another edict that was given by Constantine after he had a vision where he saw that he could conquer his rival, Maxentius, if he put the first two Greek letters of Christ's name, chi and rho, on the shields of his soldiers. Constantine did this and won the battle of Milvian Bridge in 312. After this victory, Constantine issued the Edict of Milan in 313, which affirmed tolerance for Christians. Constantine's coming to power signaled an enormous shift in the relationship between Christianity and politics. No longer a persecuted sect, Christianity was now a tolerated religion that supported the Roman government and benefited from access to political power.

Constantine's embrace of Christianity was not the first by a political ruler. According to tradition, the king of Armenia, Tiridates III, converted to Christianity in 301 and thereafter established Christianity as the state religion in his kingdom. However, Armenia did not wield the power and influence of the Roman Empire. Constantine's benevolence ushered in an era where Roman imperial power was exercised over Christian theology and practice. Clergy were granted special privileges and became a distinct class who also held importance in civic life. In 321, Constantine declared

Sunday "the venerable day of the Sun" and made it an official day of rest. Sunday was now recognized by both the military, who worshipped the sun god on that day, and Christian civilians, who recognized Jesus's day of resurrection as their Sabbath.

Constantine began the process of remaking Rome into a Christian city for political purposes. While doing this he also established a new Rome in 330 at the Greek colony of Byzantium on the Bosporus, which was dedicated to Christ and named Constantinople. Constantine permanently connected Christian theology with imperial politics when he called for the first ecumenical council of the church at Nicaea in 325 in an attempt to resolve theological controversies among his empire's Christians. In fact, Roman emperors or Byzantine emperors called for the first seven ecumenical councils of the church, formally linking Christian theology with political power. Byzantine church leaders fought to ensure theological unity, and the emperors took decisive roles in determining theological orthodoxy. In the East, this close relationship between church and state was labeled *symphonia* (harmony) and shaped all aspects of Byzantine culture and society from art and architecture to literature and the law code.

In the western half of the Roman Empire, as political power shifted to the East, the bishop of Rome, the pope, acquired more political power. By the time of Augustine of Hippo (354–430), Roman imperial power in the West was nearing its end. As Rome went into decline some blamed Christians for the empire's failure to maintain power. In response to this criticism, Augustine wrote what became one of the foundational texts on Christianity and politics, *The City of God Against the Pagans*. In this book, Augustine refuted the notion that Christianity was at fault for the fall of Rome to invaders and proclaimed that Christians made the best citizens. Augustine's writings on the relationship between Christianity and politics were extremely influential over the coming centuries.

In the late fourth century, through various decrees, Theodosius I (*c.* 346–95; r. 379–95) ensured that Christianity became the official state religion of the empire. In the period that followed, the western half of the Roman Empire faced an onslaught of invaders. Each managed to chip away at Roman imperial authority and reconstruct a political system that adapted Roman ideas with tribal customs and their understanding of Christianity. From this diverse context was forged the foundation of medieval religion and politics. One of the notable changes involved the development of the bishop of Rome's power over civil life. Pope Gelasius I (d.496; r. 492–6), writing to the Roman Emperor Anastasius I (*c.* 430/1–518; r. 491–518) in 494, asserting that the authority of the priesthood was ultimately more important than the power of earthly rulers because "they have to render an account in the divine judgment even for the kings of men" (Wilken 2012: 170).

Another important development in this period was the biblically based notion of kingship. Drawing on the Old Testament idea of God appointing and directing the actions of kings who led their chosen people, kings soon became seen as essential to the salvation of their subjects. The conversion stories of kings became the conversion stories of peoples. King Clovis I (*c.* 466–511; r. 481–511), for example, ruler of the

Franks, made a battlefield conversion to Christ (c. 496/8) and was subsequently baptized with 3,000 of his soldiers.

Baptism, a Christian sacrament, became important for linking Christianity with the royal power of Frankish kings, as they were baptized after coronation. Baptism also became essential to the concept of **Christendom**. As infant baptism, a practice dating to the second century, became widely used in the fifth and sixth centuries a socioreligious identity for all Christians was forged. Christendom was conceived as a union of church and state with Jesus as the invisible head, while the emperor and the pope functioned as his earthly representatives.

In the eastern half of the Roman Empire, the Byzantine Empire faced an ongoing struggle against the military advances of the Persians and, later, Muslims. Due to these pressing threats, theological unity was viewed as crucial for obtaining political and social stability. The most important of the Byzantine emperors was Justinian I (c. 483–565; r. 527–65). Although his law code became foundational for civil law in the medieval West, his intent was to end heresy and theological division in the East. Owing to the work of missionaries, Byzantine Christianity spread beyond the confines of political borders into eastern Europe, where Russians, Serbs, Bulgarians, and other Slavic peoples embraced Eastern Orthodox Christianity.

Over the ensuing centuries and mainly due to the rise of Islam, the remnant of the Byzantine Empire finally collapsed in 1453. Moscow replaced Constantinople as the center of Orthodox Christianity. The Russian monarch Ivan the Great (1440–1505; r. 1462–1505) adopted the title tsar (*caesar*) and married Zöe, niece to the last of the Byzantine emperors. Their marriage united the Russian people with Byzantium. The Russian church proclaimed the Tsar head of both church and state. The spiritual and temporal power of the tsar remained steadfast until the Russian Revolution in 1917.

The close connection between temporal power and spiritual power in Europe was strengthened when Pope Leo III (d.816; r. 795–816) proclaimed Charlemagne (742/7–814; r. 768–814) "Holy Roman Emperor" on Christmas Day in 800. This action affirmed a God-ordained monarch in the West. Charlemagne appointed bishops, called church councils, developed church law, and oversaw what became orthodox teaching and practice.

After the death of Charlemagne, at the Council of Paris (829), the bishops decreed that they had the power to rule on matters of the Christian faith. They made clear that secular rulers must rule justly through human laws, but also that monarchs were first and foremost accountable to God and, therefore, obligated to uphold the laws and beliefs of the church.

From the eleventh through the fourteenth centuries, the Roman Catholic Church and the Holy Roman Empire embraced this idea of dual rulership, which closely linked the power and authority of the church with the power and authority of the Holy Roman Emperor. Church leaders argued that the church had charge over both the spiritual and the temporal spheres by claiming them as jurisdictions that were subordinate to their legitimizing power. Bernard, the abbot of Clairvaux (1090–1153), tried to limit this extension of power by arguing that the church could only claim authority over the spiritual.

The battle for temporal power between the Holy Roman Emperor and the papacy came to a head during the Investiture Conflict. The fight between Pope Gregory VII (1025–85; r. 1073–85) and Emperor Henry IV (1050–1106; r. 1056–1106) was about whom, either as pope or monarch, had the power to make someone a bishop. Although

FIGURE 6.3 *Martin Luther transformed the concept of Christendom through his religious reforms that changed the relationship between church and state.* Source: *Wikimedia Commons.*

FIGURE 6.4 *Frederick the Wise, Prince-elector of Saxony, was crucial to the survival of Martin Luther and his reforming efforts. Portrait by Lucas Cranach the Elder, c. 1530–5.*
Source: *Wikimedia Commons*.

the conflict was eventually resolved at the Concordat of Worms in 1122, the Investiture Conflict revealed that monarchical power had separate functions from the papacy, though those functions could still result in power being exercised over the church.

In the aftermath of the Investiture Conflict, Pope Urban II (c. 1035–99; r. 1088–99) further complicated the role of the papacy in politics by using his spiritual leadership to encourage laypeople to pick up arms and fight. He wanted to help the embattled Byzantine Empire stymie the growing power of the Muslims in the East. Urban II's call for crusade resulted in a series of Christian pilgrim armies flowing into the Middle East over the subsequent centuries. New crusader kingdoms were established and holy war was used as a redemptive tool.

As the Crusades defined one element of Christianity and politics during the medieval period, Thomas Aquinas (1224/5–74), a Dominican, reframed Christian theology through the ideas of the ancient Greek philosopher Aristotle. Aquinas argued that the common good is the goal of political rule. He believed the common good could be achieved through unity, the ability of the people to "procure the necessities of life," and by promoting a virtuous citizenry. Aquinas also asserted that kings should be subject to the pope, but that the pope's influence should be limited to morals and theology. Aquinas's thought was the high point of medieval theorizing about the relationship between Christianity and politics (Aquinas 1982: 9).

Although there were many attempts at reforming the Roman Catholic Church before him, on October 31, 1517, Martin Luther (1483–1546), a German Augustinian monk, priest, and university professor, challenged the use of **indulgences** by posting his Ninety-Five Theses on the Castle Church door in Wittenberg. Luther believed that the church had neglected its pastoral role in favor of amassing wealth through the selling of indulgences. After posting his theses, Luther started a political firestorm that shook Christendom. In one of the most dramatic moments in world history, Luther stood his ground against the Holy Roman Emperor, Charles V (1500–58; r. 1519–56), and church leaders at the Diet of Worms in 1521. Luther, already excommunicated by the Roman Catholic Church, defended his reform efforts but soon discovered his critique was too much for either church or state. Condemned by the emperor, Luther was forced to rely on his prince, Frederick III (1463–1525; r. 1486–1525), more commonly known as "Frederick the Wise," and other sympathetic princes for support and protection.

Reformers who followed in the wake of Luther, such as Ulrich Zwingli (1484–1531) in Zurich, and John Calvin (1509–64) in Geneva, relied on civil authorities to legitimize, protect, and promote their reforms. In England, Henry VIII (1491–1547; r. 1509–47), playing on growing nationalism, used reform to separate himself from the obligations of marriage. He divorced his wife Catherine of Aragon (1485–1536; r. 1509–47) and reformulated Christianity into a state-owned church—the Church of England. As king, Henry declared himself the supreme head of this new church in defiance of the pope and the Roman Catholic Church.

The most unsettling shift in Christianity and politics occurred with the Anabaptists. Originating in Zwingli's Zurich, they rejected infant baptism in favor of adult believer's baptism. This simple act undermined both Protestant and Roman Catholic notions of Christendom by rejecting infant baptism. This alteration to baptism, though intended to imitate Christ's example in the New Testament, sent shockwaves throughout Europe as a sign of a radical rejection of the political and cultural status quo. Anabaptist leader Michael Sattler's *Schleitheim Articles* (1527) rejected many commonly held Christian practices such as serving in government, taking oaths, and engaging in warfare. Politics and political leaders were a necessity in any empire or kingdom, but true Christianity, for the Anabaptists, was found in rejecting involvement in the government or politics. Anabaptists were too subversive for either Roman Catholics or Protestants and were brutally killed by both for their understanding of the faith.

Not all sixteenth-century reforms of the church and the state erupted out of deeply held Christian convictions. Niccolò Machiavelli (1469–1527) supported the idea that religion must be subordinate to the state, and that the government must uphold the rule of law. His most important writing was a book he dedicated to Lorenzo de' Medici (1492–1519; r. 1513–19) entitled *The Prince*. In this treatise about politics and the human condition, Machiavelli assumes that all people are corrupt and that to be successful a ruler must act on this fact. The only thing that matters in the end is that the ruler maintains and expands his power. To achieve this end, the ruler must use whatever means necessary to accomplish their goals without concern for justice, mercy, truth, or any other ideal that may make them appear weak. For Machiavelli, politics had nothing to do with Christianity but was merely a way to retain power.

Because of the turmoil that erupted due to the reformations of the sixteenth century, a desire for religious unity arose within city-states and kingdoms. **The Peace of Augsburg (1555)** affirmed "whose realm, (use) his religion" (*cuius regio, ejus religio*), but this treaty between Charles V and Lutheran princes failed to resolve the deeper religious divisions. Protestants and Catholics continued to view each other as heretical. Christianity was now a powerful element in the machinations of state politics.

Protestants and Catholics alike saw religious like-mindedness as necessary for the flourishing of governments and cohesive societies. The resulting sectarianism manifested itself in persecution and wars that raged from the sixteenth through the seventeenth century. The worst of these wars was the Thirty Years' War (1618–48). This war revealed just how dangerous politics—centered on religion—could be as the fighting brought about unprecedented death and devastation. The Thirty Years' War began in 1618 as a Protestant revolt in the Kingdom of Bohemia, with the "Defenestration (throwing out of a window) of Prague." In the ensuing years, the war became a continent-wide religious fight. The war ended with the Peace of Westphalia (1648) that once again affirmed the idea "whose realm, (use) his religion."

The divisiveness fostered by sectarianism seemed to work against the notion of the common good, which was being reconceptualized by new economic and market forces. For example, throughout the seventeenth century the Dutch Republic showed the way forward as they embraced the expansion of trade and a new breadth of religious tolerance. This enabled them to flourish economically and culturally creating the Dutch golden age.

In England, Charles I (1600–1649; r. 1625–49) inherited the accumulated frustrations of Puritan dissenters who had first voiced their unhappiness with Protestant reforms during the reign of Elizabeth I (1533–1603; r. 1558–1603). Charles' inability to maintain a middle way through the religious divisions inherited from his predecessors, along with financial issues, resulted in open revolt by the Puritans. Even though religious unity was far from being achieved among the disparate groups involved in the rebellion, Puritan military leader Oliver Cromwell (1599–1658; r. 1653–8) defeated royalist forces and concluded his drive for power with the execution of Charles I. After disbanding Parliament, Cromwell proclaimed himself Lord Protector and established a "Godly Commonwealth" that once again revealed how dangerous the mixing of sectarian Christianity and politics could be for the people. In the aftermath of Cromwell's tyranny, Parliament restored the monarchy in 1660 with Charles II (1630–85; r. 1660–85). However, Parliament ensured that control over religion shifted from the monarchy to the people when Charles' brother James II (1633–1701; r. 1685–8)—an acknowledged Roman Catholic—was removed from power in 1688. In James' place Parliament invited William III (1650–1702; r. 1689–1702), prince of Orange, and his wife Mary II (1662–94; r. 1689–94), James' Protestant daughter, from the Netherlands to rule. Proclaimed the "Glorious Revolution," the peaceful shift in power made certain that Protestantism and constitutional monarchy would define England's future.

French King Louis XIV (1638–1715; r. 1643–1715) decided that Roman Catholicism would be the only form of Christianity practiced in his realm. French Protestants, known as Huguenots, fled after the **Edict of Nantes (1598)** was revoked in 1685. The French king could rest assured that religious infighting would not undermine his divine right to rule as a Catholic monarch. This was by no means an assertion of religion over state, but rather the use of religion by the king to enforce his will on the nation. Christianity, in fact, was losing more and more ground to people who wanted to significantly lessen, if not obliterate, the role of religion in society.

The Enlightenment challenged long-held assumptions about Christianity's relationship to politics. Enlightenment thinkers argued that reason would reveal the laws that God had set into motion in nature and in society. John Locke (1632–1704) and Gotthold Ephraim Lessing (1729–81) each forwarded differing notions of religious tolerance, while Francois-Marie Arouet de Voltaire (1694–1778) rejected all forms of oppression, whether they originated from the monarchy or, more abhorrent to him, the Roman Catholic Church. In terms of the connection between Christianity and politics, the Enlightenment undermined church-state unity. Increasingly, due to the popularity of emotional expressions of Christianity embraced by both Roman Catholics and Protestants in the seventeenth and eighteenth centuries, religion was perceived as being contrary to reason.

The American Revolution and the French Revolution radically altered the place of Christianity in modern politics as religion was either separated from the government, as in America, or made subservient to the government, as was the case in France. In their revolt from Great Britain, the Americans embraced a new vision of church and

FIGURE 6.5 *Napoleon Bonaparte crowns himself emperor while Pope Pius VII watches.* Source: *Wikimedia Commons.*

state that, in principle, tolerated all religions and sects so long as they submitted to the collective good of the nation.

In America, the freedom of religion was made a constitutional right and there would be no state church or preferred form of religious practice. These high ideals were not easily lived out. Roman Catholics, along with other religious groups, often experienced violent persecution from Protestants as the nation grew. However, the separation of church and state set a precedent in world history that enshrined religious liberty as a constitutional right.

The French Revolution that began in 1789 did not mark a shift to religious liberty. Rather, the revolution resulted in a wholesale attack on Christianity and the replacement of religion by politics. The church was perceived as a buttress to the monarchy and oppressive. The revolution made the church subservient to the nation, and a secular priesthood of politicians arose in its place. In one of the more startling examples of political power usurping the church, Napoléon Bonaparte (1769–1821; r. 1799–1814/15) coronated himself emperor of France while the pope watched helplessly. In a similar fashion, the Latin American revolutions that followed in the early nineteenth century, the place of the Roman Catholic Church was openly challenged by those wanting to see reason, order, and progress become more influential than religion.

Throughout the nineteenth century, as new governments were formed in independent states, Christianity was still viewed as being necessary for social cohesion and national identity. In Berlin, Johann Gottlieb Fichte (1762–1814) wanted "to cultivate the eternal in the temporal" by encouraging Germans to find unity and liberation through a militaristic and pious devotion to a single German nation-state (Fichte 1922: 132). Patriotism as a form of religion marked a turning point in the relationship between Christianity and politics in the nineteenth century that would have profound consequences. These ideas drew upon the notion of **civil religion** promoted by Jean-Jacque Rousseau (1712–78) in his book *The Social Contract* (1762). For Rousseau, "a society of true Christians would not be a society of men." Therefore, a replacement faith that "is purely civil" must be formulated to form a "social conscience, without which it is impossible to be either a good citizen or a loyal subject." Civil religion, in fact, denotes a shift toward a politics that is no longer Christian but draws on religious ideas and language to support the nation (Rousseau 1968: 182–6).

The nineteenth century also saw civil religion make headway alongside new political and intellectual visions that aimed to remove Christianity from society and politics altogether. Ludwig Feuerbach's (1804–72) *The Essence of Christianity* (1841), claimed that God was simply "the projected personality of man." He argued that people should stop contemplating an afterlife and instead focus on this world (Feuerbach 1854: 224). Drawing on Feuerbach's critique and the work of G.W.F. Hegel (1770–1831), Karl Marx (1818–83) and Friedrich Engels (1820–95) proposed a communist model of politics that was completely materialistic. Communism, as a form of universal politics, is an ideology that offers salvation here on Earth. In the nineteenth century, many thinkers, like Marx and Engels, believed that the world was finally being disenchanted from superstitions and societies were moving away from the archaic and irrelevant claims of religion. Described as secularization—a term with many definitions—the word came to describe the usurping of religion in areas of society, culture, and politics where religious faith once played the leading role.

While Christianity and politics were on divergent paths in the nineteenth century, belief in Christianity was not disappearing. Not even important scientific works such as

Charles Darwin's *The Origin of Species* (1859) could overcome religion entirely. Rather, Christianity remained vital and important in the lives of millions of people around the world. Christianity expanded through the efforts of missionaries working in India, China, Asia-Pacific, the Middle East, and across the continent of Africa. Indigenous peoples were often confronted by European imperialism cloaked in a culturally captive form of Christianity. Nevertheless, indigenous people embraced the hope Jesus provided and the seeds for the global growth of Christianity were sown.

As the twentieth century dawned, European governments found in Christianity a useful ally until the First World War radically altered that relationship. During the cataclysmic violence and social turmoil of that war, monarchies capitulated, empires collapsed, and colonized subjects no longer believed that European civilizations personified the crowning glory of human achievement. What came in the wake of the global tragedy was the rise of mass politics liberated from what remained of the alliance between Christianity and politics that had supported elite power for centuries. This was most pronounced in Russia after the Bolsheviks assumed power in 1917 and established the Soviet Union. The soviets soon seized monasteries, churches, schools, and even sacramental vessels from the Russian Orthodox Church to enrich the government. Resistance to the atheistic soviets by clergy and laypeople resulted in arrests, imprisonment, and executions. Though the soviets ruthlessly attempted to eradicate Christian belief, popular devotion to the Orthodox Church remained strong throughout Russia and even Protestants, most notably evangelicals, increased in the number of adherents.

Between the two world wars in Europe, Christianity faced many new challenges including the rise of totalitarian regimes that demanded absolute loyalty to the state. In Fascist Italy, the Roman Catholic Church supported Benito Mussolini's (1883–1945; r. 1922–43) regime and signed a concordat to retain influence over society. Similarly, the Vatican signed a concordat with Nazi Germany to protect the church. Adolf Hitler (1889–1945; r. 1933–45) took the agreement to be an endorsement of his regime. Tragically, many Protestants theologians, pastors, and laypeople who were committed to the racist ideology of the Nazi Party reimagined the biblical text, the identity of Christ, and the place of Judaism in Christian theology and, ultimately, the place of Jews in the world. The subsequent mass murder of millions of European Jews and others under totalitarian and collaborationist governments throughout Europe brought to light, once again, the grave danger of making Christianity subservient to politics.

Despite the human tragedy of the Second World War and the accompanying Holocaust, Christianity in the postwar world continued to grow and expand as vibrant Indigenous churches arose in former European colonies. In the United States, the war years brought Protestants, Roman Catholics, and Jewish believers together to fight against the Axis Powers. In the subsequent Cold War years, the Judeo-Christian tradition was further affirmed as an essential element in the American fight against the Soviet Union and the global spread of atheistic communism.

With the end of European imperial aspirations in Africa after the Second World War, postcolonial governments were influenced by the rise of dynamic forms of indigenous

FIGURE 6.6 *After Apartheid ended in South Africa, Archbishop Desmond Tutu helped guide the nation through a process of forgiveness, reconciliation, and restitution.* Source: *Wikimedia Commons.*

Christianity. The Africanization of Christianity that followed decolonization led to the explosive growth of churches throughout the continent. With this expansion, African Christians transformed the nations they resided in through "the establishment of a democratic culture both within church and state" (Ranger 2008: 6).

In South Africa, Desmond Tutu (1931–), a church leader, along with Nelson Mandela (1918–2013) and others fought against the racist, pro-white Apartheid policies of the South African government. In the mid-1990s, after Black South Africans elected Mandela president, Tutu headed the Truth and Reconciliation Commission that held the South African government and white South Africans accountable for the violent oppression of Black South Africans. These efforts were part of a peaceful transition in political power that sought to bring forgiveness and reconciliation.

Liberation theology powerfully linked Christian theology with politics in Latin America. Liberation theologians associated the origins of social and economic justice with the life of Bartolomé de Las Casas (1484–1566). De Las Casas courageously argued that the Spanish monarchy should protect Indigenous peoples from abuses by conquistadors, which resulted in the issuing of the "New Laws of 1542." Applying the idea of **praxis** (active involvement) from Marxist thought along with the insights from number of Catholic theologians, Gustavo Gutiérrez (1928–) and other Latin American theologians sought to "interpret the gospel as well as Scripture within the context of social and economic oppression" (Gonzalez 2010b: 521). Arguing that God preferred the poor, liberation theologians came to see political action as essential for correcting the evil social structures that oppress the poor. Liberation theology attempted to reorient the Roman Catholicism's spiritual focus on curing souls toward the solving political and economic problems. They intended to build the kingdom of God on earth. Curiously, liberation theology did not transform Latin American societies as hoped, though the movement did spark similar theologies of liberation around the world based on sexuality, gender, race, ethnicity, and nationality.

One new form of Protestant practice did appeal to the spiritual and personal needs of the people in Latin America. Pentecostalism spread rapidly throughout the continent as it has in recent decades in Asia and Africa. Promoting the transformation of the individual through a personal encounter with the Holy Spirit, Pentecostalism restored hope to individual lives, families, and neighborhoods. As one shrewd observer noted, "the Catholic bishops may want to encourage a preferential option for the poor [...] but the poor seem to have a preference for the pentecostals" (Cox 1995: 176).

In recent decades Christians in the Americas have embraced political parties and politicians to bring about change. In Latin America Roman Catholicism remains the dominant form of Christianity and is even, in some nations, recognized as the official religion of the state. In response to this situation evangelicals throughout Latin America have embraced political involvement to challenge the status quo. Similarly in the United States, Christians, regardless of denomination, have allied themselves with politicians and political parties that align with their convictions.

Christians in Africa, the Middle East, and Asia, have faced different challenges depending on which nation they live in. In some places, governments have openly persecuted Christians as they try to eradicate the influence of Christianity on society. Since the September 11, 2001, terrorist attacks and the subsequent global war on terror tensions have been heightened between Christians and Muslims throughout the world. And, of late, the communist government ruling China has begun to close Christian churches and persecute Christians whom they view as a threat to their power.

In 1906, an African American holiness preacher, William J. Seymour (1870–1922), led the Azusa Street Revival in Los Angeles, California, that became the wellspring for global Pentecostalism. Seymour's services were apolitical, focused on receiving the baptism of the Holy Spirit evidenced by speaking in tongues, and hoped to see racial reconciliation and the Gospel brought to all the peoples of the earth. Over the course of the twentieth century, Pentecostalism has reshaped world Christianity by promoting an exuberant piety with a strong emphasis on evangelism. Regardless of culture, language, race, ethnicity, and nationality, Pentecostals are transforming the world's religious landscape. In the coming century this dynamic form of practice is projected to become the dominant expression of Christianity globally. Pentecostals in Asia, Africa, Latin America, and elsewhere will have to discern how their Spirit-led practice of the faith will shape their involvement in politics in the decades to come.

FIGURE 6.7 *Yoido Full Gospel Church in South Korea, one of the largest Pentecostal churches in the world with approximately 800,000 members.* Source: *Wikimedia Commons.*

The relationship between Christianity and politics will continue to be contextually dynamic reflecting the influence of the politics and culture of world societies. In democratic societies, politicians will continue to try to win the votes of Christians, while Christians will remain committed to influencing policies and laws. In nations that have authoritarian regimes or where religious diversity is not tolerated, Christians will continue to face alienation and persecution. As has been the case over the past two millennia, Christians will continue to struggle to define the relationship between politics and the kingdom of God, between earthly powers and their spiritual hope in Christ.

Further Reading and Online Resources

Bays, D.H. (2012), *A New History of Christianity in China*, Malden, MA: Wiley-Blackwell.
Burleigh, M. (2005), *Earthly Powers: The Clash of Religion and Politics in Europe from the French Revolution to the Great War*, New York: HarperCollins.
Lehmann, D. (1996), *Struggle for the Spirit: Religious Transformation and Popular Culture in Brazil and Latin America*, Cambridge, UK: Polity Press.

McClendon, G.H. and R.B. Riedl (2019), *From Pews to Politics: Religious Sermons and Political Participation in Africa*, Cambridge, UK: Cambridge University Press.

Stanley, B. (2018), *A World History of Christianity in the Twentieth Century*, Princeton, NJ: Princeton University Press.

Wald, K.D. and A. Calhoun-Brown (2018), *Religion and Politics in the United States*, 8th edn., Lanham, MD: Rowman & Littlefield.

References

Aquinas, Saint T. (1982), *On Kingship, to the King of Cyprus*, trans. G.B. Phelan, rev. with intro. and notes I.K.T. Eschmann, Toronto: Pontifical Institute of Mediaeval Studies.

Bell, M. (2017), "The Biggest Megachurch on Earth and South Korea's 'Crisis of Evangelism'," *The World*, May 1. Available online: https://www.pri.org/stories/2017-05-01/biggest-megachurch-earth-facing-crisis-evangelism (accessed June 27, 2020).

Cox, H. (1995), *Fire from Heaven: The Rise of Pentecostal Spirituality and the Reshaping of Religion in the Twenty-first Century*, Reading, MA: Perseus Books.

Digeser, E.D. (2000), *The Making of a Christian Empire: Lactantius and Rome*, Ithaca, NY: Cornell University Press.

Feuerbach, L. (1854), *The Essence of Christianity*, trans. M. Evans, London: John Chapman.

Fichte, J.G. (1922), *Addresses to the German Nation*, trans. R.F. Jones and G.H. Turnbull, Chicago: Open Court Publishing.

González, J.L. (2010a), *The Story of Christianity*, vol. 1, *The Early Church to the Reformation*, 2nd edn., New York: HarperOne.

González, J.L. (2010b), *The Story of Christianity*, vol. 2, *Reformation to the Present Day*, 2nd edn., New York: HarperOne.

Gregory, B.S. (2012), *The Unintended Reformation: How a Religious Revolution Secularized Society*, Cambridge, MA: The Belknap Press of Harvard University Press.

Jenkins, P. (2011), *The Next Christendom: The Coming of Global Christianity*, 3rd edn., Oxford: Oxford University Press.

Kalu, O. (2008), *African Pentecostalism: An Introduction*, Oxford: Oxford University Press.

Manschreck, C.L. (1974), *A History of Christianity in the World: From Persecution to Uncertainty*, Englewood Cliffs, NJ: Prentice-Hall.

McGee, G.B. (2010), *Miracles, Missions, and American Pentecostalism*, Maryknoll, NY: Orbis Books.

Ranger, T.O., ed. (2008), *Evangelical Christianity and Democracy in Africa*, Oxford: Oxford University Press.

Rousseau, J.-J. (1968), *The Social Contract*, trans. and intro. M. Cranston, London: Penguin Books.

Sherman, A.L. (1997), *The Soul of Development: Biblical Christianity and Economic Transformation in Guatemala*, New York: Oxford University Press.

Smith, B.H. (1998), *Religious Politics of Latin America, Pentecostal vs. Catholic*, Notre Dame, IN: University of Notre Dame Press.

Wall, H. de (2008), "Corpus Christianum," in H.D. Betz, D.S. Browning, B. Janowski, and E. Jüngel (eds.), *Religion Past and Present: Chu-Deu*, vol. 3, *Encyclopedia of Theology and Religion*, 4th edn., Leiden: Brill. http://doi.org/10.1163/1877-5888_rpp_SIM_03244.

Wilken, R.L. (2012), *The First Thousand Years: A Global History of Christianity*, New Haven, CT: Yale University Press.

Glossary Terms

Christendom (corpus Christianum) The medieval concept for describing the unification of church and state based on baptism.

Civil religion A concept used to describe politics in a kingdom, state, or nation that ennobles them with a religious or sacred element. Originally a concept associated with Plato, it encourages a religious view of the government and the destiny of a people attributed to the gods of a city-state in ancient Greece. More recently, it involves ascribing transcendent meaning to state or public ceremonies, phrases (e.g., "God bless America"), and collective ideas and values to provide a unifying, spiritual identity for citizens and the government.

Edict of Nantes (1598) Signed by King Henry IV on April 13, 1598, the edict ended the French wars of religion that pitted French Roman Catholics against French Protestants, known as Huguenots. The Huguenots could freely practice their religion, with some exceptions, as well as receive equal treatment under the law.

Indulgences An official method used by the Roman Catholic Church for transferring the extra merits of grace from Christ and the saints to ordinary Christians. This was done to forgive Christians of their sins and reduce their time in purgatory—a transitory place where purification occurs before entering heaven. Indulgences were granted to those on crusade, who viewed relics, or did other pious acts. In the sixteenth century indulgences were sold to fund the building of St. Peter's Basilica in Rome.

Peace of Augsburg (1555) A religious agreement reached on September 25, 1555, between Holy Roman Emperor Ferdinand I and the German Elector princes at Augsburg. Allowed for both Lutheran and Roman Catholic forms of Christianity to exist in the German kingdoms based on the religion of the ruler. Those who did not affirm the religion of their ruler could sell their lands and emigrate to other lands more suitable to their religious views. The agreement did not include Calvinists.

Praxis A concept that dates to Aristotle and gained momentum in the modern era through the work of Karl Marx who used the term to describe revolutionary action that brings change. In liberation theology, praxis is action informed by an ethical mandate demanding conformity to a specific understanding of social justice regarding the poor and the oppressed.

7

Eastern Orthodox Christianity: A Vital Tradition

Gaelan Gilbert

Sometime in 1796 in northwestern mainland Alaska, at the mouth of the Kuksokwim River where it empties into the Bering Sea, a Russian Orthodox priest-monk named Juvenaly beached his small boat. He stood and began to speak to a settlement of Yup'ik inhabitants in what is now the village of Quinhagak. The local shaman, seeing Juvenaly's pectoral cross and perceiving the threat of a rival, forbade him from speaking, and ordered him to be killed "in a hail of arrows" (Oleksa 1998: 114). A later report adds that, just before his death, Juvenaly seemed to the villagers to be chasing away flies with his hand. This suggests the missionary monk was blessing his attackers with a gesture they had not seen before: the sign of the cross.

So begins the history of Orthodox Christianity on the soil of North America. The account of Juvenaly's death was passed on orally by the inhabitants of Quinhagak for generations, and eventually recounted around 1890 to John Kilbuck, a Protestant missionary. Long before Kilbuck arrived, the Orthodox Christian faith had been embraced indigenously across broad swathes of Alaska. The work of other Russian missionaries among the Aleuts and Tlingits, and eventually in Anchorage, bore much fruit. Two key figures in the Alaskan mission were Fr. Herman (d. 1837) and Metropolitan Innocent (d. 1879), both since canonized as saints. Having arrived in 1794, Fr. Herman remained on Spruce Island, near Kodiak, for forty-three years, living with and teaching the people, until his death in 1837.

In 1867, the Russian Empire sold the territory of Alaska to the United States of America for a price of $7.2 million ($109 million today). The Orthodox Christian presence that had been established in Alaska came under hostile scrutiny from Protestants like Kilbuck. While the assimilationist method of Protestant missionaries in Alaska effaced native languages and forced attendance at residential schools, Orthodox Christian missionary principles emphasized cultural respect and linguistic immersion leading to trust and eventual conversion (Erickson 2008: 35–6).

Although the hostile welcome received on the shores of the Kuksokwim was mostly an exception, it nonetheless serves as an analogy for prevailing attitudes toward the Orthodox Church in North America: that of a foreign, misunderstood rival. In part, this has to do with the fact that the Orthodox Church is a relatively new arrival. The Roman Catholicism and Protestantism brought by Spanish explorers and Puritan pilgrims established themselves much earlier. Waves of Orthodox Christian immigrants did not begin to flood the eastern seaboard until the second half of the nineteenth century.

To this day, the Orthodox Church remains what some consider the "best kept secret" of Christianity in America. It is by far a minority among the religious confessions here, with a membership of about one million, or 0.26 percent of the total population (Krindatch 2018: 24). Its relative hiddenness warrants an examination of this "vital tradition." This article offers a basic introduction to the Orthodox Church, exploring the sources of Orthodox Christian tradition, surveying notable milestones and figures in the history of Eastern Christianity, and closing with observations on the Orthodox Church globally and in North America today.

The Orthodox Church: Tradition and History

To speak of Eastern Orthodox Christianity is to speak of the Orthodox Church. Without reference to the concrete, continuous witness of the charismatic institution of the church, an Orthodox Christian would say, talk about Christianity quickly becomes incoherent. The second-century church father Tertullian put it succinctly: *unus Christianus, nullus Christianus* (a lone Christian, [is] not a Christian). The Orthodox Church exemplifies this ancient understanding of lived faith as grounded in concrete community.

This has local and universal dimensions. With regard to the former, the Eucharistic ecclesiology of the Orthodox Church has its roots in the earliest Christian communities. For Orthodox theologians from Ignatius of Antioch to John Zizioulas, those gathered around every altar, visible and invisible, are an instantiation of the universal body of Christ. At the same time, larger ecclesiastical structures are important for stability and continuity. From the early centuries, five patriarchates emerged in urban centers where the church was firmly established: Rome, Constantinople, Jerusalem, Antioch, and Alexandria, each with a large jurisdictional territory. While still grounded in the ancient patriarchates, the Orthodox Church over the last several centuries has reticulated into a family of self-headed churches whose territories now mostly mirror national boundaries, in Greece, Russia, Serbia, Romania, Bulgaria, Ukraine, Georgia, Poland, Albania, and the Czech Lands and Slovakia. Today, the ancient and modern configurations preserve a healthy balance: each patriarchate maintains jurisdiction over its ancient territory, but mission and migration have led to the bestowal of autocephaly, typically by the **Ecumenical** Patriarchate, upon synods of bishops in newly evangelized regions, such as North America.

The Orthodox Church is thus a diverse yet unified body of Christians who share a tradition of belief and practice stretching back to the earliest Christian communities. Orthodox Christians consider their church the Church of Jesus Christ, visibly founded by the Holy Spirit at Pentecost. Measured with the criteria of apostolic succession, the Orthodox claim to be the church founded at Pentecost is strong; one can trace the lineage of its bishops all the way to the *episkopoi* in the New Testament. The Orthodox Church adheres to a common creed (the Nicene-Constantinopolitan), worships with a common set of rites (the Liturgies of St. John Chrysostom, St. Basil, and St. Gregory Dialogus), administers seven sacraments, and grounds itself in a rich understanding of tradition (*paradosis*), in which scripture, church councils, **patristic** writings, liturgical worship, and lived sanctity all bear manifold authoritative witness to the truth of Jesus Christ's saving death and bodily resurrection.

A Vital Tradition

The word "Orthodox" derives from the Greek term *orthodoxa*, which implies both "right belief" and "right worship," and this is precisely what one finds in the Orthodox Church: an emphasis on the mutuality of belief and worship, authority and experience, doctrine and doxology. A fourth-century teaching from Evagrius Ponticus puts it thus: "he who prays is a theologian, and a theologian is one who prays" (*153 Chapters on Prayer*, ch. 60). This maxim, like the better-known Latin dictum *lex orandi, lex credendi*, indicates that spiritual experience is itself a form of doctrinal authority. At the same time, certain criteria are needed for assessing the validity of experience. This interwoven history of ascetic spirituality and patristic theology continues to have immense dynamism as a living link across the centuries.

Metropolitan Kallistos Ware, in *The Orthodox Church*, notes that "the distinctive characteristic" of the Orthodox Church is its "sense of living continuity with the Church of ancient times," a sense that "is summed up for the Orthodox in the one word—Tradition" (1976: 203–4). Tradition derives, essentially, from the inspiration of the Holy Spirit. The conditions for its embodied expression, however, depend on multiple sources of authority whose interrelationship constitutes the framework for the inspired life of the church. This does not mean that the Orthodox Church is ossified or static, however. As Panagiotis Bratsiotis says, "loyalty to tradition does not simply mean slavish attachment to the past and to external authority, but a living connexion with the entire past experience of the Church" (1964: 23). Jaroslav Pelikan notes that even for the church fathers, "the truth was changeless [...] but the experience of it was dynamic and variable" (1977: 31). Thus when Orthodox Christians speak of Tradition, "[it] means the books of the Bible; it means the Creed; it means the decrees of the Ecumenical Councils and the writings of the Fathers; it means the Canons, the Service Books, the Holy **Icons**—in fact, the whole system of doctrine, Church government, worship, and art which Orthodoxy has articulated over the ages" (Ware 1976: 204).

EASTERN ORTHODOX CHRISTIANITY: A VITAL TRADITION

While the Orthodox Church sees many aspects of Christian life as elements of tradition, the caveat is that such things must harmonize with the apostolic rule of faith, which takes scripture, the canon of writings assembled by the church in the third century, as a critical basis. After all, "not everything received from the past is of equal value," and so "there is a difference between 'Tradition' and 'traditions': many traditions which the past has handed down are human and accidental—pious opinions

FIGURE 7.1 *Icon of Christ the Pantocrator, Sinai, c. fifth century.* Source: *Public Domain.*

(or worse), but not a true part of the one Tradition, the essential Christian message" (Ware 1976: 205). As one Church Father at the Seventh Council of Carthage put it, "the Lord says, 'I am the truth'; He said not, 'I am the custom'."

Yet it is the truth that establishes customs. We see Christ himself inaugurating the sacramental traditions of baptism and Eucharist in scripture (Mt. 28:19–20; 26:26–8; Mk 14:12–25; Lk. 22:7–20). In these passages, Jesus commands the repetition of actions he first performs. The words, "do this in remembrance of me," embody the mimetic imperative for Eucharistic worship and, more broadly, for tradition (*paradosis*). A few decades later, Saint Paul intentionally echoes the words of Jesus: "for I received from the Lord that which I also delivered [*paredoka*] to you: that the Lord Jesus on the same night in which He was betrayed took bread" (1 Cor. 11:23). Other passages, such as Jude 1:3, lend further insight into the apostolic conception of tradition maintained by the Orthodox Church.

In harmony with scripture, the ecumenical councils produced doctrinal decrees and canons that convey the boundaries of the apostolic faith, compile patristic precedent for scriptural interpretation, and in the canons, offer practical guidelines for living a Christian life. In the Orthodox Church, there are seven ecumenical councils: (1) First Council of Nicaea in 325; (2) First Council of Constantinople in 381; (3) Council of Ephesus in 431; (4) Council of Chalcedon in 451; (5) Second Council of Constantinople in 553; (6) Third Council of Constantinople in 681; and (7) Second Council of Nicaea in 787. These seven councils exemplify the paradigm of synodal conciliarity as the highest inspired setting for determinations of theological doctrine, with the council of Jerusalem in Acts 15 as model precedent. Along with scripture, the ecumenical councils are considered infallible in their Spirit-led decisions and decrees. The Nicene Creed is the best example of such a decree, and its careful deployment of a philosophical, non-biblical term (*homousios*) to describe the inner Trinitarian life constitutes a milestone in the maturation of canonical doctrine, achieved conciliarly.

After the councils, the church fathers have pride of place; their lives and writings constitute an indispensable witness to the truth of the Gospel, as expressed in the fourth-century notion of consensus patrum, or the "shared mind of the fathers." Pelikan notes that "the fathers of the church were, by definition, 'those who have handed down the dogma to us by tradition' (Max.Schol.C.h.1.2), but the councils were a primary channel for that tradition." Ultimately, these three—scripture, councils, fathers—are the fountainheads of Orthodox Tradition: "in any complete enumeration of the means of instruction in Christian doctrine, the Scriptures of the Old and New Testament, the doctors of the church, and the councils all had to be cited" (Pelikan 1977: 23).

Numerous "unwritten" practices have also been passed down in the life of the church. In Saint Basil's words, "of the beliefs and practices whether generally accepted or publicly enjoined which are preserved in the church, some we possess derived from written teaching; others we have received delivered to us 'in a mystery' by the tradition of the apostles; and both of these in relation to true religion have the same force" (*On the Holy Spirit*, XXVII.66). Some are embodied forms of piety, for instance facing east in prayer or making the sign of the cross. Regarding prayer, the Orthodox Church has

FIGURE 7.2 *Icon of the First Ecumenical Council in 325* CE. Source: *Public Domain.*

always seen the high standard of "unceasing prayer" (1 Thess. 5:16) as a vital aim, especially through the Jesus Prayer (cf. Mk 10:47). Fasting, as emphasized by Jesus and prescribed in the canons, is a type of **ascesis** or training of a person's free will through voluntary abstinence in preparation for sacramental participation and seasonal feasts of the church. Other unwritten, lived elements are simply the cumulative response to the Gospel's call to virtue and holiness: humility, repentance, and love of neighbor. Those who have attained this live on as the communion of saints, visibly and materially present in relics and iconography, alongside those who still struggle. Among

FIGURE 7.3 *Icon of the Theotokos.* Source: *Public Domain.*

FIGURE 7.4 *The Church of Hagia Sophia (as a mosque, in the nineteenth century).* Source: *Public Domain.*

the saints, the Theotokos ("God-bearer")—the Greek name for Mary who gives birth to—has special place of honor. Veneration (but not worship) of saints, their relics, icons that depict them, and the presence of the divine image in every person are ways that Orthodox tradition affirms the dogma of the Incarnation, and the capacity of material creation for bearing divine grace.

Iconography is part of a long-standing emphasis on beauty in worship that encompasses church architecture, poetic hymnography, and monophonic chant. Such beauty often spills over from worship into evangelism. A well-known passage in the Russian Primary Chronicle describes the report of the emissaries of Vladimir of Kiev, who in 987 had visited a number of regions, seeking the true faith, but to no avail. Then they arrived in Constantinople:

> Then we went on to Greece, and the Greeks led us to the edifices where they worship their God, and we knew not whether we were in heaven or on earth. For on earth there is no such splendour or such beauty, and we are at a loss how to describe it. We know only that God dwells there among men, and their service is fairer than the ceremonies of other nations. For we cannot forget that beauty.
>
> (*The Russian Primary Chronicle*, 111)

This experience of beauty in Orthodox worship ultimately leads to the conversion of the Slavic peoples under Vladimir, which is considered the moment of Russia's Christianization. In Orthodox worship, heaven and Earth are united, Christ's Incarnation is extended through the Spirit, and "God dwells [...] among men." As Andrew Louth puts it, "the heart of the Christian faith is not something simply conceptual: it is a fact, or even better, an action—the action, the movement, of the Son sent into the world for our sakes to draw us back to the Father. And it is this movement that the **liturgy**, with its dramatic structure, echoes and repeats" (1983: 89). The ethos or *phronema* of the Orthodox Church—its ancient, apostolic faith, its transformative spiritual practices, its adherence to biblical truth and patristic wisdom, and its majestic and dignified worship—reflect this dynamic tension between movement and structure, charisma and institution, God and man.

A Two-Millennia History

A Christian Imperial Commonwealth Is Born

While the beauty experienced by Vladimir's emissaries was transcendent, it was also the fruit of the civilization known to us as Byzantium. For over a millennium, it was the cultural center of Christendom. Its scholarly and intellectual output enriched all of Christendom. Its military prowess, vast wealth, and strategic diplomacy kept Islamic forces from pushing west, arguably enabling the emergence of western Europe. Understood by the inhabitants of its imperial commonwealth be the capitol of the Christian Roman Empire, the city of Constantinople, originally called "New Rome," was founded by Emperor Constantine I in 330. Its walls were not breached until the reign of Constantine XI, approximately eleven centuries later, in 1453.

In recent years, scholars have come to revise their understanding of Byzantium's founding emperor. Constantine's Edict of Milan in 313 is increasingly recognized as a milestone not only in the relationship of Roman power and the Christian faith, but as a landmark policy of religious liberty. Constantine's legal reforms helped protect slaves, women, and children. The scores of churches he commissioned, from the Aula Palatina in Trier to the Church of the Resurrection in Jerusalem, suggest that Constantine's conversion was a sincere basis for reshaping late antiquity in light of the Gospels and the crucified Lord they proclaim.

The only emperor who rivals Constantine's legacy is Justinian. His sixth-century reconquest of northern Africa and Italy from barbarians, his construction of the largest church in the world (at the time), *Agia Sophia* (Holy Wisdom), and his compilation of Roman civil law, the *Corpus Iuris Civilis*, not to mention the Ravenna mosaics, mark the high points of his contribution to Western civilization. It would also be remiss not to mention Empress Irene, whose convening of the Seventh Ecumenical Council in Nicaea to defend the veneration of icons against iconoclasm ensured their central place in the aesthetics and piety of Eastern Christianity to this day.

Nicaea, the Cappadocians, and Saint John Chrysostom

As monarchs such as Constantine, Justinian, and Irene show, religion and politics were closely linked in Byzantine society. For the Orthodox Church, however, theological truth has always outweighed political expedience. On historical occasions when the state has contravened the Gospel, the latter ultimately triumphed. Yet when state power has defended the Faith, the results have also borne enduring witness to God's truth. Consider the Council of Nicaea, the First Ecumenical Council. It was convened by Constantine in 325 to combat the heresy of Arianism, which taught that Christ was less than fully God, and thus that "there was a time when Christ was not." On the northern coast of Asia Minor, 318 bishops spent months in study and deliberation, but it was to be the arguments of a lowly deacon named Athanasius that overcame Arius. The council ratified the Nicene Creed as the definitive formulation of faith affirming Jesus Christ as "of one essence" with God the Father.

The later fourth century would see a further flowering of sophisticated theological argument. The region of Cappadocia gave birth to Saint Basil the Great, his brother Saint Gregory of Nyssa, and Saint Gregory Nazianzus. These scholarly bishops wrote in a variety of genres—scriptural exegeses, orations, treatises, disputations, poetry, and monastic rules—about a range of topics, yet one proved predominant: the Trinity. Especially dedicated to defending the personal identity of the Holy Spirit, the Cappadocian fathers devoted immense rhetorical and philosophical acumen to theological purpose.

They are perhaps only matched in articulation by their friend Saint John Chrysostom, who like Gregory Nazianzus served as patriarch of Constantinople. His moniker, "golden-mouthed" (*chrysostomos*), was well deserved; records attest him interrupting his homilies to insist the congregation cease their applause. Yet his life, like that of so many in Christian history, bears witness to the persecution faced by those who denounce abuses of power. Exiled twice by an empress, John maintained a strong, sober faith. Aside from his voluminous scriptural commentaries and letters, he is the seminal source for the Divine Liturgy that has been corporately prayed by Orthodox Christians every Sunday for the last 1,600 years.

Monasticism and Byzantine Mystical Theology

With Constantine's legalization of faith in Christ, the martyrdom of the first centuries ended. Partly in response to the rapid, widespread adoption of Christianity by the empire, a new form of radical devotion to the Christian ideals of poverty and self-denial emerged: monasticism. Taking form in the Egyptian desert with Saint Anthony and Saint Pachomius, the hermetic and coenobitic forms of monasticism soon began sprouting across Europe. This was partly enabled by textual transmission; Saint Basil wrote his *Small Asketikon* for communities in Asia Minor, but it was brought west by Saint Rufinus

FIGURE 7.5 *Simonopetra Monastery, Mount Athos.* Source: *Author/Gaelan Gilbert.*

and Saint John Cassian. Over a century later, Saint Benedict of Nursia would build on (and mention) Basil's monastic rule in founding Monte Cassino. Western monasteries in Italy, Gaul, and the British Isles continued to draw vitality from roots in the east. The Egyptian and Palestinian deserts, Saint Sava's in Jerusalem, Saint Katherine's in Sinai, the Studite monastery in Constantinople, the monastic communities of Mount Athos in Greece, and Trinity-Saint Sergius and Optina monasteries in Russia comprise a rough genealogy of monastic centers in the Orthodox Church. The most significant, Mount Athos was founded in the tenth century on a 27-kilometer peninsula in northern Greece, and is home to over twenty large monasteries and hundreds of smaller sketes.

Alongside monasticism, Byzantine Christianity also developed a high intellectual life. Although Justinian closed the Platonic Academy in Athens in 529, the classical liberal arts flourished in Byzantium's unique Greco-Roman-Christian culture. From the fifth to the ninth centuries, figures such as Dionysius the Areopagite, Maximos the Confessor, and John of Damascus are representative of the marriage between faith and learning. Dionysius forged a mystical emphasis on apophasis, or negative theology, insisting that divine infinity forestalls any exhaustive categorical statements about God. Moreover, in his writings "the external, structural elements of the Church were spiritually interiorized, creating a new ecclesial reality that was both dynamic and static, [...] structural and existential, [...] institutional and mystical" (Constas 2019: 6). Building on Dionsyius, Maximos the Confessor further elaborated the cosmic implications of salvation in Christ, defending key insights from the Council of Chalcedon. As the preeminent Byzantine philosopher-theologian, his *Mystagogy* is a masterful synthesis "in which the movement of the liturgical drama reflects the movement of human beings and indeed of all creation toward their final consummation in God" (Constas 2019: 7). Saint John of Damascus, writing in eighth-century Damascus from the caliph's court, penned the first systematic exposition of patristic doctrine along with the pivotal defense of iconography against the iconoclasm that, through the indirect influence of Islam, prevailed in Constantinople in the eighth and ninth centuries. Theorizing the nature of pictorial representation and differing modes of veneration, Saint John appeals to Christ's incarnation, understood as the entrance of God into visible embodiment, as a basis for religious imagery.

From the tenth to the fourteenth centuries, Saint Symeon the New Theologian, Saint Gregory Palamas, and Saint Nicholas Cabasilas exemplify the late Byzantine theological mind. Saint Symeon's writings reflect poetically on the mystical encounter with God in personal, noetic prayer. Emphasizing the distinction between God's essence and His energies, Saint Gregory Palamas defended hesychasm by contending against Barlaam of Calabria that human persons can experience communion with the Uncreated Light (rather than, in the West, created grace). Cabasilas, finally, carries on the legacy of Dionysius and Maximos in exalting liturgical worship and the sacramental life. Orthodox theology in the Byzantine period is at once mystical and scholarly, rooted in personal experience and inherited, patristic teachings.

The Great Schism (1054) and the Fall of Constantinople (1453)

Between the ninth and thirteenth centuries, there was a growing estrangement and ultimately a break between Eastern and Western Christianity. The Schism of 1054 had two particular issues at its heart: papal claims of universal jurisdiction and the *filioque*. Latin for "and the Son," the *filioque* was a sixth-century addition to the Nicene

Creed. Adding anything to the Creed without the decision of an ecumenical council was unthinkable in the Greek East, which furthermore disagreed with the theological consequences of doing so. Political developments aggravated doctrinal disagreement. The crowning of Charlemagne in 800, the overreaches of Pope Nicholas I in the midninth century, Pope Sergius IV's statement of faith in 1009 with the filioque added, the mutual anathemas of Cardinal Humbert and Patriarch Michael Cerularius in 1054, and perhaps most of all the 1204 sack of Constantinople by Western Crusaders all led to what has become a sustained break between Rome and the Eastern church. While the 1054 anathemas were mutually lifted by Pope Paul VI and Ecumenical Patriarch Athenagoras in 1964, the Roman Catholic Church and Eastern Orthodox Church are not in sacramental communion, and still differ on the filioque and other doctrinal sticking points, such as *ex cathedra* papal infallibility and the immaculate conception.

Four centuries later, on May 29, 1453, after years of siege with massive, new artillery, Mehmet II and his Ottoman army entered as conquerors into Constantinople. The body of Emperor Constantine XI, who was last seen plunging into the fray as invaders streamed through the breach in Theodosius's land walls, was never found. Since the seventh century, Islamic forces had pushed westward and set their sights on various Christian territories, but especially "the City," which they were ever unable to conquer—until 1453. For the next four centuries, Ottoman rule had varying impacts on the Orthodox peoples, known as *Romioi* or *Rumi* (Romans). While Orthodox merchants in the Phanar district of what came to be called Istanbul tended to fare well enough, rural villagers and clergy—from northern Romania to Cairo, from Serbia to Jerusalem—endured intermittent oppression and persecution.

Yet Christian Byzantium had an heir apparent. With a northern consolidation of power in Moscow under Ivan III, who had wed Zoe Paleologos of the imperial line, Russia emerged in the fifteenth century as a bastion of Orthodox faith and culture. Wallachia also provided financial and political support for Christians under Ottoman rule. Despite the Old Believer controversy and Peter the Great's secularizing reforms, the late eighteenth-century labors of Nikodemos Agiorites and Paisius Velichkovsky in compiling and translating the Philokalia spurred a deepening of monastic piety and influence, which spanned from Mount Athos and the "Kollyvades" fathers in Greece to the starets of Optina and Pochaev in Russia. The twentieth century was another matter: the First World War destabilized the Balkans, and in the aftermath of the Bolshevik revolution, hundreds of Orthodox churches and monasteries were destroyed. The Soviet regime killed more Eastern Christians in seventy years than all the ancient persecutions combined, with conservative estimates of around twelve million.

The Orthodox Church Today

Global shifts in the last thirty years have significantly impacted the Orthodox Church. After the collapse of the Soviet Union, Orthodox-majority countries in the Eastern Bloc have witnessed a massive revival of faith, affirming once more Tertullian's insight that

FIGURE 7.6 *Trinity-St. Sergius Monastery, Sergiyev Posad, c. 1890.* Source: *Public Domain.*

"the blood of the martyrs is the seed of the church" (*Apologeticus* 13). A number of studies in Russia between 1991 and 2008 "show the share of Orthodox Christians more than doubling from 31% to 72%, while at the same time, the share of religiously unaffiliated adults declined from a majority in 1991 (61%) to 18% in 2008," according to a 2017 study (Pew Research Center 2017). With a global Orthodox Christian population of approximately 200 million today, about half live in Russia.

Returning to the North American context, the Russian mission continued to stabilize and grow until 1867, when Alaska was sold to the United States. Yet the Herculean missionary efforts of figures such as Metropolitan Innocent (Veniaminov) and Fr. Jacob (Netsvetov) had planted deep seeds. To this day, the Orthodox faith endures among the Indigenous population of Alaska. Further south, between 1870 and 1920, almost 30 million immigrants came to North America, many from Orthodox countries. This had a huge impact: "massive immigration was transforming what had begun as a small mission to America into a large but fragmented collection of ethnic parishes intent on giving newcomers a shelter from America" (Erickson 2008: 41). Many thought they were coming to foreign shores only temporarily, and their resistance to cultural assimilation shaped the ethos of the parishes they organized.

A key figure at the turn of the century, Bishop Tikhon (Bellavin) tried to foster the multiethnic character of the Orthodox Church in America, while forging broader administrative unity. Advocating for auxiliary dioceses to help sustain "peculiarities in canonical structure, in liturgical rules, in parish life" (Erickson 2008: 49), Tikhon also insisted that priests learn English for ministry and outreach. The turn of the century was a dynamic time. The first consecration of an Orthodox bishop in the western hemisphere occurred in 1904 when Tikhon elevated Fr. Raphael (Hawaweeny) to the episcopal ranks, planting the seeds of the Antiochian Orthodox Christian Archdiocese. Around the same time, missionary priests such as Fr. Sebastian (Dabovich) and Fr. Nicola (Yanney) tirelessly ministered to their far-flung flocks, whether Serbians on the west coast or Arabs in the rural heartland. Also notable was the return of Greek Catholics or "Uniates." Between 1889 and 1909, through the efforts of Fr. Alexis (Toth), over 163 parishes left the "Unia" and rejoined the Orthodox Church.

Due to geopolitical instabilities and Islamic extremism, Orthodox immigration to North America has continued, but increasingly without a sense of temporary relocation. This, along with an influx of converts, has led to active cooperation across ethnic jurisdictions in North America, as seen in a number of "pan-Orthodox" organizations: the Assembly of Canonical Orthodox Bishops of the United States of America, the Orthodox Christian Mission Center (OCMC), International Orthodox Christian Charities (IOCC), the Fellowship of Orthodox Christians United to Serve (FOCUS), and the Orthodox Christian Fellowship (OCF), a college campus ministry. Orthodox monasticism

FIGURE 7.7 *Orthodox clergy in a worship service (bishop, priests).* Source: *Author/Gaelan Gilbert.*

has also arrived in the western hemisphere, in large part through the efforts of a recently reposed Athonite elder, Fr. Ephraim (Moraitis), who founded a quarter of the eighty monasteries now in America. Conversions from other traditions have caught up with immigration as a primary factor in church growth, which over the last century has kept pace with total US population growth (Krindatch 2018: 3, 21, 24). The Orthodox Church is thriving and growing, in the United States and worldwide.

Bishop Tikhon's insistence on fostering cultural-ethnic particularity alongside a deeper commitment to the apostolic faith defines the unique ethos of the Orthodox Church, even while an administrative complexity lingers on. Unflinching theological unity, a fraternal spirit of love, a shared tradition of worship and practice, and the locally embodied yet transcendent reality of sacramental Communion are the visible contours of unity in the Orthodox Church. Amidst history's vicissitudes, God preserves and guides His church, raising up saints from within it even now. The Orthodox Church offers in this respect precisely what we have tried to explore above: a vital tradition that, through the prayers of its saints and in the lives of its members, endures as a mystical witness to the crucified and resurrected Lord Jesus Christ, looking forward in hope to His coming and saying with the Spirit, "Come!"

Further Reading and Online Resources

Clendenin, D.B. (2005), *Eastern Orthodox Christianity: A Western Perspective*, Grand Rapids, MI: Baker Academic.

Fitzgerald, Fr. T. (1996), "The Orthodox Church: An Introduction," *Greek Orthodox Archdiocese of America*. Available online: https://www.goarch.org/-/the-orthodox-church-an-introduction (accessed November 5, 2020).

Hieromonk, G. (2020), *The Orthodox Faith, Worship, and Life*, Columbia, MO: Newrome Press.

Lossky, V. (1997), *The Mystical Theology of the Orthodox Church*, Crestwood, NY: St. Vladimir's Seminary Press.

McGuckin, J.A. (2020), *The Orthodox Church: A New History*, New Haven, CT: Yale University Press.

Schmemann, A. (2018), *For the Life of the World*, Crestwood, NY: St. Vladimir's Seminary Press.

Ware, K. (2019), *The Orthodox Way*, Crestwood, NY: St. Vladimir's Seminary Press.

References

Bratsiotis, P.E. (1964), "The Fundamental Principles and Main Characteristics of the Orthodox Church," in A.J. Philippou (ed.), *The Orthodox Ethos – Studies in Orthodoxy: Essays in Honour of the Centenary of the Greek Orthodox Archdiocese of North and South America*, 23–33, Oxford: Holywell Press.

Constas, M. (2019), "Saint Maximus the Confessor: A Bridge between the Churches," Presented at Notre Dame Seminary.

Cross, S.H. and O.P. Sherbowitz-Wetzor, trans. and eds. (1953), *The Russian Primary Chronicle: Laurentian Text*, Cambridge, MA: Medieval Academy of America.

Erickson, J.H. (2008), *Orthodox Christians in America: A Short History*, Oxford: Oxford University Press.

Krindatch, A. (2018), "Fast Questions and Fast Answers about the Geography of Orthodoxy in America," *Assembly of Canonical Orthodox Bishops of the USA*. Available online: https://www.assemblyofbishops.org/assets/files/studies/2018-12-FastQuestionsAndFastAnswersAboutOrthodoxGeography.pdf (accessed November 5, 2020).

Louth, A. (1983), *Discerning the Mystery: An Essay on the Nature of Theology*, Oxford: Clarendon Press.

Oleksa, M. (1998), *Orthodox Alaska: A Theology of Mission*, Crestwood, NY: Saint Vladimir's Seminary Press.

Pelikan, J. (1977), *The Spirit of Eastern Christendom (600–1700)*, Chicago: University of Chicago Press.

Pew Research Center (2017), "Religious Belief and National Belonging in Central and Eastern Europe," May 10. Available online: https://www.pewforum.org/2017/05/10/religious-belief-and-national-belonging-in-central-and-eastern-europe/ (accessed November 5, 2020).

Schmemann, A. (1971), "A Meaningful Storm: Reflections on Autocephaly, Tradition, and Ecclesiology," *SVSQ*, 15 (1/2): 1–27.

Strickland, J. (2019), *The Age of Paradise: Christendom from Pentecost to the First Millenium*, Chesterton, IN: Ancient Faith Publishing.

Ware, T. (1976), *The Orthodox Church*, Harmondsworth, UK: Penguin Books.

Yannaras, C. (1973), "Orthodoxy and the West," in A.J. Philippou (ed.), *Orthodoxy: Life and Freedom*, 130–47, Oxford: Studion Publications.

Glossary Terms

Ascesis This word, originally Greek, implies the spiritual practice of measured continence or abstinence, performed through fasting, prayer, and self-denial. The Greek sense is that of an athletic training, and Paul's emphasis in his epistles on "running the race" or "fighting the good fight" are representative references to *ascesis* in the NT.

Ecumenical Historically, the *oikumene* was equivalent to the known, civilized world. Anything beyond its borders was considered to be barbarian territory. In this study, "ecumenical" is used in this historical sense as a synonym for "universal" to refer both to the set of seven definitive church councils of the first millennium, as well as to the "Ecumenical Patriarch," the archbishop of Constantinople, whose jurisdiction traditionally had a more "universal" scope in possessing oversight of missionary endeavors to "barbarian" lands, though never to the extent of infringing of other, already established episcopal sees. Ecumenical in the more modern sense of inter-Christian relations is not used in this study, though it is increasingly common in Orthodox Christian parlance.

Icon A sacred image of Jesus Christ or the saints that is used to adorn the interior of churches and homes, created according to proscribed elements of style and materials. A sophisticated approach to venerating icons emerged in response to the eighth-century iconoclasm, which maintains that in revering or kissing icons, one is not worshipping the image but instead giving due honor to the prototype of the image, namely, Christ himself.

Liturgy In the Orthodox Church, the Divine Liturgy is the name for the Eucharistic worship service, as opposed to "Mass" in the West. The Greek word *leitourgia* etymologically implies a "work" (*ergon*) of the "people" (*laos*). There are three primary texts of the Liturgy used in Orthodox worship, and each is associated with its seminal authorial source: the Liturgy of Saint John Chrysostom, the Liturgy of Saint Basil, and the Liturgy of Saint Gregory Dialogus, sometimes referred to as the Liturgy of the Pre-Sanctified Gifts.

Patristic This adjective is used to refer to the writings of the church fathers, who receive a special emphasis in the theology of the Orthodox Church. While occasional errors are acknowledged in the writings of a number of church fathers, the collective witness of patristic texts possesses an automatic and fixed position of authority in matters of doctrine and practice.

8

Roman Catholicism: A Tradition in Transition

Todd Hartch

During a prayer service in Bogotá in 2004, a student from one of Colombia's most prestigious universities entered into a trance-like state, "closing her eyes, swaying back and forth with her arms crossed over her chest, and, depending on the type of music, displaying an expression that mixed joy and distress." Later, she "lay flat on the ground and then doubled herself over, in the style of a Muslim in a mosque," staying in this position for a long time. When a more up-tempo song started, she stood up and, in the midst of other swaying and clapping worshippers, "began a liturgical dance in front of the crucifix." An anthropologist who witnessed this Charismatic Catholic event had a hard time reconciling the student's left-wing politics, politically correct attitudes, and commitment to rationality with her religious fervency and self-abandon (Ospina Martínez 2004: 42).

At St. Francis of Assisi Church in Portland, Oregon, in 2019, elderly women dressed in white gathered before **Mass**. Some held large photographs of the poor and the homeless. Others displayed placards with the words, "Catholic Women Strike." Others wore shirts that said "Jesus resisted the Pharisees" and "Question authority." During the Mass, the women raised the large photos and interrupted the "prayers of the faithful." After the official end of the Mass, one woman walked to the front of the church and began singing. Remaining members of the congregation pulled out maracas and tambourines and joined in. Then a gray-haired woman went to the pulpit and said, "We are being abused in the church by this priest and this archbishop." The heart of the matter, it seems, was that the parish's new pastor, a Nigerian priest named George Kuforiji, had restored the official Catholic **liturgy** at St. Francis, doing away with various local "progressive" variations. He had removed photographs of the poor and homeless from the sanctuary, had thrown out the "rainbow" vestments that a previous priest had used, and had insisted on the traditional terms "Father, Son, and Holy Spirit," rather than "God and Creator" (Talbot 2019).

Both the prayer service in Bogotá and the Mass in Portland are part of the global communion of the Catholic Church, whose more than 1.3 billion members make up the largest single Christian church and largest religious body in the world. Together, the Charismatic prayer service and the interrupted Mass hint at the spiritual, liturgical, and

FIGURE 8.1 *Painting of Our Lady of Guadalupe, San Miguel de Allende, Mexico.* Source: *Craig Lovell/Getty Images.*

theological complexity within what is theoretically a united body of believers. The Charismatic event points to a constant process within Catholicism, the generation of new spiritual movements and practices, in this case a new form of spirituality derived from the Protestant Pentecostal movement and popular styles of electronic and amplified music. This form of Charismatic Catholicism has proved especially influential in Latin America, where perhaps 75 million Catholics practice their faith in this manner, but it is just one of the recent spiritual adaptations in a region that has long featured various "folk" versions of Catholic spirituality.

Around the world and throughout an almost 2,000-year history, these local and national spiritualities have had a complex relationship with Catholic **orthodoxy**, that is, with the official doctrine of the Catholic Church. In Mexico, for example, devotion to the national patron saint, Our Lady of Guadalupe, was somewhat suspect in the sixteenth century, but eventually became so intertwined with Mexican Catholicism that it would be virtually impossible for a Catholic leader in that country to deny the reality of Mary's 1531 appearance. On the other hand, devotion to "Santa Muerte" or "Saint Death," common among drug dealers and other criminals, is condemned by Catholic bishops and will never be accepted as mainstream or orthodox.

The Portland Mass points to another dominant reality in contemporary Catholicism: deep divisions over the proper direction of the church and, sometimes, even over the definition of Catholicism itself. These divisions do not always follow expected lines and often challenge religious and cultural stereotypes. In Portland, for instance, it was the African priest who was the enforcer of orthodoxy and the elderly North American parishioners who were the liturgical innovators and the ecclesial rebels. There are, of course, rebels and innovators in the Global South, but in the Catholic Church the developing world is not necessarily more radical than the developed countries. In the developed countries, older Catholics can be more revolutionary than younger Catholics. To understand Catholicism today—specifically, to understand how the religion is changing and adapting to modernity and how such efforts have led to conflict and division—it is necessary to look at some major events and developments in the church over the past 150 years.

Vatican I and Vatican II

The Catholic Church has had twenty-one **ecumenical councils**, which are meetings of the world's bishops to deal with issues of great importance. The last two councils, the First Vatican Council (1869–70) and the Second Vatican Council (1962–5), addressed the church's response to **modernity**. At Vatican I, the council fathers took a confrontational stance, asserting that the modern world's rejection of divine authority had plunged it into "the abyss of pantheism, materialism, and atheism," and that many modern men and women "strive to destroy rational nature itself, to deny any criterion of what is right and just, and to overthrow the very foundations of human society." Rather than adapt to the changes around them, the bishops reaffirmed traditional

Catholic teaching in a range of areas and, as previous councils had done, issued "**anathemas**," or solemn declarations of rejection and excommunication. For instance, they asserted that in matters of faith and morals "that meaning of Holy Scripture must be held to be the true one, which Holy Mother Church held and holds, since it is her right to judge of the true meaning and interpretation of Holy Scripture," a rejection of the kind of modern biblical scholarship that had produced heterodox interpretations of scripture. They said of anyone who denied that scripture was divinely inspired, "let him be anathema" (Catholic Church [1870] 1990a).

Vatican I also dealt with the role and powers of the pope. To the dismay of more liberal clerics, the council fathers adopted a robust definition of papal powers that includes the doctrine of "*papal infallibility*." The concept is that, in certain specific

FIGURE 8.2 *Bishops gathered at the Second Vatican Council, 1965.* Source: *Keystone-France/Getty Images.*

situations, a pope cannot err when "he defines a doctrine concerning faith or morals to be held by the whole Church." Although this power of infallibility was far more than Catholic liberals such as the British historian Lord Acton wanted to admit, it was not an unlimited power of prognostication or doctrinal innovation, much less an assertion of papal impeccability (inability to sin). Infallibility applied only to public definitions of doctrine, which could only be based on "the Sacred Scriptures and the apostolic traditions." The council fathers specifically rejected the possibility of a pope using his gift of infallibility to propose "some new doctrine" (Catholic Church [1870] 1990b). Still, the council's definition of papal infallibility amounted to a strengthening of the papacy and an assertion of its supernatural nature. In the wake of the French Revolution, the Revolutions of 1848, and the rise of democratic nationalism throughout Europe, the Catholic Church was unflinching in hanging onto its traditional teachings and its monarchical leader, now with recognized supernatural abilities.

The Second Vatican Council took a more welcoming and optimistic stance toward modernity. Pope John XXIII, who announced the council in 1959, rebuked the "prophets of doom" who saw something especially pernicious in the modern age. In fact, he believed that the human family was "on the threshold of a new era" and that "with the opening of this Council a new day is dawning on the Church, bathing her in radiant splendor." As the council began in 1962, he announced, "the sun in its rising has already set our hearts aglow" and "all around is the fragrance of holiness and joy." He saw the central purpose of the council as sharing "the sacred heritage of Christian truth" with the modern world, but not through anathemas and denunciations. He wanted Christian doctrine "reformulated in contemporary terms" so that "a new enthusiasm, a new joy and serenity of mind" could emerge. In other words, the new council would differ from previous ones in its language and approach. The new language would be "more consistent with a predominantly pastoral view of the Church's teaching office" (John XXIII 1962).

True to John XXIII's hopes, Vatican II issued no anathemas and made no new doctrinal definitions. Instead, it released sixteen documents on topics as diverse as education, religious liberty, and ecumenism. The length of the combined collection of documents far exceeded the length of the documents from any previous council, and, again as John XXIII had hoped, they tended to take a more welcoming approach toward modernity, especially when contrasted with Vatican I. "The joys and the hopes, the griefs and the anxieties of the men of this age, especially those who are poor or in any way afflicted, these are the joys and hopes, the griefs and anxieties of the followers of Christ": so began the document on the church's relationship with the modern world. The council fathers made clear that they were trying to carry forward the work of Christ, which was "to rescue and not to sit in judgment." To do this, the church had "the duty of scrutinizing the signs of the times and of interpreting them in light of the Gospel" and of working for a social order "founded on truth, built on justice and animated by love." Although they also asserted that only in Christ could the "mystery of man" be understood and that Christ "fully reveals man to himself and makes his supreme calling clear," the phrase "scrutinizing the signs of the times" in later years was often interpreted in a secular sense, dropping the idea of interpretation "in light of the Gospel" and presuming an accommodation to the main ideologies and trends of the age (Catholic Church 1965b).

Another important theme from the council was the reform of the liturgy, which is the formal worship of the church. The council called for the "full and active participation" of all Catholics in the liturgy, first through better instruction about its meaning and then through revision of the rites to make them simpler, more clear, and more scriptural. To this end, Latin would remain the language of the liturgy, but more translations of parts of the Mass into local languages were encouraged, especially in "the readings and directives" and "some of the prayers and chants" (Catholic Church 1963). Other notable actions of the council were a description of the church as the "people of God" (Catholic Church 1964) and a declaration of a human right to religious freedom based in "the very dignity of the human person" (Catholic Church 1965a).

It was difficult, at the time of the council, for most Catholics to gain a clear sense of what was happening in Rome and what, exactly, the various documents meant for the church. Unlike previous councils, Vatican II took place in a global media spotlight in which bishops, their theological advisors, and reporters from all over the world, some barely conversant with Catholic theology, felt compelled to offer their interpretations of what was taking place in the council. Media reporting on the council often gave the overriding impression that great changes were taking place and new possibilities were opening up, but it was less clear what those changes and possibilities actually were.

Generally, the first place where Catholics in the pews experienced the impact of the council was in the liturgy. In 1970, Catholics around the world began participating in a new form of the Mass. The commission that had carried out the council's call for a reform of the liturgy had gone beyond the actual words of the council. Instead of "the readings and directives" and "some of the prayers and chants" being translated into the vernacular, the entire Mass would now be offered in Spanish or Japanese or English or whatever the local language was. Furthermore, instead of the modest simplification that many council fathers had been expecting, the new Mass eliminated entire sections of the old liturgy, completely reformulated the set of assigned Bible readings, and introduced a number of options at various places in the Mass. Most notably, the center of the Mass, the Eucharist (where Catholics believe that bread and wine become the body and blood of Christ), would have no one set prayer but could be offered in several different ways, depending on the choice of the celebrant.

The implementation of the new Mass came as a shock to many older Catholics, especially if it was accompanied by folk music and other manifestations of popular culture. But beyond the controversies and tensions that developed in some parishes, the new liturgy suggested to many Catholics that Catholicism was more open to change than they had previously imagined. For some, this sense of change extended beyond liturgical practices to doctrine itself. If the Mass itself could change, they wondered, would the male priesthood or the indissolubility of marriage be next?

Thus, in Europe and other developed parts of the world, the post-Vatican II era was full of questions about the nature of the Catholic Church and how much it could change. Divisions grew between three main groups. There were those, often styled liberals or progressives, who espoused "the spirit of Vatican II" and believed that the most significant aspect of the council was that it had opened the doors of change; they expected that the church would make more dramatic changes in the future, not just in disciplinary and liturgical areas but in areas of doctrine and morality. A more conservative group believed that the true spirit of the council was found in the actual documents of the council and that Catholic doctrines could not be changed. A still more conservative group, usually referred to as traditionalists, believed that the council had been a mistake and that its innovations were unnecessary or even heretical.

Unnoticed by many Catholics in Europe and North America, as they argued over these issues, were two profound developments. First, by almost every measure—Mass attendance, baptisms, first Communions, marriages—Catholic participation in the developed world was dropping and many Catholics were leaving the church altogether. The reforms of Vatican II had been designed to make the church more accessible to the modern world, but they not only failed to attract non-Catholics to the faith but also proved ineffectual in holding onto those who were already Catholic. By 2015, it was a truism that the second largest denomination in the United States was "former Catholics," since the approximately thirty million former Catholics outnumbered the Southern Baptists, the country's second largest religious community (Pew Research Center 2015a). Second, during the twentieth century the demographic center of the Catholic Church shifted to the Global South. While Catholics of the global north were arguing about the legacy of Vatican II, or simply leaving the church, the very nature and composition of the worldwide Catholic community was being transformed.

New Centers

Globally, the shift has been quick and dramatic. In 1910, 82 percent of all Christians lived in the so-called Global North (Europe, North America, Australia, New Zealand, and Japan). Today more than 60 percent of Christians live in the Global South, or the world outside of the Global North (Pew Research Center 2011). For Catholicism this change brought prominence to Latin America, the new demographic center of the religion. Today about 40 percent of all Catholics live in Latin America and almost half of all Catholics live in the Americas. Of the six nations in the world with the largest Catholic populations, the two largest (Brazil and Mexico) are in Latin America, as is number six (Colombia). The only European nation in the top six, Italy, has fewer Catholics than the United States and the Philippines (Pew Research Center 2011). In other words, although Catholicism still has its institutional center in Rome, it would be a mistake to think of the religion as primarily European. The vast majority of today's Catholics are (and future Catholics will be) Asians, Latin Americans, and Africans. Almost all of the religion's demographic growth is coming from outside of Europe, as is most of the religious dynamism. The current pope, Francis, is an Argentine, and future popes could well come from Africa and Asia.

FIGURE 8.3 *Archbishop Oscar Romero in 1979.* Source: *Alex Bowie/Getty Images.*

Although Latin America has suffered from a shortage of priests for centuries, in the past few decades lay Catholics have become increasingly active and have assumed many leadership roles. They have started evangelizing and have joined many different "ecclesial movements," such as Focolare and the Neocatechumenal Way, that provide teaching, guidance, and community. Others have joined "base ecclesial communities" in which Catholics study the Bible and apply its teachings to their neighborhoods. Most impressively, by 2012 Latin America had 1.8 million lay catechists and over 300,000 lay missionaries (Center for Applied Research in the Apostolate [CARA] 2014).

Latin American Catholicism also has had a major influence beyond its own borders. The military governments of the Cold War era were oppressive, violent, and corrupt. In response, bishops, priests, religious sisters, and lay Catholics committed themselves to justice and peace, setting an example for Catholics around the world. Movements of resistance to injustice and aid to the suffering sprang up all over the region and almost every nation boasts its heroes and martyrs who were willing to die in defense of the most vulnerable. Most famous of these is El Salvador's Archbishop Óscar Romero (1917–80), assassinated at the altar during Mass. He was recognized as a saint in 2018. Liberation theology, a reworking of Catholic theology that focused on justice and prioritized the poor, spread from Latin America around the world and was a stimulus to the social thought of Pope Francis.

A second influence of Latin American Catholicism came from migration to the United States and Europe. As Mexicans, Central Americans, and others moved north or crossed the Atlantic, they brought with them new beliefs and practices. In the United States, where one-third of all Catholics are now Hispanic, migration has led to a "Latinization" of Catholicism, not just in terms of demographics but also in religious practices (Pew Research Center 2015a). Most notably, non-Latino Catholics now give a great deal of attention to the Virgin of Guadalupe, who has a large shrine in the diocese of La Crosse, Wisconsin, and is honored with paintings, statues, and murals in countless churches around the United States. Some Latin American immigrants

FIGURE 8.4 *Catholic Mass in Harare, Zimbabwe, 2018.* Source: *Dan Kitwood/Getty Images.*

view their new homes as mission fields. In Portugal, for instance, Brazilian Charismatic Catholics are leading some of their Portuguese hosts back to the church (Hartch 2014: 196–206).

If Latin America is the current center of global Catholicism, tomorrow's center is Africa. Although only one million or two million Catholics lived in Africa in 1900, by 1980 the number was more than fifty-eight million (CARA 2014). By 2015, the Catholic population of Africa had reached 222 million and was expected to reach 460 million by 2040 (Holy See 2017). If current trends continue, since the European Catholic population seems to be flat or shrinking and the Catholic population of the Americas is growing at a slow rate, Africa could eclipse Latin America as the continent with the largest Catholic population by the early twenty-second century. By 2050, the Democratic Republic of the Congo will have almost double as many French-speaking Catholics as France itself (Allen 2009: 175). Africa's rise is not simply a matter of demographics: African Catholics tend to be more religiously active than Catholics in Europe and the Americas. Where only 20 percent of European Catholics and 29 percent of American Catholics attended Mass at least once per week in 2010, among African Catholics the rate of attendance was 70 percent (CARA 2014).

Asia is in a different situation, largely because more than two billion of its people live in China, still an officially atheist, communist nation, and India, where Hinduism dominates the religious and cultural landscape. Asia also hosts the holy cities of Islam on the Arabian Peninsula and large, predominantly Muslim nations such as Turkey, Iraq, Iran, and Indonesia. In other words, the ideological, religious, and cultural barriers to the expansion of Christianity in the region are significant.

Although this is an article about *Roman* Catholicism, it should be mentioned that the global Catholic Church includes twenty-three particular churches (often called the Eastern Catholic churches), in addition to the Roman or Latin Church. The vast majority of Catholics—about 98 percent—are Roman Catholics. Large majorities of the Catholics in Northern and Western Europe, the Americas, and Africa are Roman Catholics. But Asia is home to many Catholics who are not part of the Latin Church. They include Maronite Catholics in Lebanon, Syro-Malabar Catholics in India, and Armenian Catholics in Armenia, whose ancient liturgies are in the Arabic, Syriac, and Armenian languages, respectively. Thus, if we look exclusively at Roman Catholics in the Middle East or India, the numbers are quite low, but if we look at all Catholics, the numbers are higher. For instance, in the nation of Israel, of the approximately 70,000 Catholics, almost all are from the Eastern Catholic churches. In India, the Syro-Malabar Catholic Church and the Syro-Malankara Catholic Church, both tracing their roots back to Saint Thomas the Apostle, include about 5 million and 400,000 members, respectively (Catholics and Cultures n.d.-a, n.d.-b).

Still, Roman Catholicism is growing in Asia. The Philippines is home to the region's largest Catholic population and to several vibrant lay Catholic movements, including Couples for Christ and El Shaddai, that have spread to many nations around the world. In China, despite years of persecution that put many priests and bishops in prison,

FIGURE 8.5 *Syro-Malabar Catholics in Bhopal, India, 2016.* Source: *Hindustan Times/Getty Images.*

there are as many as ten million Catholics (Holy Spirit Study Centre 2018). In India, where persecution is less systematic but sometimes more violent, the Latin Church grew steadily during the twentieth century and today boasts about fifteen million believers, in addition to the five or six million members of the Syro-Malabar and Syro-Malankara churches (Catholics and Cultures n.d.-a). South Asia (India, Nepal, and Sri Lanka) now boasts more members of the Jesuit religious order than the United States, which is significant because the Jesuits, who have been losing members in the United States and Europe for decades, are highly trained priests who often become scholars, teachers, and influential leaders (Gaunt 2015).

Catholicism in the Era of Globalization

The massive growth of Catholicism in the Global South, as important as it is, has not soothed the tensions of the post-Vatican II era. In fact, the globalization of Catholicism means that the disagreements that permeate European and North American Catholicism have spread to the Global South. To make a gross generalization, Catholics of the Global South tend to be conservative on issues of personal and sexual morality and liberal or progressive on political and economic issues (Allen

2009: 23). But the ubiquity of social media and the education of many future priests and leaders of the developing world in Italy, the United States, and other northern countries, means that northern issues have become world issues. Thus, Catholics in Peru, South Africa, and the Philippines are having many of the same debates that Catholics in Germany and the United States are having. On the surface, these debates often concern sexuality and reproduction—homosexuality, transgenderism, divorce, remarriage, abortion, and contraception have all received attention in recent years—but the deeper issue is a theological one. On the one hand, there is the long tradition that Catholic doctrine can develop—that is, become more clear and specific—but cannot reverse itself. For instance, the First Vatican Council declared "that meaning of the sacred dogmas is ever to be maintained which has once been declared by Holy mother Church, and there must never be any abandonment of this sense under the pretext or in the name of a more profound understanding" (Catholic Church [1870] 1990a). In 1910, Pope Pius X required that all clergy take an oath against modernism in which they rejected the idea that "dogmas evolve and change from one meaning to another different from the one which the Church held previously" (Pius X 1910).

On the other hand, Pope Francis seems to have a different view of doctrine. His 2016 apostolic exhortation on the family, "Amoris Laetitia," although not entirely clear,

FIGURE 8.6 *Pope Francis in San Cristobal de Las Casas, Mexico, 2016.* Source: *RONALDO SCHEMIDT/Getty Images.*

appears to permit the "divorced and remarried" to receive Communion even if they are participating in an ongoing sexual relationship outside of their original marriage (Francis 2016: n329, n351). If this is indeed the intention of the document, Francis is not merely allowing for new pastoral options; such a policy would imply either that sexual activity outside of the original marriage is not a mortal sin or that persons engaging in mortal sins can still receive Communion. Either interpretation would indicate a change in what had previously been seen as settled doctrine. His actions on the death penalty are similar. In 2018, Francis changed the section of the *Catechism of the Catholic Church* on the death penalty, so that it said that the death penalty is "inadmissible" because it is "an attack on the inviolability and dignity of the person" (Catholic Church 2019: s. 2267). In May 2019, Francis said, "I have clearly stated that the death penalty is unacceptable, it is immoral. Fifty years ago, no, but there has been a better understanding of morality" (Schmitz 2019). A practice that appears to be endorsed by the Old Testament, the New Testament, and the tradition of the Catholic Church, has now become "immoral." Beyond the specific issues of cohabitation and the death penalty, the more fundamental issue is that Francis and his allies are advancing a new doctrinal paradigm. They believe that doctrine can change, not simply in the sense of growing in clarity or in application to new areas, but in the sense of complete reversal, in the sense of redefining as immoral something that previously had been taught to be moral.

Although it is impossible to predict the future of Catholicism, the southward shift of the religion means that the resolution of its most serious disagreements will take place in a church dominated by Latin Americans and Africans. In the coming decades, more and more Catholic bishops will be from the Global South, but it is not only the bishops who will decide these issues. The church also affirms the importance of "the sense of the faithful," which is the idea that "the holy people of God shares also in Christ's prophetic office" and therefore "cannot err in matters of belief." The whole people of God, including lay Catholics, has been given "supernatural discernment in matters of faith" (Catholic Church 1964). Consequently, the future of Catholicism will be worked out in the Global South, by African bishops, Latin American Charismatics, members of Filipino ecclesial movements, Indian Jesuits, and a whole host of lay and ordained Catholics, who will, somehow, try to tell a new chapter of the Catholic story while staying faithful to what has gone before.

Further Reading and Online Resources

de Mattei, R. (2012), *The Second Vatican Council: An Unwritten Story*, Fitzwilliam, NH: Loreto Press.

Hartch, T. (2014), *The Rebirth of Latin American Christianity*, New York: Oxford University Press.

Sanneh, L. (2003), *Whose Religion Is Christianity? The Gospel beyond the West*, Grand Rapids, MI: Eerdmans.

References

Allen, J. (2009), *The Future Church: How Ten Trends Are Revolutionizing the Catholic Church*, New York: Doubleday.

Catholic Church ([1870] 1990a), "Dei filius," in N.P. Tanner (ed.), *Decrees of the Ecumenical Councils: Trent to Vatican II*, vol. 2, New York: Sheed & Ward.

Catholic Church ([1870] 1990b), "Pastor aeternus," in N.P. Tanner (ed.), *Decrees of the Ecumenical Councils: Trent to Vatican II*, vol. 2, New York: Sheed & Ward.

Catholic Church (1963), "Sacrosanctum concilium," *Second Vatican Council*. Available online: http://www.vatican.va/archive/hist_councils/ii_vatican_council/documents/vat-ii_const_19631204_sacrosanctum-concilium_en.html (accessed November 5, 2020).

Catholic Church (1964), "Lumen gentium," *Second Vatican Council*. Available online: http://www.vatican.va/archive/hist_councils/ii_vatican_council/documents/vat-ii_const_19641121_lumen-gentium_en.html (accessed November 5, 2020).

Catholic Church (1965a), "Dignitatis humanae," *Second Vatican Council*. Available online: http://www.vatican.va/archive/hist_councils/ii_vatican_council/documents/vat-ii_decl_19651207_dignitatis-humanae_en.html (accessed November 5, 2020).

Catholic Church (1965b), "Gaudium et spes," *Second Vatican Council*. Available online: http://www.vatican.va/archive/hist_councils/ii_vatican_council/documents/vat-ii_cons_19651207_gaudium-et-spes_en.html (accessed November 5, 2020).

Catholic Church (2019), *Catechism of the Catholic Church*. Available online: http://www.vatican.va/archive/ENG0015/_INDEX.HTM (accessed November 5, 2020).

Catholics and Cultures (n.d.-a), "India." Available online: https://www.catholicsandcultures.org/india (accessed November 5, 2020).

Catholics and Cultures (n.d.-b), "Syro-Malabar Catholic Church Celebrates India's Ancient Roots in Christianity." Available online: https://www.catholicsandcultures.org/eastern-catholic-churches/syro-malabar-catholic-church (accessed November 5, 2020).

Center for Applied Research in the Apostolate (CARA) (2014), "Global Catholicism: Trends & Forecasts." June 4.

Francis, Pope (2016), *Amoris Laetitia*, March 19. Available online: https://w2.vatican.va/content/dam/francesco/pdf/apost_exhortations/documents/papa-francesco_esortazione-ap_20160319_amoris-laetitia_en.pdf (accessed November 5, 2020).

Gaunt, T.P. (2015), "By the Numbers: Jesuit Demography," *Nineteen Sixty-four*, January 9. Available online: https://nineteensixty-four.blogspot.com/2015/01/by-numbers-jesuit-demography.html (accessed November 5, 2020).

Hartch, T. (2014), *The Rebirth of Latin American Christianity*, New York: Oxford University Press.

Holy See Press Office (2017), "L'Annuario Pontificio 2017 e l'Annuarium Statisticum Ecclesiae 2015," April 6. Available online: https://press.vatican.va/content/salastampa/it/bollettino/pubblico/2017/04/06/0222/00505.html (accessed November 5, 2020).

Holy Spirit Study Centre (2018), "Provisional Statistics of the Catholic Church in China," December 31. Available online: http://hsstudyc.org.hk/en/china/en_cinfo_china_stat18.html (accessed November 5, 2020).

John, XXIII Pope (1962), "Opening Address to the Council," in *The Encyclicals and Other Messages of John XXIII*, 423–35, Washington, DC: TPS Press.

Ospina Martínez, M.A. (2004), "Apuntes pare el Estudio Antropológica de la Alabanza Carismática Católica," *Convergencia*, 11 (3): 31–59.

Pew Research Center (2011), "Global Christianity – A Report on the Size and Distribution of the World's Christian Population," December 19.

Pew Research Center (2015a), "America's Changing Religious Landscape," May 12.

Pew Research Center (2015b), "U.S. Catholics Open to Non-Traditional Families," September 2.

Pius, X Pope (1910), "The Oath against Modernism," *Papal Encyclicals Online*, September 1. Available online: https://www.papalencyclicals.net/Pius10/p10moath.htm (accessed November 5, 2020).

Schmitz, M. (2019), "Women Deacons and the Church's Confusion," *Catholic Herald*, May 16. Available online: https://catholicherald.co.uk/magazine/women-deacons-and-the-churchs-confusion/ (accessed November 5, 2020).

Talbot, P. (2019), "Reverence and Resistance in One of Portland's Oldest Catholic Churches," *The Oregonian*, August 11.

Glossary Terms

Anathema From a Greek word that refers to items that were "set aside" or "separated." It appears frequently in the New Testament to indicate someone who was expelled from the body of believers for heresy or serious moral failures. In later years, the church used anathema as a synonym for the most serious form of excommunication, the kind based on the gravest crimes. Many ecumenical councils promulgated sentences of anathema on anyone who committed certain crimes or who held certain opinions. The Second Vatican Council is notable for its absence of any anathemas in any of its documents.

Ecumenical council A meeting of the Catholic bishops from the entire world to address an issue or issues of great importance to the church. Because of the cost and difficulty of gathering bishops from around the world in one place, ecumenical councils usually occur only in times of crisis. The most recent three ecumenical councils are the Council of Trent (1545–63), the First Vatican Council (1869–70), and the Second Vatican Council (1962–5).

Liturgy The official prayer and ceremony of the Catholic Church (or of other Christian bodies). The most well-known example of the liturgy is the Mass, but the liturgy also includes other prayers and rituals such as baptism, funeral services, and the daily prayers required of all priests and deacons. The liturgy, which has a set form, should be distinguished from private prayers and devotions whose form is not set by the church.

Mass The central Catholic liturgical ritual. It consists of two parts: the liturgy of the Word and the liturgy of the Eucharist. The first part includes prayer and readings from the Bible. The second part is a representation of Jesus Christ's sacrificial death on the cross, in which Catholics believe that the bread and wine used in the ritual become the actual body and blood of Christ. Mass is offered daily in most Catholic churches. Catholics are required to attend Mass on Sundays and Holy Days.

Modernity In a strictly chronological sense modernity refers to the period of history after the Middle Ages, but it is often used in a qualitative sense to describe philosophical suppositions and political and economic practices that have assumed prominence in the West and then around the world over the past five centuries. Often included in descriptions of this second type of modernity are the following characteristics: secular forms of political power; industrial economies based on commodities and private property; weakening of social hierarchy; secularization of culture; and general "disenchantment" of every aspect of society. Modernity in this second sense favors bureaucratic structures over families and tribes; it prefers scientific approaches and therapeutic motivations over tradition and custom.

Orthodoxy Literally, "right belief." For Catholics, orthodoxy signifies an acceptance of the official teachings of the Catholic Church. As a proper noun, the term is also applied to the Eastern churches that are separate from the Catholic Church, such as the Greek Orthodox Church.

Papal infallibility A Catholic doctrine that asserts that the pope cannot err when, speaking as pope (not in a private capacity) and intentionally binding all Catholics (not just some part of the church), he makes a clear and definitive statement about an issue of faith or morals. In other words, this doctrine is extremely specific and does not assert that popes do not sin or that popes can predict the future. Private opinions of any sort and the vast majority of public statements would not be eligible for infallibility; to exercise this ability would have to make a conscious effort in a very specific set of circumstances. The theory behind the doctrine is that it is one of God's gifts to the church and that it enables Catholics to have a final arbiter in matters of faith and morals.

9

Protestantism: 40,000 and Still Counting

William T. Purinton

Birthing

It seemed the whole world had its sights on a single day in a small city in Germany, all to celebrate the 500th anniversary of the birth of the Protestant Reformation. If that single date (October 31, 1517) was the birth of Protestantism, there were, at least, birth pangs that lasted for centuries before the posting of Martin Luther's Ninety-Five Theses on the church door (bulletin board). So, we will both go back in time, long before the sixteenth century, all the way back to the first, and we will travel from Germany all the way to Palestine and begin the movement that is now "40,000 and still counting."

If it is really a count of 40,000 separate parts within one religious body called Protestantism, there needs to be a means of determining when it began and explaining how it either grew to such a phenomenal number or divided to create such a multitude. First, it is fair to say it is a case of growth through division, and not by multiplication or even simple addition. As a movement that grew in numbers through dividing, we ask the questions: How is it possible that a movement established to be a single body has morphed into such a schismatic number? Were the very seeds of discord that created so many divisions (or denominations) sown during the first century, perhaps within the very text of the New Testament and other early Christian writings? And, if there are many sects/divisions within a church that is called to be one, is the plurality forced to conform to a standard **orthodoxy** or is there a freedom to view various expressions of one faith as all valid forms?

The first century CE, rather than the sixteenth century, begins our story, because the pattern of an apostolic orthodoxy will be carried on through the next sixteen centuries, and will become a case of the Protestant reformers in the sixteenth century matching the early church's standard, with the language of the Renaissance borrowed in word but not in meaning. The Renaissance was a call to get back to the sources (*ad fontes*), meaning a return to the greats in classical literature, but within the Reformation context it was a return to the greats in biblical literature, meaning the apostolic standard of the New Testament. So, let us look back far enough and "back track" in our study of Protestantism, and let our attention begin with a look at the New Testament and the earliest Christian writings to determine whether or not unity is found within diversity, as Dunn and other New Testament scholars have attempted to prove through their research and writing.

While we can hear Jesus praying that his disciples would all be one (Jn 17:21), only decades later, the church in Corinth would be divided, with multiple schisms related to personality cults. Dunn uses this case study and others from the New Testament writings to "suggest that the picture of a wholly unified primitive Church belongs more to the realm of dogmatic wishful thinking than to historical reality" (Dunn 2006: 25). Thus, Dunn argues from the New Testament itself that early Christianity produced diversity rather than unity and, along with Walter Bauer, proposed that heresy preceded orthodoxy, meaning that orthodoxy was not primarily engaged in affirming the truth but resisting the non-truths. While this might appear to be a concluded argument from both the New Testament and early Christianity, other scholars have been vocal in affirming the need to rediscover the place of truth and unity, over diversity (Köstenberger and Kruger 2010).

After the New Testament documents came a series of church councils, seven were called "**ecumenical**," and with these assemblies of piety were written creeds and confessions. While it attempted to clarify what people in churches believed, it also caused levels of confusion and a series of divisions. Those divisions in the first centuries of the common era can be termed "turning points" or, as Mark Noll also calls them, "the critical moments" (Noll 2012: 2). These turning points can mark a positive movement or a progression forward, but again, the church was split into two over every turning point and further divisions occurred over each council's decision to affirm one belief over another, so we need to continue adding to the number of divisions.

The sixteenth century continues to mark the start of Protestantism with its first pillar: Martin Luther (1483–1546). Underneath the pillar stands a foundation of three levels from the fourteenth and fifteenth centuries: the prophetic preaching of John Wyclif (1320s–1384) and Jan Huss (c. 1372–1415); the invention of moveable type (Gutenberg); and Christian humanism (Erasmus). Together they shaped the contours of Protestantism for centuries as a religious movement that placed a priority on preaching, the printed word, and the larger reform of culture, and all three are embodied in the reforms of Martin Luther himself.

While all three foundations are technically not Protestant, Wyclif and Huss can be viewed as "pre-reformers," meaning they lived before the sixteenth century, but their religious reforms were similar in language and delivery to those of Luther and Zwingli, and just as threatening to the Roman Catholic Church, and one could say, just as effective. Wyclif initially unleashed his reforms in England and they spread throughout

FIGURE 9.1 *Jan Huss, a Czech reformer, was martyred in July 1415.* Source: *Wikimedia Commons*.

Europe. "The new Czech heresy, underway in Prague by 1403 with Huss as its leader, gathered the forces of Czech political and social discontent around it" (Ozment 1980; 165). The cost for Huss was execution/martyrdom in July 1415.

It was Luther's second attack on the Roman Catholic Church, his Ninety-Five Theses placed as a challenge to ferment theological debate—one, single event that is commemorated globally as Reformation Day. Luther's protest was posted originally in Latin, but it was soon translated into German and copies were sent all over Germany. The Ninety-Five Theses were challenges to the Roman Catholic abuse of indulgences. While the pope was trying to build the Basilica of St. Peter, the Dominican John

(Johann) Tetzel (1465–1519) was traveling all over the kingdom selling **indulgences**, and for that Luther could not remain silent or complacent.

While the Protestant Reformation was starting in Germany, it soon developed, in some ways through the influence of the printed page, and spread to the other nations of Europe, with less influence in some and more in others. For the early sixteenth century, Protestantism was centered in Germany and Switzerland (in both German and French). The actual term "Protestant" was coined in 1529 at the Speyer Reichstag when Catholics voted to rescind protection that had been granted previously to Luther and his followers. Those who stood in opposition to this decision were called "Protestants."

Luther remains the pioneer of Protestantism and John Calvin (1509–64) became a builder of second-generation Protestantism, with a name other than Lutheran, it goes by the name "**Reformed**." The Protestant Reformation had begun in Geneva with the preaching and pastoral work of William (Guillaume) Farel (1489–1565), but it would continue to expand and develop under Calvin's lead. With Calvin's reform centered in Geneva, he would write *The Institutes of the Christian Religion* as a systematic theology and develop the church community there. Except for a three-year exile to Strasbourg (1538–41), Calvin spent the rest of his life in Geneva, Switzerland. His years in Geneva were both fruitful and decisive, as Protestantism continued to be defined by movements toward orthodoxy and away from heresy (heterodoxy). One single case during Calvin's lifetime was the life and death of Michael Servetus (1511–53). Born in Spain, trained as both a theologian and physician, Servetus's anti-Trinitarian (unitarian) theology became apparent when he wrote two theological treatises, teaching that the doctrine of the Trinity was neither in the early church or in the Bible.

Already, Servetus had escaped the Inquisition in Spain by changing his name to Michel de Villeneuve, settling in Lyons and Paris. That is where he began his study of medicine, having served as court physician to the Archbishop of Vienna (1541–53). Intrigued with the theological discourse of Calvin's *Institutes,* Servetus began to write his own work, a refutation of Calvin. When Servetus arrived in Geneva to hear Calvin preach, he was arrested and later tried for heresy. Calvin's opponents, called the Libertines, supported Servetus. Calvin himself called for some measure of mercy: beheading rather than burning. On October 27, 1553, Servetus was burned at the stake. His final words were, "Jesus, thou Son of the Eternal God have mercy on me." A Trinitarian would have said, "Jesus, the eternal Son of God." After the death of Servetus, Calvin's authority in Geneva was nearly absolute. Servetus was a heretic; the Catholics and Protestants were agreed on that (Hillerbrand 2007: 133–7). But on other major beliefs in Christianity, Protestants were not able to agree among themselves.

One major belief that divided Protestants in the sixteenth century was the view of Christ's presence in Holy Communion. This was the main disagreement between Luther and Zwingli, as they discussed it at the Colloquy of Marburg. Thus, with views of Holy Communion as a dividing line, there were two major groups of Protestants, "Reformed" and "Lutherans," with a third one, Anglicans, growing (in addition to the Anabaptists). While Communion divided, a major component of Augustine's theology had been adapted by both Luther and Zwingli: **predestination**. So prominent was predestination in Reformed theology, that the 1559 edition of Calvin's *Institutes* has four chapters devoted to the doctrine.

By the end of the sixteenth century, Protestantism had further divided and, one could say, diversified. There was no monolith called the Protestant Reformation, but rather there were national and denominational expressions of reform that were outside the Roman Catholic and Orthodox Christian traditions. Reformations included German (Lutheran), Swiss (Reformed), Anabaptist (Mennonite), and English (Anglican), along with the birthing of a Catholic reformation that would include the Iberian (Spanish and Portuguese) Carmelites and Jesuits. As different as each reformation was from its neighbor, there would be further renewal in the seventeenth century, with three primary movements: Unitarianism, Pietism, and Puritanism. All three were vital and contributed toward the transatlantic movement of people and ideas, as European Protestants found new homes in the New World.

Building

On the Continent and in Britain, Protestantism attempted to define itself according to the Bible as a renewal movement, or simply, a reform movement. But when do you call the reform complete and abandon any further change? In a sense you never cease reforming but find various expressions of division that enhance the truth of your own theological position, that shows others what you believe exactly. Three will be discussed in this section: Unitarianism, Pietism, and Puritanism. First, we look at Unitarianism.

Unitarianism was expressed, as we read earlier, by the theological thought of Michael Servetus, and his view of God as one and not triune, and it became his own death sentence in Geneva. This perhaps is an isolated case study of unitarian theology. It would be an Italian uncle and his nephew that propagated the message of Unitarianism throughout Europe and on to the form that would arrive in the New World. Fausto Sozzini (1539–1604) and nephew Laelio Sozzini (1525–62) would travel Europe and teach the message of Unitarianism, spreading it through Christian communities. One of the reasons that Unitarianism was attractive was because of the growing religious conflict that was dividing not only the church but European society as well. People were choosing sides, which did not prosper unity but rather promoted division. While Unitarianism became popular in Bohemia (Czech Republic) and Poland, it would go on through English translation of the Racovian Catechism to Britain and from there to the Americas. One goal of Unitarians was to promote understanding and tolerance, far beyond the usual level in seventeenth-century Europe.

After Unitarianism, we move on to Pietism. Pietism was a direct response to the formal dogmatism of theologians and the rationalism of professors of religion. There was a new quest to find the heart of Christianity and to have a vital piety. Philipp Jakob Spener (1635–1705) is called the "father" of Pietism. He wrote *Pia desideria*

(Pious desires) and discussed the priesthood of believers and placed less emphasis on the division between laity and clergy. In the area of theological education, Spener recommended that all students of theology be tested to make sure that they are "true Christians." Published in 1675 (in Frankfurt), *Pia desideria* had six "simple proposals": (1) the intensive study of the Bible, (2) more laity involvement in the church, (3) an emphasis on the practical (rather than intellectual), (4) to show love (charity) in religious discussions, (5) a reorganization in theological education and a more intense devotional life among students and faculty, and (6) a revival of preaching (with an aim to edify).

More easily recognized among the reforming Protestant groups is Puritanism, but the popular form is not the genuine and historical group. Puritanism goes back to the closing of Catholic monasteries in England (1535), when a new way was opened to experience the Christian life. For the "hot Protestants," a return to the Bible meant more than a few theological adjustments, it involved a radical conversion to Christ and a consistent and faithful lifestyle.

John Hooper (1495–1555) was a former Cistercian monk who became first a Protestant and later a Puritan in 1540. It was through reading several theological treatises by Ulrich Zwingli (1484–1531) that he became convinced to adopt the harder road of Puritanism, a Protestantism with stripped altars, where everything Catholic in form or tradition had been removed. For Hooper and the other Puritans, Zurich (Zwingli)

FIGURE 9.2 *The Separatist Pilgrims seeking Zion in New England.* Source: *Oscar Gerson/ Wikimedia Commons.*

and not Wittenberg (Luther) was worth following. And following Zwingli's stripped-down liturgy, the *Book of Common Prayer* was abandoned due to its failure to turn away from all that either smelled or looked like a Catholic. To become "purified" all of the old elements of liturgy and devotion must be purged from the true faith. There was to be no Mass, no prayer books, no real presence in Communion. While Anglicans were becoming a "via media," they attempted to maintain much of the Catholic tradition, while Puritans pushed it away and marched on to Zion, that city on a hill, which many Puritans could only see on the other side of the Atlantic. "Puritanism's most long-lasting religious contributions, its stern, demanding practical divinity that offered guidance about staying on the narrow path to heaven and following the duties God expected of his people while on earth" (Winship 2018: 5). With these three groups serving as reform movements within Protestantism in the seventeenth century, we can discern the proposed changes in what people believed and how they practiced their faith.

Yet there were still other spiritual renewal movements within Protestantism, as new traditions began (Quakers and Moravians) and even more within the Roman Catholic tradition (Jansenists, Quietists, Sacred Heart), Orthodox tradition (*Doukhobors*), and within Judaism (*Hasidism*). So many spiritual stirrings within the seventeenth and eighteenth centuries that Ted Campbell could put them together and label them as "the religion of the heart" (Campbell 1991). But the real challenge is having a renewed and fervent spirituality in the midst of secularization, when rationalism rules the mind and anticlericalism and atheism are on the rise.

Awakening

During the eighteenth century, when North America and Europe were experiencing the Enlightenment with its waves of religious doubt and dissent against established religion, revival occurred in churches and in individuals to such a large scale that it was dubbed "the Great Awakening." The Great Awakening was a transatlantic spiritual awakening that moved over the British colonies and created a sense of both religious and political unity that people were considering themselves to be a nation, ahead of any independence movement. The spiritual experience of being "born again" was echoed from the south to the north along the Atlantic coast by the preaching of George Whitefield (1714–70).

Whitefield found that churches were closing their doors to him and his message of being "born again." As a result, Whitefield started preaching outdoors or doing "field preaching," as it was called. For Whitefield, it was preaching without notes, an extempory message (Kidd 2014: 64–9). To many of the cultured despisers, it was scandalous to hear an Oxford graduate preaching outdoors to the least educated of all. But the scandal was related to Whitefield's evangelical view: the power of the cross can reach all the way to the lost. When Whitefield crossed the Atlantic and preached throughout the thirteen colonies in North America, his words were heard by the masses, so that his preaching was "multidenominational" and the hearers were "multiracial," including African slaves in the American South.

Jonathan Edwards (1703–58) was a philosopher, theologian, preacher, and missionary. After his ordination as a Congregational minister, he became an associate pastor at Northampton, Massachusetts, serving under the senior pastor Solomon Stoddard (his maternal grandfather). When Solomon Stoddard died in 1729, Edwards became the senior pastor of one of the largest churches in New England.

In the wake of the Great Awakening, members of Edwards's congregation who were considered errant beyond repair were converted and had expressed a genuine faith in Christ, the signs of true revival were starting to rise (Marsden 2008: 45–8). Edwards put his theological view on religious conversion into a sermon that he preached in 1734, titled "A Divine and Supernatural Light."

As important as both Whitefield and Edwards were to the Great Awakening, they have been viewed as the core both intellectually and evangelically, but there is always a periphery. Where there is a center, there are also margins. One of the persons who lived on the margins of revivalism was James Davenport (1716–57). Often overlooked by historians and maligned in the process of writing history, Davenport was caricatured as embodying all the excesses of revivalism, its rank emotionalism and extreme anti-intellectualism. Of course, leading a book burning of all the popular authors opposed to him might convince many of Davenport's extreme beliefs and behavior (Kidd 2007: 151–2).

FIGURE 9.3 *Methodists in prayer.* Source: *Pavel Svinyin/Wikimedia Commons.*

In the end, the Great Awakening divided churches and denominations into "new lights" (pro-revival) and "old lights" (anti-revival). While Jonathan Edwards was the most prominent voice on the "new lights" side, Charles Chauncy (1705–87) was the most powerful voice on the side of the "old lights," as part of the Congregational establishment in Boston. Pastor of First Church, Boston, Chauncy wrote *Seasonable Thoughts on the State of Religion in New England* (1743) and preached a sermon "An Unbridled Tongue a Sure Evidence, that our Religion is Hypocritical and Vain," all aimed at Edwards and the Great Awakening. "Chauncy denounced all those who 'will presume proudly to take to themselves the sole prerogative of the omniscient God, by looking into the hearts of their neighbors, and judging them carnal, unregenerate men'" (Kidd 2007: 120–1).

As an overview of the entire Great Awakening and the rise of evangelicalism in the eighteenth century, Mark Noll first states the worst: "This new evangelicalism neglected, caricatured and distorted the inherited traditions of Reformation Protestantism," and then he sees the best as giving "needed revitalization to English-speaking Protestant Christianity" (Noll 2003: 292).

Advancing

The advancing of the nineteenth century was Protestantism's evangelistic push west in North America and its missionary movement to the ends of the earth. The move west was embodied in the early nineteenth century with the itinerant evangelism of Francis Asbury (1745–1816). At the end of the Revolutionary War and the start of the United States of America as a new nation, the older established denominations in New England (Congregationalists and Episcopalians) were being pushed aside in the move west and the newcomer Baptist and Methodist churches were in the front of the migration (Finke and Starke 2006).

To activate North American Protestantism's global movement, voluntary associations were formed, helping to organize the churches and unite the mission. Some of them were the American Board for Foreign Missions (1810), the American Bible Society (1816), the American Colonization Society for liberated slaves (1817), the American Society for the Promotion of Temperance (1826), and the American Antislavery Society (1833). What would later divide conservative and liberal Protestants in the twentieth century, formed an active alliance for the promoting of both individual conversion and social reform. The abolition movement, however, shared by many Protestants in the North would become a cause for division in the mid-nineteenth century, in the wake of the American Civil War (1861–5). In 1837, the Presbyterian Church divided over slavery, as they had already separated over the issue of revival. The Methodist Church divided in 1844, and by 1939 it would be united again: north and south. The Baptists divided in 1845 and have yet to be reunited. Further, at the outbreak of hostilities in 1861, the Episcopalians divided.

Another part of moving west was the streamlining of spirituality, to find what a church and denomination truly stood for, what is the most important part of their Protestant identity. For many Methodists the doctrine of entire sanctification or holiness was cited as being most central to Methodism. Methodists had organized the National Camp Meeting Association for the Promotion of Holiness in 1867, with their first

FIGURE 9.4 *First Baptist Church of Morelia, Mexico.* Source: *Alejandro Linares Garcia/ Wikimedia Commons.*

meeting in Vineland, New Jersey. Combined with a religious experience of holiness was an outreach to the urban poor, thus the holiness churches grew up in the cities and included the Salvation Army, the Wesleyan Church, the Church of the Nazarene, and the Church of God (Anderson, Indiana). Another group rose in the early nineteenth century with a call for church unity coupled with a restoration plea, attempting to return to the New Testament church model. For frontier Baptists, Congregationalists, Methodists, and Presbyterians the act of dividing the church was contrary to the restoration plea. This restoration movement or Stone-Campbell movement would also take the names Churches of Christ, Christians, and Disciples (Conkin 1997: 1–56).

Overall, the nineteenth century was marked by a geographic expansion that Kenneth Scott Latourette, the great church historian and long-time professor at Yale University, would call the "Great Century of Missions" (1792–1914). Many evangelical Protestants mark the beginning of the modern missionary movement with the voyage of William Carey (1761–1834) from Britain to India in 1792, and the first step for Americans was when the Congregationalists in the United States founded the American Board of Commissioners for Foreign Missions and sent Adoniram Judson (1788–1850) to India and later Burma. The real beginning, however, was when a freed slave and loyalist moved to Canada and would later depart for Jamaica as a foreign missionary in 1782, ten years before Carey and thirty years before Judson. His name was George Liele (1750–1820).

The move south of the border is significant for North American Protestants and marked Mexican Protestantism as being unique, "outside the mainstream of Catholic society." Not only "outside," but Protestants in Mexico were identified with political and social liberals and Masons as being one and the same (Baldwin 1990: xi). As early as 1839, and not too long after Mexico's independence from Spain (1821), Protestants were looking at Mexico as a ripe field of harvest.

Finally, the Mexican Constitution of 1857 made the religious practice of Protestantism legal and curtailed the government's persecution of Protestants, but it would not be able to change the public's sentiments concerning Protestantism. "Protestant missionaries went into the Southwest convinced of the importance of their mission. Theirs was a continuation of the battle between Protestantism and Catholicism and Protestantism had to win" (Martínez 2006: 26). Now we will view twentieth-century Protestantism.

Questing

The first decade of the twentieth was marked by global revivals, but in North America it started in Topeka, Kansas, on January 1, 1901, and had such an impact on Protestantism that some have termed the next one hundred years: the Century of the Holy Spirit. As Protestantism expanded globally there was a real need to reach the poor or, as H. Richard Niebuhr called them, the "disinherited" (Niebuhr 1929: 26–76). Niebuhr was pointing out that American denominations were shaped by economic, racial, and social forces, and not merely by what people believed (or theology). Of course, even with this novel way to view Protestant denominations, not everyone wants to be called "disinherited," or even "poor," but inequalities were as present among Protestants as any other social or religious group. At the very bottom were the radical holiness and evangelicals who would become the Pentecostals in the twentieth century, their expressive worship and practice of speaking in tongues had given them such religious slurs as "holy rollers" and the "tongues people."

Pentecostalism began in Topeka, Kansas, at the Bethel Bible College, where a group of around thirty studied the Bible as their only textbook with their only professor: Charles Fox Parham (1873–1929). He was born in Iowa and moved to Kansas with his family in 1878. Parham served as a Methodist pastor and joined the holiness movement, and by the turn of the century he became a catalyst for the theological birth of Pentecostalism. From Topeka through southern Kansas and down to Houston, Texas, Parham taught and practiced Pentecost or, as it was called, "Apostolic Faith." One of Parham's students in Houston was William Joseph Seymour (1870–1922), his most prominent student was sitting in the hallway because of his skin color. Jim Crow laws in the American South did not allow the education of white and Black students in the same classroom, integration would not come to American schools until the 1960s, at this time schools in the South were all segregated.

Seymour was invited to Los Angeles to lead a holiness congregation, so he asked for Pastor Parham's blessing as he journeyed west. His ministry was not to last long with the holiness church, since the experience of speaking in tongues was not accepted by them. The next place of ministry was the front porch prayer meeting at 214 Bonnie Brae Street in Los Angeles, and then on to 312 Azusa Street, a place so small it was overlooked, just as the manger in Bethlehem.

Unlike other segments of Protestantism, this new wave would experience "for one of the few times in American history, blacks and whites, men and women, joined in complete equality in exhilarating and exhausting religious services" (Conkin 1997: 299).

But, even with such ecstasy, there was a coming down from the peak, at times almost a crash, when Pentecostals, like all other Protestants before them, began to divide. A united movement was now a long series of denominations, separated because of race (Black and white) and doctrines (sanctification and divine healing).

Protestantism in North America was ready to divide in half between fundamentalists and modernists by the 1920s. Princeton Seminary professor J. Gresham Machen (1881–1937) left to found Westminster Theological Seminary (1929), the Independent Board for Presbyterian Foreign Missions (1933), and the Orthodox Presbyterian Church (1936). Baptists would divide over the line that separated Fundamentalist/Evangelical from modernist/liberal and created their own new denominations, including the Conservative Baptist Association of America (1947) and the General Association of Regular Baptists (1932). With all the separating in the 1920s and 1930s, it would seem to be an appropriate time to form organizations that strive for unity and not division. There were six organizations that formed in the twentieth century to express ecumenicity.

FIGURE 9.5 *A small Pentecostal (full gospel) church in Seoul.* Source: Will Purinton.

The first three of the six organizations in North America are in the United States: the mainline Protestant Federal Council of Churches of Christ in America (1908, later renamed National Council of Churches 1950), evangelicalism's National Association of Evangelicals (1942), and Fundamentalism's American Council of Christian Churches

(1941). Canada has experienced an organic union with the merger of mainline Protestant denominations in 1925 to form the United Church of Canada, and the Evangelical Fellowship of Canada (1964) continues in relationship with the World Evangelical Alliance. Mexico has only one Protestant church that is a founding member of the World Council of Churches (1948), and that is the Methodist Church of Mexico.

While the United States has three distinct groups that continue to exist in relationship with one another and with their larger like-minded global partners, the experience in Canada was less antagonistic and more irenic. "The brisk advance of church union among Methodists and eventually among Methodists, Congregationalists, and some Presbyterians to form the United Church of Canada in the 1920s required doctrinal accommodation" (Phillips 1996: 34).

While the Ecumenical movement continues to follow its global agenda of both seeking peace and justice in the world and of pursuing reconciliation and unity among churches, there has been a backlash among evangelicals who see the ecumenical direction as steering clear of the Gospel and traditional confessions of the faith. What has emerged is a "New Ecumenism." Two of the advocates of this view are Timothy George and the late Thomas C. Oden. For Oden, the way forward begins with the ancient path or the "old ecumenism, one grounded in the scriptures and the apostolic tradition" (Howard and Noll 2016: 324). One fruit of the "New Ecumenism" is the document *Evangelicals and Catholics Together* (1994), which contrary to Fundamentalism and more conservative evangelicalism, views Roman Catholics as being truly Christian.

References

Baldwin, D.J. (1990), *Protestants and the Mexican Revolution: Missionaries, Ministers, and Social Change*, Urbana: University of Illinois Press.
Campbell, T.A. (1991), *The Religion of the Heart: A Study of European Religious Life in the Seventeenth and Eighteenth Centuries*, Columbia: University of South Carolina Press.
Conkin, P.K. (1997), *American Originals: Homemade Varieties of Christianity*, Chapel Hill: University of North Carolina Press.
Dunn, J.D.G. (2006), *Unity and Diversity in the New Testament: An Inquiry into the Character of Earliest Christianity*, 3rd edn., London: SCM.
Finke, R. and R. Starke (2006), *The Churching of America, 1776–2005: Winners and Losers in Our Religious Economy*, New Brunswick, NJ: Rutgers University Press.
García, A.L. and J.A. Nunes (2017), *Wittenberg Meets the World: Reimagining the Reformation at the Margins*, Grand Rapids, MI: Wm. B. Eerdmans.
Hatch, N.O. (1989), *The Democratization of American Christianity*, New Haven, CT: Yale University Press.
Hillerbrand, H.J. (2007), *The Division of Christendom: Christianity in the Sixteenth Century*, Louisville, KT: Westminster John Knox.
Howard, T.A. and M.A. Noll, eds. (2016), *Protestantism after 500 Years*, New York: Oxford University Press.
Irvin, D.T., ed. (2017), *The Protestant Reformation and World Christianity*, Grand Rapids, MI: Eerdmans.

Jacobsen, D. and W.V. Trollinger, Jr., eds. (1998), *Re-Forming the Center: American Protestantism, 1900 to the Present*, Grand Rapids, MI: Eerdmans.

Kidd, T.S. (2007), *The Great Awakening: The Roots of Evangelical Christianity in Colonial America*, New Haven, CT: Yale University Press.

Kidd, T.S. (2014), *George Whitefield: America's Spiritual Founding Father*, New Haven, CT: Yale University Press.

Köstenberger, A.J. and M.J. Kruger (2010), *The Heresy of Orthodoxy: How Contemporary Culture's Fascination with Diversity Has Reshaped Our Understanding of Early Christianity*, Wheaton, IL: Crossway.

Marsden, G. (2008), *A Short Life of Jonathan Edwards*, Grand Rapids, MI: Eerdmans.

Martínez, J.F. (2006), *Sea la Luz: The Making of Mexican Protestantism in the American Southwest, 1829–1900*, Denton: University of North Texas Press.

Niebuhr, H.R. (1929), *The Social Sources of Denominationalism*, New York: Henry Holt.

Noll, M.A. (2002), *The Old Religion in a New World: The History of North American Christianity*, Grand Rapids, MI: Eerdmans.

Noll, M.A. (2003), *The Rise of Evangelicalism: The Age of Edwards, Whitefield and the Wesleys*, Downers Grove, IL: InterVarsity.

Noll, M.A. (2011), *Protestantism: A Very Short Introduction*, New York: Oxford University Press.

Noll, M.A. (2012), *Turning Points: Decisive Moments in the History of Christianity*, 3rd edn., Grand Rapids, MI: Baker.

Ozment, S. (1980), *The Age of Reform, 1250–1550: An Intellectual and Religious History of Late Medieval and Reformation Europe*, New Haven, CT: Yale University Press.

Phillips, P.T. (1996), *A Kingdom on Earth: Anglo-American Social Christianity, 1880–1940*, University Park: Pennsylvania State University Press.

Winship, M.P. (2018), *Hot Protestants: A History of Puritans in England and America*, New Haven, CT: Yale University Press.

Glossary Terms

Ecumenical "The whole world" and an expression of a desire to foster Christian unity through both dialogue and church union. When it is capitalized and placed before movement, it refers specifically to the World Council of Churches and its regional associations.

Indulgences Religious merits that a person receives for the remission of sins when they perform a religious act. You can erase the penalty for your sins by performing a religious ritual. Indulgences had been part of the Roman Catholic Church's system for a long time and remain even to this day. However, the abuse that Luther was wanting to correct was the selling of indulgences. Instead of actually going on a pilgrimage and praying at a religious shrine, you pay for the certificate that says you went there.

Orthodoxy A faithful adherence to the teachings of the Bible and the church, as delivered through historic creeds and theological confessions.

Predestination Having been fore-ordained or established ahead of time by God's divine action or decrees. God has the knowledge and power sufficient to plan ahead for the guidance of persons to salvation according to his will.

Reformed The theology and churches historically connected with Zwingli, Knox, and Calvin, and are commonly referred to as Calvinist, differing from Lutheran.

10

Global Christianity: The Future of the Faith

William T. Purinton

Sources and History

Christianity emerged from the roots of first-century Judaism, and along with Islam, all three religions are connected closely to literary texts based upon prophetic messages. For Christianity and Judaism this means sharing a book of writings, and for Christianity it involves a new covenant/testament being connected with the former one. The first four books in the New Testament are called the Gospels, containing the words of Jesus and his final message to his disciples. The very pulse of evangelism and the drive to conversion lies in the instructions that Jesus gave to his disciples at the time of his departure. This final message is recorded in all four Gospels and the book of Acts and is called the Great Commission. Although the language differs from text to text, the mission remains the same: to spread the message from person to person until all the nations are reached or continue in the journey of disciples until they reach the ends of the earth (Tennent 2010: 130–57). Out of the five texts (Mt. 28, Mk 16, Lk. 24, Jn 20, Acts 1), we will focus our attention on two, Matthew and Acts, to highlight the phrases "all nations" and "ends of the earth." These are both key literary expressions of the ongoing outward expansion of Christianity, to extend from a limited area in western Asia to cover all the continents on the planet. While we might call this "mission" or "evangelization," it is the very heart of Christianity and not a novelty or an appendage. But when "missionaries" are considered within the larger framework of religious history, we can either see them as a living link toward the birthing of global Christianity or as the main impediment in the process of the globalization of Christianity. It might be a "spoiler," but this article will view the role of missionaries as "midwives" in the birthing of global Christianity. But, as vital as their role is, they merely are assisting in the process and not initiating. Now, we look at the five key mission texts.

Our first mission text from the end of Matthew gives these words from Jesus: "Go therefore and make disciples of all nations, baptizing them in the name of the Father and of the Son and of the Holy Spirit, and teaching them to obey everything that I have commanded you. And remember, I am with you always, to the end of the age" (Mt. 28:18–20, NRSV). The actual imperative is to make disciples, and baptizing and teaching are two processes by which disciples are made. Within the Christian mission is a going and a reaching out to others, to connect them with his body (baptize) and assist them to mature in their faith (teach). So, within the Matthew text of the Great Commission we have a call to becoming followers (disciples), which entails "evangelization" (going), "assimilation" (baptizing), and "education" (teaching). In a fuller view, disciples are followers of Jesus who form a community and do mission, so making disciples is simply a process of repeating this formula (Flemming 2015: 15–16).

An important textual note should be made with the word "all nations" in Matthew's Great Commission, since our modern word "nation" can carry the meaning of a distinct people and ethnicity, but it more often relates to a political grouping, known as a "nation-state." We are reminded that "nation derives from the *political* structuring of the world-system" (Balibar and Wallerstein 1991: 80, emphasis in the original). But the usage in the New Testament relates exclusively to nations as peoples. The Greek phrase "of all nations" is "panta ta ethnē," which has been translated as "all gentiles," but in the context of Matthew's entire usage of the phrase conveys more the meaning of "nations" or "peoples" (Meier 1977: 102). This has both geographical and cultural understandings, going beyond diverse lands or spaces to include human beings with their various unique ethnicities.

This concept of ethnicity was utilized fully by the missiologist Donald A. McGavran (1897–1990), long-time professor at Fuller Theological Seminary and founder of the Church Growth School, when he proposed the evangelism of "peoples groups" and the further development of "homogenous units," meaning distinct ethnic groups should remain separate for maximum growth potential (McGavran 1955). While the "church growth" model has not remained unchallenged by those who advocate multicultural churches, it does represent a case of intentional blending of social science with biblical texts for an enhanced mission.

After the four Gospels, we turn to the Acts of the Apostles to hear again the Great Commission text, this time with prescribed geographical zones for evangelism. "But you will receive power when the Holy Spirit has come upon you; and you will be my witnesses in Jerusalem, in all Judea and Samaria, and to the ends of the earth" (Acts 1:8, NRSV). The narrative of the remaining twenty-seven chapters of Acts follows the pattern of evangelism from where they were (Jerusalem), through the present geographical region to the zone of "others," and finally to the "ends of the earth," another key biblical phrase found in the prophets to emphasize the farthest reach of mission. But, prior to any evangelism, Acts 1:8 states that spiritual empowerment will be given to all disciples for world mission. Power was neither for the political restoration of Israel nor for the defeat of Rome. Further, it was not in supernatural abilities to see the future. Only one reason was given for the descent of the Holy Spirit on Pentecost, and that was to enable the fearful to assert publicly and powerfully the Resurrection of Jesus and his gift of salvation to the nations, extending both his love and forgiveness (Barrs 2001: 20).

Culture, Class, and Caste

In the journey of mission there are bumps along the way, borders to cross, and steps to climb. The cultural distances involved are stretched out both vertically and horizontally, meaning that culture is something that changes over geographical space, while class and caste are lined up on a vertical plane, thus mission ends up being in both directions. From here to there, and from high to low, but in the context of the third millennium, it easily can be the other way, from there to here and from low to high.

Let's talk about culture first. In North America, race (or simply skin color) seems to be the primary distinction that identifies one group as being different from another and tends to set it in opposition to that other side. But in other parts of the world, it can be linguistic markers that identify one group and set it against another, or cultural identities related to a geographical region or to an ethnic group that we might call a "tribe." Still, others are set against one another based upon economic status, so that inequalities are marked by economics rather than nation or region or ethnicity. In addition, **caste** is tied up with both religion and culture and does not carry with it a permanent economic status, you can be from a "low" caste and be "high" on the economic scale. Furthermore, due to the caste system's identification with Hinduism, many Protestant missionaries in India resisted it as being "incompatible with Christian life and doctrine" (Kooiman 1989: 172).

Within North America, we can quickly state three model identities and how they express two sides of one nation. In the United States, it is easily described in terms of "black" and "white" (Jennings 2010). The entire world is aware of how divided the United States is over race, and how it was divided politically and engaged in a civil war in the 1860s over the issue of slavery. In Canada, we are quick to remember the bilingual signs, both English and French, and acknowledge that the two bordering provinces of Quebec and Ontario are representative of two distinctive and, often, contrary cultures within one nation. But the divide was not simply between English and French, with the later arrival of Irish, Italian, Polish, and Portuguese Catholics to Canada, it became more diverse and complicated as a nation of both religious and cultural pluralism (Scott 2012: 50–8). In Mexico, the dividing line has been geographical, with northern and southern regions of the nation as expressive of both liberal versus conservative, or pro-government versus anti-government, and even in some cases Protestant versus Catholic. In addition to that marked regionalism are the cultural/racial identities of mulatto, mestizo, and the groups that have not been mixed and remain in stark contrast with one another. Perhaps, illustrative of this has been the

FIGURE 10.1 *Student choir at the Asian Center for Theological Studies and Mission (Yangpyeong, South Korea).* Source: *Photograph by and © William Purinton.*

revolt centered in the southern province of Chiapas, where Indigenous peoples have been struggling against the central government for both human rights and for political recognition, while many in the region turned toward Protestantism/**evangelicalism** for salvation and hope (Stoll 1990: 85–7).

The differences in language and customs are only a part of the cultural grid of life. Communication itself rests upon the foundation of culture, and when it fails, words are misunderstood and misconstrued, and it can involve more than words: the very gestures of our hands and expressions on our face can be understood as communication. But beneath all the layers of cultural expression is the foundation of the very words of scripture that carry Christianity beyond borders and has had significant cultural impact upon the peoples of the world.

Bible translation has its roots in American Christianity in the seventeenth century with the work of John Eliot (1604–90). Serving as an evangelist to Native Americans, Eliot was called "Apostle to the Indians" and translated the Bible, completing both the Old (1663) and New Testaments (1661) in the Algonkian language.

Although there were Roman Catholic translations of the Bible from the sixteenth century on, the work to produce vernacular translations was pioneered and sustained by Protestants, both mainline and evangelical. One example is North American

Protestant missionaries working together for several decades in the late nineteenth century to produce the Korean translation of the Bible, putting the finishing touches on it by 1910 for publication the following year. Two Presbyterian missionaries in Korea, one Canadian and the other American, were given the task of focusing on biblical translation. The Canadian Presbyterian James Scarth Gale (1863–1937) had arrived in Korea in late 1888 as a missionary supported by the University of Toronto's YMCA. Later, he transferred his mission affiliation to the Presbyterian Church in the (northern) United States and became active in both evangelism and literary studies, translating John Bunyan's *Pilgrim's Progress* into Korean in 1895 (Oak 2013: 108–14). The Bible translation committee included at various times three Korean Christian leaders (Mun Kyung-ho, Kim Myung-jun, and Chung Tong-myung) and representatives of the two American Presbyterian denominational missions and the Northern Methodist mission. Although, in the end, not all missionaries were satisfied with the results of the first Korean-language New Testament and Bible publications, but they were in agreement that the Hangeul script (Korean alphabet) was superior for the purpose of Bible translation, since it was a truly phonetic writing system that preserved the sounds of the Korean language well, and—perhaps not understood fully by the missionaries—it allowed illiterate people who were otherwise "uneducated," not being able to read

FIGURE 10.2 *St. Peter and St. Paul's Church, Ganghwa Anglican Church in Korea was consecrated in 1900 by Bishop Charles Corfe.* Source: *Photograph by and © William Purinton.*

Chinese literary script, to read God's word for themselves. Thus, a Bible translation opened wide a world of learning along with a door of salvation. Another important aspect of Bible translation is that working with words and trying to connect the first century with the present, meant a bridging of both time and culture. When one considers the cultural world of Hellenism and Judaism in the first century and the multitude of contemporary cultures today, there had to be a way for the Christian religion to fit within each global culture and not to misshape either the culture or the religion to make that fit. The process of "fitting" or the agricultural metaphor of "being planted" within a culture can be called indigenization or inculturation, but within the area of theological studies it is termed **contextualization**.

While a number of mainline Protestant missionaries were engaged in Bible translation throughout the nations of the world, it would remain a small part of their entire ministry. Only with the rise of the Summer Institute of Linguistics and Wycliffe Bible Translators, founded in 1942 by William Cameron Townsend (1896–1982), would Bible translation take a prominent position within evangelical missions in North America. Further, again, allied with the task of preparing for a truly global Christianity, translating the Bible into the thousands of languages in the world meant that "minority" ethnic groups would have the Bible in their own "tongue" and would be equipped through literacy education for an increased role in their nation ruled by a "majority" language and culture.

Bible translation and literacy education might appear to be an indirect means of "empowering" the powerless in the majority world, but the primary role of missionaries to evangelize and start churches contributed also toward a rising social position for the marginalized, including the scheduled castes (untouchables/Dalit) and the working classes. The writings and revival preaching of Charles Grandison Finney (1792–1875) addressed the emotionalism of people from the working classes in his meetings: "trimming of the 'rough edges' of revivalism also entailed taming ecstatic religious behaviors" (McCloud 2007: 132). Again, it was the words of the Bible that inspired ministers and missionaries to reach out to the poorest of the poor and those words provided the encouragement to rise above poverty and to struggle against marginalization. But at times it worked the other way, with religious instruction on how both race and class are divinely created.

Within North America, the nineteenth and twentieth centuries were times of mass immigration and the beginning of the twentieth century marked a time of urban social unrest. Christianity's response was in a myriad of forms, some reactionary and others progressive. One that has remained in the annals of religious history and contributed toward an even more holistic view of ministry was the Social Gospel.

The Social Gospel movement was birthed in the practice of ministry to the poor, first by the congregationalist Washington Gladden (1836–1918) and later by the Baptist Walter Rauschenbusch (1861–1918). It was the theologizing done by Rauschenbusch that gave birth to *Christianity and the Social Crisis* (1907) and *A Theology for the Social Gospel* (1917), two primers for an activist Christianity in response to a world in transition. These books were written upon the theological foundations laid already in the 1880s: "Divine Immanence" (God is always present) and "Incarnationism" (God has

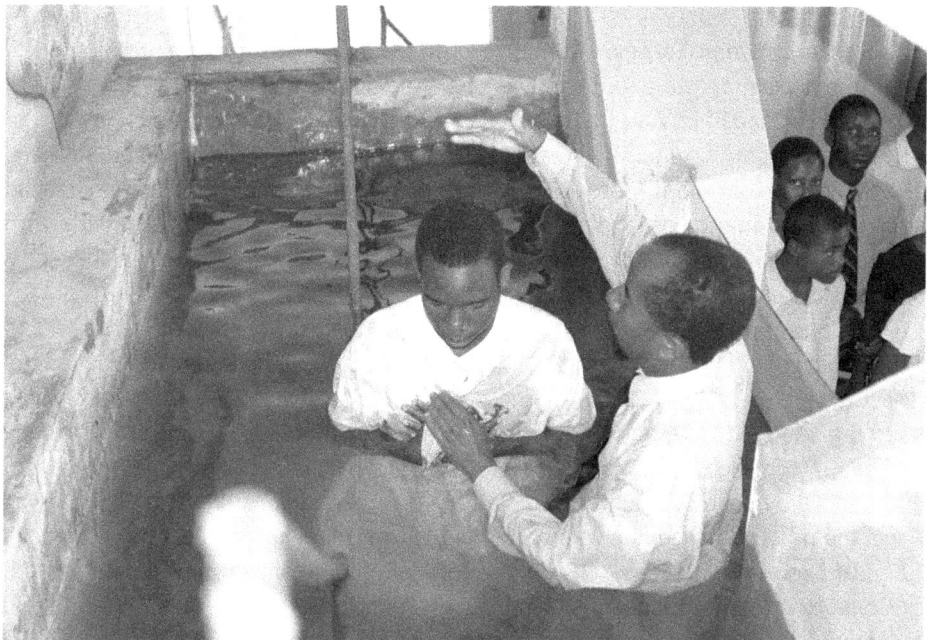

FIGURE 10.3 *Adventist baptism in Mozambique.* Source: *Creative Commons, Public Domain.*

an intimate relationship with humanity) (Phillips 1996: 8). In addition, Rauschenbusch's writings would lay a future foundation for the liberation theologies of the 1970s, in all their various global expressions: African, Asian, Latin American, and North American.

Within the various contexts of global mission, conversion can happen to individuals but there were also people movements that erupted with entire communities being transformed into Christians. But who was it that responded to the message? When you set up a continuum of socio-economic classes or status, you will find those at the bottom socially and economically hear and believe the message, that act of God reaching down to sinners, and when you reach down that far you will find the poor and the marginalized.

Beyond the Nations

Mission was becoming global as early as the first century, even on the day of Pentecost, when there were people from the Jewish **diaspora** gathered in Jerusalem to observe the religious feast from three continents: Africa, Asia, and Europe. From that initial encounter, African Christianity would continue through the centuries to be shaped and to further shape global Christianity (Daughrity 2018: 132–45). The same holds true for both Asia and Europe.

The sixteenth century—a hundred years of global exploration and discovery—was a race between Portugal and Spain to reach the lands of Africa, Asia, and the Americas to claim territory for their own king, with due recognition of the pope's claim upon each monarch. Roman Catholic missions to Africa and Asia were first led by the mendicant orders, including Franciscans, Dominicans, Carmelites, and Augustinians. These religious orders of men and women led the way through the centuries ahead as mission became global and not merely national or continental. But it was the birth of the Society of Jesus (SJ) and the mission of Francis Xavier that indicates the global turn for Roman Catholic Missions.

The Society of Jesus, or the Jesuits, was cofounded by Ignatius of Loyola (1491–1556) and Francis Xavier (1506–52). Ignatius was a Basque Spaniard who was a disabled veteran of the military, having been injured in the leg by a cannon ball. He used the Latinized form of his name Ignatius of Loyola and was converted in mid-life and had to commence his studies at an elementary school, but he managed to learn Latin and progressed through university studies, graduating from the University of Paris, the most esteemed university for the study of theology. Ignatius developed the *Spiritual Exercises* (1548) as a 28–30-day cycle of meditations on the life and passion of Christ designed to prepare Jesuits through spiritual discernment, with the help of a director to guide the seeker through a series of reflections on Christ, all designed to bring about a fuller understanding of oneself in relationship to Christ.

While the Spanish and Portuguese empires were in heated competition to possess the lands of the New World, the Jesuits brought forth a corps of missionaries and educators who were Spanish, Basque, and Portuguese to show unity for mission and took a fourth vow of loyalty to the papacy. Chief among the first wave of missionaries was Francis Xavier who conducted mission in south India, the Maluku Islands, Borneo, Japan, and died as he was about to enter China for evangelization. It was during his brief 2.5-year mission to Japan that a total of one thousand people were converted, but that first one thousand were only seeds sown, since within the next twenty years the Jesuit mission in Japan—never more than nine priests during that time—would witness a harvest of thirty thousand converts (O'Malley 1995: 77).

The nineteenth century—Kenneth Scott Latourette's "Great Century"—was a hundred years of both Protestant and Catholic missions to the nations of the world, with the United States taking the lead in the number of missionaries sent overseas. But when one looked at the European colonial powers and their holdings throughout Africa, Asia, and Latin America, it seemed that all the control yielded from the sixteenth century would be lost during the nineteenth century. The "Great Century" of Protestant missions was acting as a preparation for words and acts of political and ecclesiastical independence and liberty. It was during this "Great Century" that the United States became even more keenly aware of the need to spread the message of complete political independence along with the Protestant call for the younger churches to become "indigenous" and less reliant upon Western mission funding.

Indeed, by the start of the nineteenth century, America had become the game-changer in the face of the colonial empires of Spain, Portugal, and France. From the time that the United States won its independence in 1783 through a prolonged war against Britain. The American victory would inspire other revolutions and wars for independence, spreading first to France (1789–99) and then back to the New World with powerful effect as the less-powerful colonies would struggle and

FIGURE 10.4 *A seventeenth-century Japanese depiction of St. Francis Xavier.* Source: *Public Domain.*

defeat the more-powerful world empires. The first, after the United States, to gain independence was Haiti in 1804, with others becoming free from Spanish colonial control, including: Chile (1810), Paraguay and Venezuela (1811), Mexico (1813), Argentina (1816), Columbia (1820), Venezuela (1821), Ecuador (1822), Bolivia (1824), and Uruguay (1825). By the second half of the nineteenth century, the once global empire of Spain had shrunk down in size to two small islands in the Caribbean: Cuba and Puerto Rico.

One of the most effective and important mission strategies of the nineteenth century was called in general "the indigenization principle." It was named the "three-selfs": self-supporting, self-governing, and self-propagating, and came through the Protestant mission theorists Henry Venn (1796–1873), Rufus Anderson (1796–1880), William Taylor (1821–1902), and John Livingston Nevius (1829–93).

Henry Venn had developed a real distaste for the "civilizing" model of Christian mission. The real antitheses to the "three-selfs" was the "three C's" of commerce, civilization, and Christianity. And coupled with a distaste for the "three C's" was a devotion to the New Testament pattern for mission, and the church in Antioch was the newly discovered template for contemporary missions.

Moving forward into the nineteenth century and reaching across the Atlantic to North America, we see Rufus Anderson, secretary of the American Board of Commissioners for Foreign Missions (ABCFM). He emphasized the crucial need for a "native ministry" capable of "self-propagation" and organized into churches, with one aim: saving the lost.

The Methodist William Taylor began following a streamlined biblical model of "self-supporting missions." Following his thirty years of evangelism, Taylor wrote *Pauline Methods of Missionary Work* (1879), listing six important elements in his plan: preaching only the pure Gospel, Indigenous leadership, unity of the Holy Spirit, faith missions, Indigenous communities of faith, and an itinerant ministry. Taylor's work was extended through East Asia by the Presbyterian missionary to China, John Livingston Nevius, to perfect the plan and to implement it throughout a nation. The "three-selfs" became the "standard" of both Protestant conciliar and evangelical mission theology. The ideal of "indigenous missions" would be heralded through all the meetings of the Ecumenical movement: Edinburgh (1910), Jerusalem (1928), Tambaram (1938), Bangkok (1973), and even extending to the evangelical meetings during the Lausanne Congress of Evangelism (1974).

In addition to the strategy of the "three-selfs" was a number of cooperative agreements signed on the mission field and endorsed by the home denominations. They were called **comity** agreements and consisted of mapping out the entire mission territory, many times, as in the case of Korea, an entire nation was divided among six mainline denominations (two Methodist and four Presbyterian). The denominations and mission agencies that failed to subscribe to the comity agreements or were not invited to participate became marginalized, but that would turn them toward a sectarian evangelism, where the entire nation, all races, all cultures, and all peoples were wide open for their evangelism.

FIGURE 10.5 *The World Parliament of Religions was held in Chicago (1893).* Source: *Public Domain.*

The future of world evangelism was not in the hands of only donors or evangelists, but the future rested in strategic meetings for visioning and planning. Those global gatherings of mission theorists and practitioners in the 1970s and 1980s would continue to chart the future of world evangelism. Included are the "AD2000 and Beyond Movement," Lausanne I (1974) in Switzerland and Lausanne II (1989) in Manila. The "AD2000 and Beyond Movement" was orchestrated by Luis Bush (1946–) with an aim to have a church for every people by the year 2000. Another key mission concept was the "10/40 Window." It was a mission geographical term coined by Luis Bush to mean "a portion of the world between 10 and 40 degrees north of the equator where 'the world's least-evangelized poor are found'" (Van Engen 2016: 151). All of these mission strategies served to turn an inward-looking church in North America away from itself and toward the global "harvest fields."

Breathing Fire

Missionaries sent to Asia were learning about the world's religions for the first time and they were learning about them firsthand. While the responses to the challenges posed by rival world religious traditions differed from mission to mission, all the way from accommodation to antagonism, perhaps the most damaging influence was when **syncretism** occurred as a "mixing" of Christianity with another religious tradition. The loss of an "exclusive" evangelical message (meaning Christ is the only savior) could lead to a view of religious pluralism, where all religions are equally valid as paths to pursue for salvation. Once you have validated all world religions as being equal, Christianity has lost its distinctive reason for evangelization and the only purpose remaining for mission is either social change or interreligious dialogue.

But the missionaries were still far removed from the homeland and world religions were still excluded from immigration to North America, due to acts of government that prevented their entering the nation. That would change in 1965 for the United States and people from Asia would begin to emigrate to America in the thousands. Long before that mass migration was the World's Parliament of Religions where Christianity met its rivals in Chicago.

Among the attendees were representatives from all the major and even minor world religions. They met as part of the World's Columbian Exposition or what would later be termed a World's Fair. Counted as present were representatives from all the world religions: Jain, Theravada Buddhism, Zen Buddhism, Pure Land Buddhism, Hinduism, Islam, Bahai, Theosophical Society, and Christian Science.

Originally planned to coincide with the 400-year anniversary of Columbus's exploration of the New World (from 1492), the start date was changed to 1893 and the reason for meeting was not to celebrate Columbus but to engage in dialogue with adherents of the world's religions. Interfaith or interreligious dialogue actually began with these meetings at the World's Parliament of Religions in Chicago. In the end, there was more favor extended toward the Asian religious traditions, others were condemned as not offering a plan for salvation (Braybrooke 1992: 27).

While the path toward a globally aware church and mission seemed to be paved back in 1893 in Chicago, there was a disruption in the 1930s, when the fundamentalist/modernist fight was starting in the major Protestant denominations in North America and a professor of philosophy was handed a job: coordinate all the investigations and reports on the current state of Protestant world missions and provide a published remedy for whatever ills they face. This was an opportunity for those opposed to evangelical missions to breathe some fire on it, not for renewal or even purification, but for its destruction.

The reports were turned into a book titled *Rethinking Missions: A Laymen's Inquiry after One Hundred Years,* edited by William Ernest Hocking (1873–1966) and published in 1932 (Hutchison 1987: 158–75). Among the report's recommendations was that Protestant missionaries should cease from evangelization and focus all their effort on education/social change. Will this be the end of world mission and a missed opportunity to create global Christianity?

Rebounding Grace

With all the books that declare a major shift has occurred, we cannot help but look quickly at the before and after picture. We want to see the promise fulfilled; all the actions completed. But how did it happen that the numbers shifted, or grace rebounded, and the church was moved from north to south and from west to east? Part of movement has to do with vehicles carrying it or driving it, but the other part is like a sailboat that moves from the wind that blows. The more the wind blows, the more quickly the sailboat travels upon the seas. What we see are people gathering, as on the day of Pentecost, and the Spirit wind blowing afresh.

The 1910 Missionary Conference in Edinburgh was a marker in time and space, to indicate the beginning of the modern Ecumenical movement and to mark the end of the unevangelized Global East and South. Efforts were made to complete the missionary task within one generation, but into a new (twentieth) century and the task was yet to be completed.

Since the *Laymen's Inquiry* was released in 1932, mainline churches were asking, even demanding, a moratorium on mission personnel being sent to the majority world, or more specifically the unevangelized nations of the world, like inside the 10/40 Window. The only people who needed to be sent were social workers or medical doctors, only people to change society for the better not to preach eternal damnation and salvation. One of the key transitions was that the flow of persons was not from north to south or from west to east, but the reverse direction was now possible. Although it was not fully responsible for making people aware, but the writing of books by missiologists has propelled mission forward and helped people to consider where they have come from and where they are headed.

Samuel Escobar's *The New Global Mission: The Gospel from Everywhere to Everyone* is one of those books that warms the heart and illumines the mind. Escobar alerts his readers that "the single-minded passion for Christ is still the driving force behind mission, but over the course of a century the composition of the missionary force has changed significantly, and changes are also coming to attitudes, methods and, of course, patterns of support for mission" (Escobar 2003: 17).

In addition to the moving out, the activation of a newly emerging mission force is the joining together for mission. The signing of the document *Christian Witness in a Multi-Religious World* (2011) signifies an end to competition in global evangelism and the beginning of mutual understanding, if not actual cooperation in the Great Commission. The position that the real world is made up of a plurality of religions has brought the church, at the least, to new readings and mutual understandings of what evangelism should be. We have come a long way from the time of comity agreements. "At a formal level, commitment to Common Witness anchors a shared commitment to proclaiming one Christ and recognizing him in the lives of Christians unlike oneself" (Robert 2016: 275).

As with bookends we can view the Bible as holding texts within it that are related to mission and extending the kingdom of God. The first canonical book, Genesis, holds the global promise made to Abraham for land, descendants, and to become a blessing to "all nations" (Gen. 12, 15, 17, NRSV). The means by which the nations would be blessed was through his numerous descendants, so God "brought him outside" and invited Abraham to "look toward heaven and count the stars, if you are able to count them [...] so shall your descendants be" (Gen. 15:5, NRSV). At the end of the New Testament, the last book called Revelation, John looks around at a "great multitude that no one could count, from every nation, from all tribes and peoples and languages, standing before the throne and before the Lamb, robed in white" (Rev. 7:9, NRSV). The bookends hold a lot of years between the beginning and the end, the start and the finish, and we can see what is in the middle by looking up and looking around. In the end, we see a graphic picture as proof that the promise made to Abraham was fulfilled through Jesus and his apostles, and there they are "robed in white."

Further Reading and Online Resources

Cardoza-Orlandi, C.F. and J.L. González (2013), *To All Nations from All Nations: A History of the Christian Missionary Movement*, Nashville, TN: Abingdon.
Daughrity, D.B. (2015), *To Whom Does Christianity Belong? Critical Issues in World Christianity*, Minneapolis, MN: Fortress.
Hunt, R.A. (2010), *The Gospel among the Nations: A Documentary History of Inculturation*, Maryknoll, NY: Orbis.
Jacobsen, D. (2015), *Global Gospel: An Introduction to Christianity on Five Continents*, Grand Rapids, MI: Baker.
Kim, S. and K. Kim (2016), *Christianity as a World Religion*, 2nd edn., London: Bloomsbury Academic.
Robert, D.L. (2009), *Christian Mission: How Christianity became a World Religion*, Malden, MA: Wiley-Blackwell.
Wuthnow, R. (2009), *Boundless Faith: The Global Outreach of American Churches*, Berkeley: University of California Press.

References

Balibar, E. and I. Wallerstein (1991), *Race, Nation, Class: Ambiguous Identities*, New York: Verso.
Barrs, J. (2001), *The Heart of Evangelism*, Wheaton, IL: Crossway.
Braybrooke, M. (1992), *Pilgrimage of Hope: One Hundred Years of Global Interfaith Dialogue*, New York: Crossroad.
Daughrity, D.B. (2018), *Rising: The Amazing Story of Christianity's Resurrection in the Global South*, Minneapolis, MN: Fortress.
Escobar, S. (2003), *The New Global Mission: The Gospel from Everywhere to Everyone*, Downers Grove, IL: InterVarsity.
Flemming, D. (2015), *Why Mission?* Nashville, TN: Abingdon.
Hutchison, W.R. (1987), *Errand to the World: American Protestant Thought and Foreign Missions*, Chicago: University of Chicago Press.
Jennings, W.J. (2010), *The Christian Imagination: Theology and the Origins of Race*, New Haven, CT: Yale University Press.
Kooiman, D. (1989), *Conversion and Social Equality in India: The London Missionary Society in South Travancore in the 19th Century*, Columbia, MO: South Asia Publications.
McCloud, S. (2007), *Divine Hierarchies: Class in American Religion and Religious Studies*, Chapel Hill: University of North Carolina Press.
McGavran, D. (1955), *The Bridges of God: A Study in the Strategy of Missions*, New York: Friendship Press.

Meier, J.P. (1977), "Nations or Gentiles in Matthew 28:19?" *Catholic Biblical Quarterly*, 39 (1): 94–102.

Oak, S. (2013), *The Making of Korean Christianity: Protestant Encounters with Korean Religions, 1876–1915*, Waco, TX: Baylor University Press.

O'Malley, J.W. (1995), *The First Jesuits*, Cambridge, MA: Harvard University Press.

Phillips, P.T. (1996), *A Kingdom on Earth: Anglo-American Social Christianity, 1880–1940*, University Park: Pennsylvania State University Press.

Robert, D.L. (2016), "One Christ—Many Witnesses," *Transformation*, 33 (4): 270–81.

Scott, J.S., ed. (2012), *The Religions of Canadians*, Toronto: University of Toronto Press.

Stoll, D. (1990), *Is Latin America Turning Protestant? The Politics of Evangelical Growth*, Berkeley: University of California Press.

Tennent, T.C. (2010), *Invitation to World Missions: A Trinitarian Missiology for the Twenty-first Century*, Grand Rapids, MI: Kregel.

Van Engen, C.E., ed. (2016), *The State of Missiology Today: Global Innovations in Christian Witness*, Downers Grove, IL: IVP Academic.

Glossary Terms

Caste An inherited social position that restricts vocational choice, residence, employment, marriage, religious gatherings, and interaction with others based upon an ascribed status by birth. It is primarily found in Hinduism but can also be seen in Buddhism.

Comity A cooperative agreement for missions in a nation that divides geographical space among the member denominations, aiding the optimal usage of personnel and finances and avoiding areas of competition. Comity agreements were signed among mainline Protestants in Japan (1876), Korea (1889), and the Philippines (1898).

Contextualization Helping a foreign idea to fit within another culture, without forcing it and without reforging it. This includes the broader idea of indigenization where a natural growth within a culture of an otherwise alien or foreign religious tradition.

Diaspora Transliterated from the Greek word; meaning "being spread out," a large group of people have migrated either voluntarily or involuntarily from their homeland for various reasons and continue to share an identity with their own people. In some cases, scholars insist that a true diaspora involves the majority of a people to migrate outside their home nation.

Evangelicalism Viewed popularly as merely being conservative Protestantism, it is more theologically diverse and socially engaged than the adjective "conservative" might describe. Evangelicalism expresses a high regard for the Bible, a strong belief in Jesus as the only savior of the world, with a need for both conversion and evangelization.

Syncretism When an attempt to contextualize loses the real content of the original message (Gospel) and becomes reshaped to accommodate and adapt to another religious system or worldview.

Index

Abrahamic covenant 64
Adam 37, 52, 82, 85
"AD2000 and Beyond Movement" 179
African Christianity 66, 115, 147, 175
Agiorites, Nikodemos 132
American Civil War 56, 162
American religious freedom 91, 112
American Revolution 111
anabaptists 23, 75, 109–10
Anastasius I 105
anathemas 141–2
Anderson, Rufus 178
Anderson, Steven L. 85
Angelus Temple (Los Angeles) 93
Anglicans 24, 73, 157, 160
anointing the sick 63
Anthony, Saint 129
Apocalypse 47
Apocrypha 74, 91
apologetics 59
apostles 3, 8, 11, 52, 81, 92, 124. *See also* Paul
apostolic succession 53
Aquinas, Thomas 67–8, 88, 98, 109
Arch of Titus (Rome) 31
Aristotle 109
Asbury, Francis 162
ascesis 125
Athenagoras 132
Augustine of Hippo 14, 64, 105
  The City of God Against the Pagans 105
  theology 157–8
Augustus, Caesar 13
Azusa Street Revival 17, 75, 92, 116

baptism 23, 63–4, 70, 74–5, 86–7, 106, 116, 124
  adventist (Mozambique) 175
  Episcopal 74
  infant 70–1, 73, 106, 109–10
  Pentecostal 75
  spirit 75–6
Baptists 162, 165
Barton, John, *A History of the Bible* 44
Basil, Saint 124, 129
  Small Asketikon 129
Bauer, Walter 155
Bebbington, David W. 56
Benedict, Saint 130
Bernard (abbot of Clairvaux) 106
Bible (Christian Bible) 18, 44–5, 47–8, 53, 64, 68, 89, 91, 145, 158–9
  in the American context 45, 56–9
  Christian ownership and polemical usage 52–3
  identification 48
  nature and purpose 44, 55–6
  sacred by usage 48
  Tanakh 45–9
  in tandem with tradition 53–4
  Ten Commandments 59
  translation 68, 70, 74, 172–4
  used above tradition 54–5
  used in Bible 49–50, 52
  women in 81–6
biblicism 58, 60
Bibliology 55
Blomberg, Craig L., *Can We Still Believe the Bible?* 59
Boleyn, Anne 88
Bonaparte, Napoleon 112–13
Book of Common Prayer 160
Bradstreet, Anne 88, 90
Bratsiotis, Panagiotis 122
Brazilian Charismatic Catholics 147
The Bridal Call 92
Bunyan, John, *Pilgrim's Progress* 173
Burning Bush 50
Bush, Luis 179
  "10/40 Window" 179, 181

Byzantine/Byzantine Empire 14–15, 106, 109
   Christianity 106, 131
   monasticism and mystical theology 129–31
   silver plate 29
Byzantium 14, 105–6, 128, 131–2

Cabasilas, Nicholas, Saint 131
Calvin, John 157
   The Institutes of the Christian Religion 157–8
Campbell, Ted 160
Campolo, Tony, *Red Letter Christians* 49
canonical 85
canonization 44, 48, 53, 55, 59, 86
Carey, William 164
Cassian, John, Saint 130
caste 171
Catechism of the Catholic Church 150
Catherine of Aragon 109
Cerularius, Patriarch Michael 132
charismatic 91
Charismatic Catholicism 140
charismatic prayer 76–8, 139
Charlemagne 106, 132
Charles I 111
Charles II 111
Charles V 109
Chauncy, Charles, *Seasonable Thoughts on the State of Religion in New England* 162
Chi Rho 103
Christendom (corpus Christianum) 24, 106, 109–10, 128
Christianity/Christians 1, 3, 10–17, 20, 24, 45, 48, 59, 81, 83, 89, 102
   beyond the nations 175–9
   culture, class, and caste 171–5
   Eastern Orthodox (*see* Eastern Orthodox Christianity)
   fortunes 14
   genius of 24, 26
   globalization of 169, 175–9
   legalization of 14
   monasticism 87
   ownership and polemical usage 48, 52–3
   and politics (*see* politics, Christianity and)
   rebounding grace 180–2
   sources and history 169–71
   syncretism 179
   widespread 17
Christians believe/belief 13, 18–20, 22–4, 85
   Bible reading 20
   forgiveness 22
   heaven and hell 18
   marriage and sexuality 24
   Nicene-Constantinopolitan Creed 19
   periods of deprivation 20
   prayer 20, 22
   reality of sin 20–1
   regular worship of God 22–3
Christian Witness in a Multi-Religious World 181
Christmas 3, 23, 106
Christology 85
Christ the Redeemer, Rio de Janeiro (Brazil) 25
Chrysostom, John, Saint 129
church and state 20, 105–6, 113, 115
church fathers 19, 53–4, 56, 122, 124
The Church of Hagia Sophia 127
civilizing model of Christian mission 178
civil religion 113
Clovis I 105
Codex Sinaiticus 47
Codex Vaticanus 47
colonialism 16–17
comity 178, 181
confession 63, 68, 70, 76, 121, 155, 167
confirmation 63, 76, 78
Congregational 81, 162
Constantine the Great 13–14, 87, 105, 128–9
   battle of Milvian Bridge, victory at 104
   Edict of Milan 104, 128
Constantine XI 132
Constantinople 14–15, 19, 105–6, 127, 128, 131
contextualization 174
conversionism 56, 58, 60
Council of Trent 67, 71, 89
COVID-19 crisis (2020) 98
Cromwell, Oliver 111
Crossan, John Dominic 49
crucifixion 3, 8, 34–5
Cyrus 28

Darwin, Charles, *The Origin of Species* 114
Davenport, James 161
David 28–30, 50, 83
Dead Sea Scrolls 29–30
de Las Casas, Bartolomé 115
diaspora 175
Diocletian 102
disciple of Jesus 11, 32–3, 38, 48, 50, 55–6, 59, 155, 169–70
Divine Immanence 174
Dunn, J. D. G. 155

Eastern Orthodox Christianity 14–15, 23–4, 87, 106
  Orthodox Church 121–2
  two-millennia history
    Christian imperial commonwealth 128
    Fall of Constantinople (1453) 131–2
    The Great Schism (1054) 131–2
    monasticism and Byzantine mystical theology 129–31
    Nicaea, Cappadocians, and Saint Chrysostom 129
  vital tradition 122–8
Easter Sunday 10
ecclesial movements 145, 150
ecumenical 121, 155
ecumenical councils 124, 140
Ecumenical movement 167, 178, 181
Edict of Nantes (1598) 111
Edwards, Jonathan 161–2
  "A Divine and Supernatural Light" 161
Eliot, John 172
Elisha 83
Elizabeth I, Queen 71, 88, 111
Engels, Friedrich 113
English Reformation 71, 90
Enlightenment 90, 94, 111, 160
Ephraim (Moraitis) 135
Episcopal baptism 74, 76
Episcopalians 76, 81, 97, 162
Erasmus of Rotterdam 70
Escobar, Samuel, *The New Global Mission: The Gospel from Everywhere to Everyone* 181
Esther 84
Ethiopian Orthodox traditions 87
ethnicity 170–1
Eucharist 22–3, 63–6, 70, 76, 124, 143
  Eucharistic celebrations 66, 74

European imperialism 114
European Reformation divisions 67–8, 70–3
evangelical/evangelicalism 49, 56, 75, 90–1, 94, 114, 116, 162, 167, 172
Evangelical revivalism 91
Evangelicals and Catholics Together 167
evangelism 116, 169–70, 173, 178–9, 181
evangelists 88, 92, 179

faith 19, 45, 49, 63–4, 82, 86–9, 110
Farel, William (Guillaume) 157
Farrow, Lucy 92
Felicitas 87
Feuerbach, Ludwig, *The Essence of Christianity* 113
Fichte, Johann Gottlieb 113
Finney, Charles Grandison 174
First Baptist Church of Morelia (Mexico) 163
First Ecumenical Council 125, 129
First Vatican Council 140–4, 149
First World War 114, 132
Francis, Pope 144, 146, 149–50
Fraser, Brooke 94
Frederick the Wise (Frederick III) 108–9
The Freedom of a Christian 68, 70
French Revolution 111, 113, 142
Fulke, William 72–3
The Fundamentals 57–8

Gaither, Bill, worship songs 94
Gaither, Gloria 93–4
Gale, James Scarth 173
Galerius 104
Garden Tomb (Jerusalem) 34
Gelasius I, Pope 105
Geneva Bible 72–3, 90
Gentiles 36–7
George, Timothy 167
Gladden, Washington 174
globalization
  of Catholicism 148–50
  of Christianity 169, 175–9
Glorious Revolution 111
"Godly Commonwealth" 111
Good Friday 10
Gospels 2, 5, 30–2, 35, 40–2, 49, 73, 169–70
Goths 14
Graham, Billy 57–8

Graham, Franklin 58
the Great Awakening 90, 160–2
Great Bible (1539) 72–3
Great Commission 10–11, 56, 169–70, 181
Greenwich Mean Time (GMT), London 16–17
Gregory Nazianzus, Saint 129
Gregory of Nyssa, Saint 129
Gregory Palamas, Saint 131
Gregory VII, Pope 107
Gutiérrez, Gustavo 115

Hebrew Bible 5, 18, 28. *See also* Tanakh
Hegel, G. W. F. 113
Helena 13, 87
Hellenism 174
Henry IV 107
Henry VIII 71, 88, 109
Hillsong United 94
Hitler, Adolf 114
Hocking, William Ernest, *Rethinking Missions: A Laymen's Inquiry after One Hundred Years* 180–1
Holy Communion 76, 157
Holy Mother Church 141, 149
Holy Orders 70, 72–3, 76
Holy Roman Empire 106
Holy Spirit 3, 19, 84–5, 116, 122, 129, 164, 170–1
homiletics 52–3
Hooper, John 159
Huguenots 111
Huldah 83
human-divine relationship 64
humanism 68
Humbert, Cardinal 132
Huss, Jan 70, 155–6
Hutchinson, Anne 90

iconography 126–7, 131
Icons 122
   Icon of Christ the Pantocrator (Sinai) 123
   Icon of the First Ecumenical Council 125
   Icon of the Theotokos 126
Ignatius of Loyola, *Spiritual Exercises* 176
Incarnationism 174
indigenization principle 178
indulgences 68, 109, 157
Investiture Conflict 107, 109

Isaiah 33, 37, 49–50, 52, 86
Ivan the Great 106

Jefferson, Thomas 49
Jefferts Schori, Katherine 96–7
Jesuits 17, 148, 158, 176
Jesus Christ 2–5, 7, 10, 18, 28, 49, 59, 65–6, 70, 84–5, 91, 106, 114, 124, 129, 182
   anointed one 30–2
   BC/AD system of dividing time 18, 23
   birth 3
   childhood 3
   disciples 11, 32–3, 38, 48, 50, 55–6, 59, 155, 169–70
   Kingdom of God 7
   repentance 7
   resurrection 10, 40, 105, 171
   "Sermon on the Mount" 7–9
   social taboos 5
   and woman of Samaria 6
Jesus Seminar 49
Jews 2, 5, 18, 28, 36–7, 114
John, Gospel of 42, 50
   Jesus 38–40
   and Synoptics 40
John of Damascus, Saint 131
Johnson, Elizabeth A. 81, 94–6
   She Who Is 95
John the Baptist 3, 70
John XXIII, Pope 142
Josephus 29, 45
Judaism 2, 13, 44–5, 48–9, 52, 160, 169, 174
Judeo-Christian tradition 114
Judson, Adoniram 164
Julian of Norwich 88, 94
   Revelations of Divine Love 88
Justinian I 106, 128, 131
Juvenaly 120

Katherine, Saint 130
Kennedy, Aimee 92
Kennedy, Minnie 92
Kilbuck, John 120
King James Bible 90–1
Kuforiji, George 138

Latin America 17, 140
   Catholicism 144–7, 150
   liberation theology 115

revolutions 113
Roman Catholicism 116
shortage of priests 145
Latourette, Kenneth Scott, "Great Century" of Protestant missions 164, 176
Lausanne I 179
Lausanne II 179
Law of Moses 65, 83–4, 86
Leo III, Pope 106
Lessing, Gotthold Ephraim 111
liberal Christianity 90
liberation theology 115–16, 146
Liele, George 164
liturgy 67, 128, 138, 143, 160
Livingston, John 178
Locke, John 111
Lombard, Peter 67
Sentences 68
Lorenzo de' Medici, *The Prince* 110
Louis XIV 111
Louth, Andrew 128
Luke, Gospel of 36–7, 50, 65, 85, 97
Jesus 37–8
Luther, Martin 16, 23, 54–5, 64, 67–8, 70, 88, 107, 109, 155, 157
defended infant baptism 71
Ninety-Five Theses 68, 154, 156

Machen, J. Gresham 165
Machiavelli, Niccolò 110
MacLean Brown, Shannon 97–8
Malleus Maleficarum 88
Mandela, Nelson 115
Mark, Gospel of 37–8, 84
story of Jesus 32–5
marriage 63, 67, 131
Martha 84
Martin, Gregory 72–3
A Discoverie of the Manifold Corruptions of the Holy Scriptures by the Heretikes of Our Daies 72
Martin Luther King Jr. memorial 44
Marty, Martin E. 56
Martyr, Justin, *Dialogue with Trypho* 53
Marx, Karl 113
Mary I 71
Mary II 111
Mass 138–40, 143–4
Mather, Cotton 90

Matthew, Gospel of 7, 22, 32, 37–8, 48, 50, 55, 70, 170
story of Jesus 35–6
Maximos the Confessor, *Mystagogy* 131
McGavran, Donald A. 170
McPherson, Aimee Semple 92–4
This is That 93
McPherson, Harold 92
Mehmet II 132
messiah (Messiah) 2, 18, 28, 48–9, 55, 102
anointed one 28–30
John's Jesus 38–40
Luke's Jesus 37–8
Mark's Jesus 32–5
Matthew's Jesus 35–6
memory of anointed one 40–2
Methodists 167
Church 162
National Camp Meeting Association for the Promotion of Holiness 163
in prayer 161
Mexican Catholicism 140
Mexican Constitution (1857) 164
Mexican Protestantism 164
Miriam 83, 98
Missionary Conference, Edinburgh (1910) 181
modernity 140, 142
Moscow 15, 106
Moses 8, 50, 64, 83
Mussolini, Benito 114
mystic 87

Nation, Carrie A. 59
nation-state 170
Nevius, John Livingston 178
The New American Sunday School Hymn Book 57
New Ecumenism 167
New England Puritans 68
New Testament 13, 23–4, 31, 45, 47, 64, 72, 88, 102, 110, 124, 150, 154–5, 170, 173, 181
criteria 48
Gospels 2, 169
Tanakh quotations and allusions 50
Nicaea 128–9
Nicene-Constantinopolitan Creed (Nicene Creed) 19, 76, 124, 129, 131–2
Nicholas I, Pope 132

Niebuhr, H. Richard 164
Noll, Mark A. 56, 155, 162
North America
    Christianity, women in 81–2, 89–98
    organizations, ecumenicity 165–7
    Orthodox Christianity 120–1
    pan-Orthodox organizations 134
    Protestants/Protestantism 16, 162, 164–5, 172–3, 180
    race 171
    sacramental belief and practice in 63, 73–6, 78

Oden, Thomas C. 167
Old Testament 18, 45, 47, 53, 59, 64, 102, 105, 150
Orthodox Christianity 67, 106, 122, 133
    Alaska 120
    Eastern
    (*see* Eastern Orthodox Christianity)
Orthodox Church
    ecumenical councils 124
    ethos/*phronema* of 128
    Eucharistic ecclesiology of 121
    today 132–5
    tradition and history 121–2
Orthodox monasticism 134–5
Orthodox tradition 54, 87, 127, 160
Orthodoxy 15, 23, 53, 122, 140, 154–5
Osteen, Joel 94
Osteen, Victoria 94
Ottoman Empire 15
Our Lady of Guadalupe 139–40

Pachomius, Saint 129
Paleologos, Zoe 132
pan-Orthodox organizations 134
papal infallibility 141–2
Parable of the Good Samaritan 5, 7
Parham, Charles Fox 165
Passover celebration 3, 8, 64
patristic 122, 131
Paul 3, 10–11, 42, 50–2, 55–6, 59, 64, 66, 68, 85–6, 97–8, 124
    vision of Christ 12–13
Paul II, John, Pope 96
Paul VI, Pope 132
The Peace of Augsburg (1555) 110
Peace of Westphalia (1648) 110
Pelikan, Jaroslav 53, 122

penance 63, 67–70
Pentecostals/Pentecostalism 73–6, 92, 116, 165
    baptism 75–6
Perpetua 87
Peter 11–12, 33–4, 55, 86
Philip 52
Pietism 158
Pilate, Pontius 8, 19, 40, 42
Pius X, Pope 149
politics, Christianity and 102, 105, 117
    American Revolution 111–12
    with Anabaptists 109–10
    Byzantine Empire 106
    church-state unity 111
    communism 113
    Enlightenment 111
    French Revolution 111, 113
    liberation theology 115–16
    during medieval period 109
    patriotism 113
    Pentecostalism 116
    Roman Empire 105
    sectarianism 110
    secularization 113
    totalitarian regimes 114
Ponticus, Evagrius 122
praxis 115
predestination 158
prerequisite 48
Protestantism/Protestants 16–17, 23–4, 54–6, 58–9, 63, 73, 81, 91, 111, 121, 154, 157, 172
    advancing 162–4
    birthing 154–8
    building 158–60
    and constitutional monarchy 111
    Great Awakening 160–2
    Methodists in prayer 161
    movement 16, 70
    in North America 16, 162, 164–5, 172–3, 180
    Pentecostal movement 140
    questing 164–7
Protestant Reformation 154, 157–8
Puritanism 158–60

Rauschenbusch, Walter 174–5
    Christianity and the Social Crisis 174
    A Theology for the Social Gospel 174

Reformed 157–8
Renaissance 155
Revelation 181–2
reverse missions 17
revivals and crusades 57
Roman Catholic Church 10, 67–8, 72, 76, 88, 96, 106, 111, 113–14, 155–6
    doctrine of transubstantiation 88
Roman Catholics/Catholicism 16, 23–4, 63, 76, 81, 87–8, 90, 98, 111–12, 116, 121, 160
    in the era of globalization 148–50
    Latin America 116
    New Centers 144–8
    teachings on sacraments 67, 74
    Vatican I and II 140–4
Rome 10, 14, 31, 105, 132, 143–4
Romero, Oscar 145–6
Rousseau, Jean-Jacque, *The Social Contract* 113
Rufinus, Saint 129
Russian Orthodox Church 114
Russian Revolution 106
Russia's Christianization 15, 20, 128, 133

Sabbath 5, 52, 105
sacramental belief and practice
    common ground in scripture 63–7
    European Reformation divisions 67–73
    in North America 63, 73–6, 78
sacraments 23, 63–4, 68, 71–3, 76, 96, 122
    anointing the sick 63, 71
    baptism 63, 70–1
    confession 63
    confirmation 63, 71
    Eucharist 63, 70–1
    marriage 63, 67, 71
    penance 63, 67, 69–71
    Roman Catholic teachings on 67, 74
Samaritans 5, 37
Samuel 28, 83
San Baudelio church (Spain), wall painting 39
Sattler, Michael, *Schleitheim Articles* 110
Sava, Saint 130
Second Temple Period 28, 84
Second Vatican Council 67, 74, 94, 96, 140–4
Second World War 114

Semple, Robert 92
Sergius IV, Pope 132
"Sermon on the Mount" 7–9, 36
Servetus, Michael 157–8
Seymour, William Joseph 75, 92, 116, 165
Simonopetra Monastery, Mount Athos 130
sins 19–20, 64
    deadly 22
    mortal 22, 150
    venial 22
A Small Pentecostal (Full Gospel) Church (Seoul) 166
Smith, Taya 94
Social Gospel movement 174
social justice 56, 76
Society of Jesus (SJ) 176
sola fide (faith alone) 67
Sola Scriptura (the Bible alone) 54, 59, 67
soteriology 85
Soviet Union 114
Sozzini, Fausto 158
Sozzini, Laelio 158
Spener, Philipp Jakob, *Pia desideria* (Pious desires) 158–9
spirit baptism 75–6
Spong, John Shelby, *The Sins of Scripture* 59
Stoddard, Solomon 161
Stone-Campbell movement 164
St. Peter and St. Paul's Church, Ganghwa Anglican Church (Korea) 173
Strasbourg 157
Sunday School movement 56, 60
Sunday School songs 57
Symeon, Saint 131
symphonia (harmony) 105
syncretism 179
Synoptic Gospels 38, 84
Syro-Malabar Catholic Church, India 147–8
Syro-Malankara Catholic Church, India 147–8

Tanakh 45–50, 55–6, 59
    apologetical source 50
    genealogical source 50
    hermeneutical source 52
    homiletical source 52
    polemical source 52
    typological source 50, 52

Taylor, William, *Pauline Methods of Missionary Work* 178
Temperance movement 59
Teresa of Ávila, Saint 88–9, 94, 98
   Way of Perfection 88
Tetzel, John (Johann) 156–7
Theodosius I 105, 132
Theotokos 126–7
Thirty Years' War 110
Thomas, Saint 147
Tikhon (Bellavin), Bishop 133–5
Timothy 55–6, 59, 85
Tiridates III 104
Townsend, William Cameron 174
Trinity 19–20, 129
Trinity-St. Sergius Monastery (Sergiyev Posad) 133
turning points (Noll) 155
Tutu, Desmond 115
   The Book of Forgiving: The Fourfold Path for Healing Ourselves and Our World 97
Tutu van Furth, Mpho, *The Book of Forgiving: The Fourfold Path for Healing Ourselves and Our World* 97
Tyndale, William 72, 88

Unitarianism 158
Urban II, Pope 109

Velichkovsky, Paisius 132
Venn, Henry 178
Virgin Mary 2, 19, 74, 87
Vladimir of Kiev 127–8
Voltaire, Francois-Marie Arouet de 111

von Bora, Katharina 70, 88
Vulgate 47, 72–3

Ware, Kallistos, *The Orthodox Church* 122
water baptism 76
Wesley, Charles 90–1
Wesley, John 90–1
Western Christianity 14, 66–7, 131
Whitefield, George 160–1
William III 111
Winthrop, John, *A Model of Christian Charity* 56
women 76, 81
   in Christian Bible 81–6
   in clerical leadership 96
   of faith in late antiquity and Latin Middle Ages 86–9
   in North American Christianity 81, 89–98
Woodworth-Etter, Maria Beulah 91–2, 94
   Marvels and Miracles 93
Woodworth, Philo Harrison 91
World Parliament of Religions, Chicago (1893) 179–80
World's Fair 180
Wycliffe, John 70, 155

Xavier, Francis 176–7

Yahweh 2, 18, 28, 83
Yoido Full Gospel Church (South Korea) 117

Zechariah 50
Zizioulas, John 121
Zschech, Darlene 94
Zwingli, Ulrich 70, 155, 157–60

www.ingramcontent.com/pod-product-compliance
Lightning Source LLC
Chambersburg PA
CBHW080245170426
43192CB00014BA/2574